iGods

iGods

HOW TECHNOLOGY SHAPES OUR
SPIRITUAL AND SOCIAL LIVES

CRAIG DETWEILER

BrazosPress

a division of Baker Publishing Group
Grand Rapids, Michigan

Published by Brazos Press
a division of Baker Publishing Group
P.O. Box 6287, Grand Rapids, MI 49516-6287
www.brazospress.com

Printed in the United States of America

Library of Congress Cataloging-in-Publication Data

Detweiler, Craig, 1964–
　　IGods : how technology shapes our spiritual and social lives / Craig Detweiler.
　　　　pages cm
　　Includes bibliographical references and index.
　　ISBN 978-1-58743-344-3 (pbk.)
　　1. Technology—Religious aspects—Christianity. 2. Social networks. I. Title.
BR115.T42D48 2014
261.5′6—dc23　　　　　　　　　　　　　　　　　　　　　　　　　　　　2013025133

13　14　15　16　17　18　19　　　　7　6　5　4　3　2　1

In keeping with biblical principles of creation stewardship, Baker Publishing Group advocates the responsible use of our natural resources. As a member of the Green Press Initiative, our company uses recycled paper when possible. The text paper of this book is composed in part of post-consumer waste.

green press INITIATIVE

Contents

Acknowledgments

While writing appears to be a solitary craft, it is built upon the work and words of others. Like research and technology, advances arise by merging previous ideas into new forms, shapes, and applications. Yes, there are moments of blinding insight, unexpected breakthroughs, and divine sparks. But they arise in an incubator formed through reading and studying, teaching and testing, reflection and prayer.

I am grateful to the communities that made this book possible. First and foremost, I am grateful for my wife-for-life, Caroline Cicero, and our children, Zoe and Theo, who endured far more of this book than they deserved to. Whatever romance they may have harbored about the glamour of the writer's life is long gone. But hopefully, in its place, they have seen there are no shortcuts when it comes to finishing a book. Despite technological advances, writing remains a long and winding road that proceeds at a snail's pace.

This book was road-tested on the Pepperdine University students in my Introduction to Media class. They are a vibrant, living laboratory, the heavy users and early adopters who helped me tailor this manuscript to their passions and needs. I am heartened by their enthusiastic response. They want to discuss these important issues and long to go deeper in their reflection and discipleship. Special thanks to Brandon Scheirman, a brilliant student and talented designer, who created all of the original illustrations for the book.

I am indebted to my editor, Bob Hosack, Lisa Ann Cockrel, and the team at Brazos/Baker Academic who embraced this concept and were remarkably patient. It is tough to finish a book about an industry that changes daily. I am attempting to craft a timely tale rooted in timeless truths. Thank you to my many partners on this endeavor.

So many books have been written on faith and science, but the relationship between theology and technology is a newer, burgeoning field. Marshall

McLuhan and Walter Ong were pioneering thinkers, way ahead of their time. Their robust Catholic faith informed their prophetic understanding of the shifts from oral to literary culture and the retribalizing effects of electronic culture. David Noble's *The Religion of Technology* offers an essential historical overview. Albert Borgmann approaches faith and technology from a philosophical point of view in the seminal *Technology and the Character of Contemporary Life*. Jacques Ellul and Ursula Franklin offered insightful critiques of the technological society, challenging the Christian community to resist the totalizing system. I am so indebted to these remarkable scholars for how they've influenced my efforts to forge a theology of technology.

I will not focus on how faith is disseminated via technology. Distinguished scholars analyzing religion on the internet include Brenda Brasher (*Give Me That Online Religion*), Heidi Campbell (*Digital Religion*), and Rachel Wagner (*GodWired*). Lynn Schofield Clark has studied the impact of digital technologies upon families (*The Parent App*). Those who have articulated how to shift church practices to coincide with technological shifts include John Dyer (*From the Garden to the City*), Jesse Rice (*The Church of Facebook*), Elizabeth Drescher (*Tweet if You Heart Jesus*), and Brandon Vogt (*The Church and New Media*). Dwight Friesen reframed our understanding of church for a networked world in *Thy Kingdom Connected*. Douglas Estes pressed forward the furthest with the implications for twenty-first-century ministry in *SimChurch*. Pastoral concerns and cautions have been articulated by Quentin Schultze (*Habits of the High-Tech Heart*), Shane Hipps (*Flickering Pixels*), and Tim Challies (*The Next Story*). Leonard Sweet recovers the early days of Christianity as a social movement in *Viral*. I am energized by the emerging scholarship of Brett T. Robinson found in *Appletopia*. Jesuit paleontologist Pierre Teilhard de Chardin's notion of the noosphere inspired Jennifer Cobb in her *CyberGrace*. She posits a world in which we evolve, thanks to technology, toward a higher consciousness, perhaps to a more Godlike calling. While this hopeful vision is attractive, it doesn't address how technology can also bewitch and blind us. Technology has given us the ability to improve our conditions but also the power to destroy ourselves via bombs or chemical warfare. We can enjoy the benefits of technology while still remaining skeptical of what happens when we become iGods of our making.

A similarly diverse spectrum—from caution to enthusiasm—is found among technologists. Nicholas Carr may bemoan *The Shallows*, our less-than-deep thinking thanks to the internet, while Clay Shirky celebrates the *Cognitive*

Surplus arising from our collective intelligence. Both messages have found broad audiences. I am intrigued by the words of warning coming from artificial intelligence researcher Jaron Lanier (*Who Owns the Future?*) and Eli Pariser of Upworthy.org (*The Filter Bubble*). They experienced the early, unchecked promise of the internet but now worry about the standardization that arises from a consolidation of power among a few techno-lords. MIT psychologist Sherry Turkle shifted from an enthusiastic embrace of *The Second Self* to a position of caution and concern in *Alone Together*. Whether coming from a specifically religious or avowedly sociological perspective, the debate about our technological shift is rampant. I appreciate both words of warning and practical advice on how to incorporate social media into church practices. But I find myself more interested in the theological questions of where technology is going. What is the *telos* of our commitment to faster, smaller, and more? How do we retain an embodied faith in a digital era?

The most advanced technologist and theologian leading this conversation is Kevin Kelly. From his work on the *Whole Earth Catalog* to his editing at *Wired*, Kelly has reported on each stage of our computing era. He suggests that the emerging question isn't where we are headed but *What Technology Wants*. I am fascinated (and frightened) by that notion. It sounds a long way from seeking the will of God or asking, "What Would Jesus Do?" Is technology a distinct entity, birthed from our need for comfort and calculation, now surpassing us in far more than chess games or Jeopardy? I vividly recall the cold, calculated horrors of HAL, the computer gone amok in *2001: A Space Odyssey*. And who wants to have their every keystroke or phone call monitored by advertisers or government agencies? Yet, I also must acknowledge how many magnificent breakthroughs in science and engineering have raised all our standards of living. Technology is increasingly shifting from something outside us to a partner and monitor inside us, an evolutionary upgrade. I am grateful that Kelly has gone before us, reassuring us that we need not fear the future, especially if theologians and ethicists work with technologists.

This book arises from ancient mysteries: Why did God give us a brain and why are we called to be fruitful and multiply? When we apply our talents to the task of planting, harvesting, and creating, we get more products, more ideas, more leisure. So are we slowly creating heaven on earth, fulfilling God's hopes for us? Or are we repeating the errors of Eden, making ourselves the center of our world in unhealthy and unsustainable ways? The short answer is "yes." The longer explanation follows.

Introduction

iGods

Nothing is permanent, but change!

—Heraclitus, 4th century BC

Resenting a new technology will not halt its progress.

—Marshall McLuhan, 1969[1]

Technology is most effective when we fail to notice it, but our faith in technology is so pervasive it is often blind. Consider an average day: We expect our alarm to go off. We believe our lights will turn on. We expect the shower to run. We trust appliances to chill our milk, heat our coffee, toast our bread, and clean our dishes. We depend on trains to run, buses to roll, our car to start. We trust our radio to play and our GPS to guide us. The elevator will carry us to our floor. Our computer will retrieve our files, print our documents, and deliver our email. The microwave can cook our lunch or reheat our dinner. Our phone can order pizza to be delivered. Our thermostat makes sure we are warm in the winter and cool in the summer. We are comfortable. We feel self-sufficient. We did not need anyone's help to make this happen. At no time did we need to pause or even consider how these appliances worked. Conveniences once well beyond the reach of royalty are now standard fare. As dutiful servants, these technologies perform their services without acknowledgment. They are virtually invisible. Thank you technology for making our life so simple. Forgive us for taking you for granted.

Our faith in technology is impatient. It does not tolerate delays. If bad weather befalls O'Hare Airport, tempers flare. When the Apple map in the iPhone5 failed to deliver results, heads rolled within the company. If our cable service is cut off (or the power goes out during the Super Bowl), Comcast will hear from us! Our faith in technology allows little room for error. We often exclude the events in the natural world (such as weather) in our expectations of technology. As psychologist Rollo May noted, "Technology is the knack for so arranging the world that we do not experience it."[2] We may not realize how our faith in technology can blind us.

Our faith in technology connects us to long lost friends. It also enables us to avoid people we'd rather text with than talk to. It is our hiding place.

Our faith in technology is so widespread that we feel we must be always available, always connected. Technology demands our attention.

Our faith in technology is so complete that we place devices into our children's hands at earlier ages and stages. We train our kids to look down rather than up.

Our faith in technology is so passionate that we rarely question the wisdom of our embrace. We text now, worry later.

Our embrace of technology is so boundless that we have poured staggering riches on those who brought us these magic devices.

Futurist Arthur C. Clarke noted that any "sufficiently advanced technology is indistinguishable from magic."[3] We marvel at the results without analyzing how the trick was accomplished. We may be tempted to bow down to the magic box, ascribing secret powers to the technology. We may also applaud the magician who performed the trick. When it comes to technology, we celebrate the icons of Silicon Valley as iGods worth emulating. We reward them for granting us superpowers. With a smartphone in our pocket, we can transcend the bodily limits of space and time. We can send and receive, buy and sell, upload and download with a swipe of our finger.

In this book, we will discuss the magic technologies that we may consider Godlike. We will also study the trails blazed by tech leaders like Steve Jobs—the original iGod. We will also consider the temptations offered by Google and Facebook and Twitter to build our digital brand, to become iGods of our making. An iGod can be a technology, a technologist, or the person bewitched by the power promised by the gadget. A healthy perspective on technology, unmasking the magic, may make us more appreciative of the craft involved. In examining how technology improves our lives, we may even come to a deeper understanding of the glory of God. In other words, a better grasp of the iGods we fashion and follow can lead us toward the God of Abraham, Isaac, and Jacob.

Perhaps we should pause more often and thank God for the gift of technology. Before we pick up a fork, we could be grateful for the toolmakers who preceded us. We may marvel at Google's internet-connected glasses, but we can also appreciate any invention that clarifies our vision—from the reading glasses that accompanied my fortieth birthday to the sunglasses that keep us from developing cataracts. When we get a flu shot, the doctors have anticipated the future of disease so effectively that they can give it to us (and protect us!) ahead of time. We don't think about our artificial hip or pacemaker; we just incorporate them into our bodies and move on as satisfied semi-cyborgs. Technology at its finest is easy to adopt, quick to implement, and bound to be underappreciated.

Comedian Louis (Louie) C. K. jokes about our sense of entitlement regarding technology. He marvels that "everything is amazing right now and nobody is happy." Louis mocks those who get impatient when they have to wait a few seconds to get a cell phone signal . . . FROM SPACE![4] The fruits of technology are often ingratitude and impatience. We don't want to be short-tempered and demanding, but we have come to expect technology to be at our beck and call. Could a deeper understanding of technology broaden our sense of appreciation? If we receive technology more as a God-given gift and privilege, could we grow in gratitude? How might stepping away from the conveniences of technology sharpen our perceptions and quicken our spirit?

This book is about how technologies entertain and enthrall us. We are tethered to our mobile devices. They comfort us when we're lonely, reassure us when we're lost, organize us when we're feeling out of control. They are an electronic security blanket, a way for families and friends to feel close despite the distances that may separate us. They offer an easy way to pass the time between things, when we are waiting for something to start or someone to show up. We can sink into our cell phone when we are bored, when we are scared, or when we are eager to share some great news. However, delight can devolve into devotion.

It is good to be connected to family and friends, but when we cannot resist the urge to check updates or upload a photo, we are veering toward idolatry. Idols serve our needs according to our schedule. When we call, they answer. They give us a false sense of being in control. But over time, the relationship reverses. We end up attending to their needs, centering our lives on their priorities and agendas. Most idols begin as good things, from a modest improvement to a lofty goal or something we long to acquire. When we gaze on our idols, we see ourselves differently. We can picture ourselves driving the car, winning the award, taking the bow. Over time, we can become so attached to the image of ourselves being reflected back at us that we lose perspective.[5] When we shift from thinking about something occasionally (a romantic relationship, a promotion, a possession, our family) to obsessing over it constantly, we are turning an idea into an idol. It becomes the thing we cling to, that gives our life purpose and meaning. Idols are anything we're so attached to that we can't imagine living without.[6] Tim Keller challenges us to take stock. What would we hate to lose and feel lost without? Where do our thoughts wander in our free time? Who or what can we not wait to check in with?

The iMac begat the iPhone and the iPad, and each one starts with me—or rather "i." They enhance our ability to connect and to serve, but they can also create an inflated sense of self, believing the entire world revolves around "me": iVoice, iWant, iNeed. The ability to broadcast ourselves from anywhere to anyone at any time gives us an electric charge. In an age of status updates, personalized shopping, and lists of followers, we are experiencing the rush of becoming iGods of our own making. Updating our profiles can be exhausting. The pressure to perform can be demanding. Why are devices designed to broaden our reach and elevate our personal brands so enslaving?

When Moses descended from Sinai with the original tablets, the crowd was dancing around a golden calf. On the long journey toward freedom out of Egypt, they had forgotten who they were and whose they were. In the first commandment, God appropriately insisted, "You shall have no other gods before me."[7] The second commandment warned against worshiping graven images (no matter how sleek, cool, or trendy they may be). Biblical history reveals how quickly the Israelites bowed down to foreign idols, shifting allegiance toward the latest innovations introduced by conquerors and kings.[8] Images of lines of people outside the Apple store awaiting the latest iPhone dance through my mind. The apostle John concluded his letter to the early church with the cautionary warning, "Dear children, keep yourselves from idols."[9] As parents, we put an iPad in our children's hands to get through road trips and plane rides. Kids can scroll before they even speak. John Calvin said, "Every one of us, even from his mother's womb, is a master-craftsman of idols."[10] As soon as we remove one, we elevate another in its place. Despite their lofty promises, idols can end up sucking the life out of us.

This book celebrates the wonders of technology and sings the praises of Apple, Amazon, Google, Facebook, YouTube, and Twitter. We will consider what important everyday problems these technologies solved and ask what is our proper relationship to these technologies. In examining why we place so much faith in their abilities, we may rediscover our original calling. We want to appreciate the gift of technology, but we also desire to put the iGods in their proper place.

Writing this book has forced me to measure my own technological devotion. We value speed and efficiency while the Bible upholds patience and kindness. When we start the day with electronic updates, we may forget how "great is his faithfulness; his mercies begin afresh each morning."[11] Where shall we express our hopes and fears? If we post our concerns on Facebook, we may forget to cast our cares on the Lord, the one who sustains us in our sorrows.[12] Should we find our comfort in a gadget or in God? If our goal or calling in life is to glorify God and to enjoy him forever, should we fill each moment of boredom with an electronic input to keep us entertained? Almost all of Jesus's most important teaching happened on the journey between destinations. After his disciples had experienced something, Jesus took the time before the next encounter to reflect on the meaning of what had just happened. He put things in context, revealed the bigger picture, and imparted eye-opening wisdom. The insights were so memorable and so deep that they were passed on via word of mouth with such clarity that they could still be gathered in the Gospels almost one hundred years later. When we go from experience to experience, from Gmail to Facebook to Tumblr to YouTube, we crowd out those moments where the Spirit may have something significant to convey. We replace God-given interludes of pause, rest, and reflection with the goat version of Taylor Swift's "I Knew You Were Trouble" (look it up on YouTube). Nobody laughs harder at "Goats Screaming Like Humans" than I do. However, it is tough to build a life around viral videos and memes. They are a welcome respite—a celebration of the weird wonder of God's creation and a quick laugh amid daunting days—but if we are going to go the distance, we need more enduring wisdom than "McKayla is not impressed" or "Charlie bit my finger."

Hyperconnected and Distracted

As a college professor, I am amazed by how stressed and overscheduled my students appear. They never seem to have enough hours in the day to get everything done. They arrive in class looking exhausted and bleary-eyed. They are often in the middle of a relational drama that is playing out in real time, either on Facebook or via instant messaging. It may be a fight with a roommate, the end of a romance, or a plea from a parent. The constant tug of electronic inputs keeps them from being focused. We are hyperconnected and easily distracted, always available and rarely present. When Jesus saw the crowds in ancient Israel, he had compassion on them, recognizing them as harassed and helpless, like sheep without a shepherd.[13] I want to alleviate my students' stress.

In my media and communication classes, I insist that students close their laptops and turn off their phones. I want to capture that elusive and essential commodity: *attention*. We can't think, learn, or get in touch with our feelings unless we've focused our attention. The social contract is clear: *be here now*. I even try to teach in a manner that defies note taking. My class is a lived experience that cannot be replicated, captured, or reduced to any other medium (although numerous efforts are under way to deliver education online, including the 2013 TED Prize winner, Sugata Mitra's "School in the Cloud"). What happens among our community of learners at Pepperdine is designed to spark thought that will reverberate until the next class session.

However, when it is time for midterms or final exams, I encourage students to bring their laptops to class. My tests are open book, open notes, open computers. They are even welcome to text message their friends. In real-world scenarios, the challenge is assimilation: sorting through too much information as quickly and wisely as possible. A timed test, surrounded by information, approximates the kind of decision making we face every single moment. With too many sources, where should we turn for advice? Which authorities do we trust, and when do we stop gathering information and start crafting it into something uniquely our own? My classroom illustrates a key tension for every person and every family: When should we immerse in and when should we withdraw from the information torrent (or is that "tyrant")?

We love our iPhones, but we fear that they are distracting us. We want our searches answered instantaneously by Google, but we feel overwhelmed by too much information. We relish the chance to connect with friends via Facebook, but we wonder how much privacy we may sacrifice via public posts. Viewed from one angle, technology may seem like a savior to so many social ills. It lifts us out of ignorance. It provides access to all. It can unite us, it can heal us, and it can make us one. Plenty of us still worry about the totalizing effects of technology. Does entrusting all our information to a few central databases and companies open up the possibility for new forms of domination? Those who have seen regimes attempt to consolidate power via disinformation worry whenever a few entities control the airwaves. We solved the problem of too much information by giving a few key companies too much of our information.

We have been swamped by a tsunami of new technologies, without pausing to consider whether they are good or bad, helpful or hurtful. Are they making us more thoughtful, more articulate, more loving? I see the benefits of technology when I can let my family know where I am or send a quick text message of support to a friend. But I also feel pulled away from them in order to check for updates and to respond to requests for information, simply because everything can happen so instantaneously. Our devices demand our attention. MIT psychologist Sherry Turkle notes how the current generation is "among the first to grow up with an expectation of continuous connection: always on, and always on them."[14] We have embraced this shift largely without considering the implications. Our basic philosophy has been summarized by William Powers: *It's good to be connected, and it's bad to be disconnected.*[15] He describes us as "digital maximalists" operating under a basic maxim, "The more you connect, the better off you are." Powers notes, "We never sat down and consciously decided that this was the code we would live by. There was no discussion, no referendum or show of hands. It just sort of happened, as if by tacit agreement or silent oath. *From now on, I will strive to be as connected as possible at all times.*"[16] I write this book because I want to pause and question that aphorism. This is an effort to step back, slow down, and take a long view of where we've been and where we're heading.

iGods

We may be tempted to eschew the electronic kingdom, skip the smartphone, and forgo Facebook. I am not a Luddite calling us to smash our machines. I love God, and I am attached to my iPhone. I believe Jesus was a techie and God calls us to count and to code. You can find me via Gmail and on Facebook, YouTube, and Twitter. I worked as a tutor in computer programming for the math department at Davidson College. I then went to film school at the University of Southern California and became a content creator rather than a technologist. I've watched Silicon Valley usurp Hollywood as the primary storyteller and mythmaker for our generation. This is my respectful response.

The only computers I've ever owned have been Macs. I remember the giddy first day that Earthlink allowed me to get online. I recall the visceral thrill generated by the simple words, "you've got mail." I still have the pullout map of the world wide web provided inside an issue of *MacWorld*. It all seemed so strange and wild and wonderful. I remember the day CarsDirect.com moved into our Southern California neighborhood. While it became an immediate internet sensation, to those of us in Culver City, it became an annoyance. How did they squeeze so many people into such a small building? Employees had to park their cars on our suburban streets and walk to work—all in order to sell more cars. Friends of mine got rich working for GeoCities before Yahoo! bought it. I've watched those same friends drop out and move to Indonesia, leaving the tech scene altogether. While some cashed out, others have continued to cash in. When one internet start-up failed, they found new suitors to invest in another.

It has been a wild two decades of booms and busts and booms, of IPOs and overnight billionaires. We have elevated new American icons to rival previous captains of industry like Andrew Carnegie, John D. Rockefeller, Thomas Edison, and Leland Stanford. These captains laid the groundwork for our twentieth-century infrastructure of steel and railways and fuel. They invested in new technologies that increased efficiency, hastened delivery, and lit up our lives. The information era has been ruled by the iGods: Steve Jobs of Apple, Jeff Bezos of Amazon, Larry Page and Sergey Brin of Google, and Mark Zuckerberg of Facebook. They beam from magazine covers as the entrepreneurs who mastered technology and transformed our lives. The entertainment industry now tells the stories of these icons who have displaced Hollywood as California's most influential export and financial engine.

The iGods got rich by solving problems created by technology such as the complexity of the original computers, the unmanageability of the internet, and the sheer excess of information. The first computers primarily processed numbers. They were designed to make it easy to calculate complex formulas for firing missiles. Armed forces needed to know how to account for the angle of the gun, the weight of the bomb, the variables of temperature and wind. Such complex algorithmic equations took too much time in the heat of battle. Computers offered an ability to calculate fast—faster than the human brain, faster than a whole roomful of women plugging the numbers into formulas far from their husbands on the front. Computers required specialized knowledge. They operated via arcane languages like Fortran. No matter how BASIC they labeled it, for the average person it was an unintelligible foreign tongue. How to make computers easy and natural, warm and humane?

Apple made computers approachable. The Macintosh even sounded like a friend, "Mac." Jobs and Apple turned a generation on to the creative power of computers, shifting computers from number processors to word processors. They encouraged people to engage in desktop publishing. We could design our own newsletters, lay out our own fanzines, publish our own novels. Blogging would follow. We started making our own designs, touching up our photos, recording our garage bands. Final Cut and iMovie turned us all into filmmakers as we edited hours of home movies into cool music videos. Visualization via computers transformed architecture and design, spawning the maker movement and 3D printing. The DIY revolution resulted in a dizzying array of media, on our computers, on the web. How do we organize all the music in our collection? What do we do with all the movies we have made? Where do we find all the books and music we'd like to buy? The iGods of Apple and Amazon got rich by solving our problem of abundance. They made billions by helping us control our millions—millions of songs, photos, and books. In a world of too much, they allowed us to find what we wanted, to make sense of too much. Our gratitude is immense. Our faith in their abilities is almost blind.

The iGods of Google and Facebook made the internet manageable. Google gave us the answers we were looking for. Facebook allowed us to gather our friends. The iGods helped us organize our calendars and promote our events. We can instantly connect with anybody at any time from anywhere. Such superpowers can be dizzying. How much do we value such services? Century-old companies that made trains, planes, and automobiles were eclipsed by start-ups that transported us across uncharted territories. Apple gave us the tools to create. Google showed us where to find what we were seeking. Amazon made it easy to buy it. Facebook allowed us to tap into the wisdom of friends. The demigods of YouTube and Twitter and Instagram turned us all into broadcasters. Yet, the creators of YouTube, Twitter, and Instagram are not viewed as iGods because they didn't solve a problem. They deepened our problems by creating even more information.

We are just beginning to grasp our ability to gather followers and attract subscribers, to find an audience via our mobile devices. Who or what is God in an era where we have acquired such reach? Sam Lessin, project manager at

Facebook, suggests, "We as a species in the last few decades have gotten three new superpowers. . . . We can literally remember anything, we can talk to anyone on earth instantly for free, and we can process huge amounts of data."[17] Will our view of God need to expand, rising above a mountain of data? Do we need a new understanding of omniscience comparable to the cloud and omnipresence rooted in "mobiquity," the ubiquity of mobile devices?

I want us to consider what to do with these newly found superpowers. Like Harry Potter and Hermione Granger, we must learn how to wield the magic wand in our hand. The rise of superhero movies may correspond to our sense of expanding horizons. Google Earth allows us to fly like Superman, zeroing in on any location we desire. Spider-Man learns that with great power comes great responsibility. The students of Hogwarts have shown us how to resist evil—it is a question of character, of wisdom. Trying on technology will involve some awkward missteps, crashes even. The netiquette of social media is still being negotiated. We've never been so close to so many. We may embarrass ourselves on YouTube. Twitter forces us to think before we tweet. Facebook should cause us to consider what it means to be a neighbor. How do we love our friends and followers when there are hundreds of them?

I am not equating Jesus's principles with business a la Bruce Barton who quipped, "Christ would be a national advertiser today, I am sure, as He was a great advertiser in His own day. He thought of His life as business."[18] However, I do want to discover what these tech and business entrepreneurs understood in order to grasp how people of faith might respond to our context with similar creativity. Christianity was a social movement rooted in powerful symbols, creative actions, and remarkable word of mouth. It was a global brand that spread without advertising. The integrity of what it offered, demonstrated by millions of transformed pagans, spoke volumes. Now, having been usurped by the cult of technology and its fervent evangelists, we must figure out how to regain our mojo, to tap into our strengths, to remember our first love.

A Theology of Technology

Technology is the realm of engineers. They crunch numbers to build bridges, make decisions, and create applications for our smartphones. Theology is seen as the province of the spiritual, a realm of intangible ideas and ultimate questions. I want to bring these two worlds together, to point out how spiritual our designs can be and how material theological concerns should be. Kevin Kelly has noted "that many people who do not believe in God somehow believe in information."[19] Technologists play god in their research all the time. As a theologian, what might I learn from technologists? As a student at Fuller Theological Seminary, I blended the seemingly incompatible realms of faith and film. I've tried to understand how God can offer revelatory moments amid seemingly profane, pop cultural means. Teaching for Fuller's Northern California campus and speaking at a Menlo Park Presbyterian Church retreat, I discovered the growing need for a theological understanding of the burgeoning tech industry. In turning toward technology, I will continue to examine our lived experiences as an expression of profound spiritual longing. Our posts on Facebook can be a form of prayer and praise. The device in our pocket can be a conduit to and from the divine. The same God who worked through ancient Babylonian and Persian kings can work through today's tech titans. By forging a theology of technology, we may even discover why large sections of the Bible focus on numbers!

David Tracy encourages a shift from theo-*logy* to *theo*-logy, a shift from the study of God driven by reason, to the *experience* of God rooted in *revelation*.[20] To respond to the age of reason, theologians became much more rational. We could look at the rise of the iGods as the triumph of computation, algorithms as Authority. However, I want to suggest that the expansion of their digital kingdom is also about material abundance. It is a lived *experience* rooted in *revelation*. We need a poetic, God-centered *theo*-logy to address an age of acceleration. Our theology must affirm the physical world amid mental, rational, and numbering functions. We are more than a gadget, and our ethics must be found in far more than an algorithm. An embodied faith rooted in the real world will enable us to resist a gnostic ascent into virtual kingdoms.

God's first command in the Bible was to be fruitful and multiply. We have been up to the task. Early church father Tertullian (AD 160–240) noted how "farms have replaced wastelands, cultivated land has subdued the forests, cattle have put to flight the wild beast, barren lands have become fertile, rocks have become soil, swamps have been drained, and the number of cities exceeds the number of poor huts found in former times. . . . Everywhere there are people, communities—everywhere there is human life!"[21] He worried that "the world is full. The elements scarcely suffice us. Our needs press."[22] Two millennia later, we are equally overwhelmed by our fruitfulness. Our knowledge, our information, our playlists have multiplied. We have filled our brains with data, but we don't know how to subdue it. Humanity gave names to all the animals in the garden of Eden, but we can no longer name everything in sight. The diversity of our world, the proximity of what's possible has overwhelmed us. Becoming like God has fried our brains. To use the metaphor of our era, our hard drives are full and threatening to crash.

Religion used to order our world. It was a way of numbering our days, making sense of the seasons. A church calendar told us what we should be thinking about. Changes in the color of the priests' vestments sent us signals: sacred times are ahead. In the wake of rampant acceleration, we have placed our faith in technology to inform us, organize us, and sustain us. We expect it to function so seamlessly that it can also entertain us at the same time. Silicon Valley is ruled by numerical efficiency that rewards faster, cheaper, smaller, and more. This techno-monarchy, mediated via electronic devices connected to the internet, has overwhelmed us with abundance.

Such abundance can be frustrating and even maddening. In Genesis 1, Father, Son, and Spirit brought order to chaos, separating light from darkness, land from sea. Having set the stage, God commanded us to be fruitful and multiply. Now, we are drowning in a sea of creativity. We have too many books, songs, shows, and stuff to choose from. We are distracted by our choices, burdened by too many friends, and overwhelmed by too many options to enjoy. So what was God's response to too much fruitfulness and creativity? Rest. He enjoyed the splendor. He spread it around. He invited us all to the party. Can we learn to admire our handiwork, to revel in all that the internet offers, to be grateful for another day, another click, another virtual connection?

Jean-Luc Marion writes in terms of excess—the overwhelming charity of God that infuses our life. He revels in the captivating presence of God that arrests our brain. Irish philosopher and storyteller Peter Rollins suggests that our sense of being overwhelmed by these challenges could be a good thing:

> A revelation worthy of the name involves *epistemological incomprehension . . .* what we have encountered cannot be understood within our current intellectual structures. Second, there is *experiential bedazzlement . . .* a type of oversatura-tion in which our experience is overcome. One is overwhelmed by the incoming and short-circuited by it. Third, there is an *existential transformation.* When a revelation occurs, the person who is receiving it is never the same again.[23]

This resonates with our experience of abundance, our sense that there is simply too much of everything to process. Rather than trying to control it, perhaps we need to learn how to simply embrace or receive it. Revelation is God's download to us. Theology is our upload in appreciative response; neither may fit in a status update or a tweet.

We obeyed God's first command; we filled the earth, but we couldn't subdue it. Adam and Eve tried to possess all knowledge, but such presumption proved deadly. Their efforts to dominate the garden of Eden got them kicked out. We face a similar temptation today. Control seems to reside in our fingertips; access to all is packed into a digital device. The flood of resulting information feels more like a form of judgment, threatening to drown us. We needed a lifesaving ark. As Noah once rescued the animals, so Apple, Google, Amazon, Facebook, and Twitter became the lifelines to keep us afloat. They appear magical (even godlike) because they solved our abundance problems. They put a filter around the flood, making the flow more manageable. Apple's computers arrived like a rainbow, assuring us that all was safe. Google extended an olive branch that told us it was safe to search. We lionize their leaders as oracles who can foresee the future, programmers on high. These technological icons became entrepreneurial idols—the iGods we adore.

The primeval prologue in Genesis concludes with a cautionary tale about attempts to become like God. Noah's offspring included Nimrod, a mighty hunter whose kingdom began with Babel. They built a tower in Babel to reach heaven and make a name for themselves before God leveled such presumption. History has come to judge such self-seeking as Nimrod's folly. Today's tech leaders built platforms to elevate our status. Apple has given us the illusion of control—packing our friends, our followers, our schedules, and our diversions into one essential device—the iPhone. We poured riches upon these techno-lords in appreciation. The iGods of Amazon, Google, Facebook, and Twitter have responded to our praise by offering us a form of divination. We can extend our brand, broaden our reach, and spread our Klout by joining the digital parade. Yes, it can be exhausting to be an iGod. The electronic din can resemble the confusion that followed Nimrod's folly. At Babel, everyone was talking, but no one could understand. They were confused.[24] The iGods continue to insist that active participation in virtual technologies ensures a lasting impact. We will make a name for ourselves; our profiles will live on. Technologists have faith in the future and confidence in progress. They await the coming of the Singularity, when machines surpass humanity, our tweets become eternal, and world peace prevails. Technology is an alternative religion where faith in progress is manifested in a faster, smarter, more efficient world. Such cyber-utopianism, reflected by rave reviews in *Wired*, seemingly knows no bounds.

The distribution of the abundance remains a problem; not everyone is plugged in. While the iGods have prospered, those outside the platforms have yet to be lifted up. Automation has decimated large segments of the former middle class.[25] The annual TED (Technology/Education/Design) conference is an admirable effort to promote "ideas worth spreading." TEDsters are committed to solving hunger, combating poverty, eradicating disease. It is an ambitious and inspiring movement rooted in human potential. I hope it sparks far more lifesaving arks than misguided towers to the sky.

Jesus showed us there was more than enough to go around. He fed five thousand people with two fish and five loaves of bread. He blended crowdsourcing with communion. We have never been closer to one another before—more aware of strife and hunger, able to respond more quickly to need. We are still growing into our calling as stewards and shepherds and cultivators. Despite the pain in our past, we are heading toward a massive party, celebrating the mystic sweet communion of Jesus and his bride, the church. So we must plant and harvest toward the great banquet, preparing the bottomless cup of wine, baking the baskets of bread overflowing.

We need a theology of abundance to deal with the outcomes of our technology, the massive fruitfulness that the Creator God baked into us. We need a theology of abundance equal to the grace and generosity found in the blood of Jesus poured out for many. We need a theology of abundance commensurate with the superabundant presence of the Holy Spirit that can flood our senses, short-circuit our rationale. Unfortunately, our economics is built on a model of scarcity, and our theology feels equally impoverished.

We've argued about who's in and who's out, separating, while God called us to simply gather everybody, two by two. The confusion that pulled us apart at Babel has been reversed by the cohesion of the Spirit, speaking to and through every tongue and tribe and nation. We've been focused on what we don't have while Jesus multiplies the two fish and five loaves he's already provided. We've been hoarding when we should have been sharing. Our technology allows us fewer claims to ignorance. The age of accountability and metrics is here. We can study the numbers, but we must remember that each number is actually a person, created by God, worthy of our attention. You are not a number or an outcome. You are not a gadget. You are far more than your social profile.

While the algorithms offer pictures of our collective behavior, discipleship still comes down to a life on a life. We are children of God, called to love and serve God's children. Let's figure out how to live out our faith in tangible ways, each hyperaccelerated day.

Key Words

Key words like *access*, *aesthetics*, *abundance*, *algorithms*, *authority*, and *authenticity* will drive our discussion. The first big hurdle on the internet was *access*. Companies like AOL and Earthlink competed to dial us into the world wide web. Smartphones gave access to people and countries that never experienced a landline. Our machines offer us more access and more computing speed at more affordable prices every day. We are so busy texting that we rarely pause to question if access is always preferable. We exchange our privacy for access, and we may be losing our sense of agency in the process.

Another key word is *aesthetics*. Steve Jobs's commitment to aesthetics turned amateurs into professionals, and the Macintosh unleashed a torrent of creativity from desktop publishing to editing home videos. Users developed an eye for design, admiring the gadgets that hold our electronic information.

We'll also discuss *abundance*. If nothing else, today's technology can be described as abundant! Communication originated as a one-to-one, person-to-person, aural activity. Then the printing press made duplication scalable, and the electronic era allowed one radio station or television network to reach millions.[26] Next Apple made computers accessible to nontechnical people, and the iPhone transformed us all into broadcasters. Never have so many people been able to create and distribute so many words and images. We are uploading our videos and updating our statuses in dizzying ways. We are inundated by too much information (of our own making). We desperately need a theology of abundance to figure out how to respond to this strange, new problem.

To solve this information overload, we have turned to *algorithms*. The engineers at Google created algorithms that gave us the ability to comb through the thicket of the world wide web. They brought order to a chaotic environment. Complex mathematical equations now drive our decision making, from what to buy, to which route to take, to whom to date. Algorithms filter our news and answer our questions.

Our traditional sources of *authority* are shifting, from people to programs, from God to Google. Google knows where to find answers, but does it understand my individual quirks and taste? Who can we trust as an authority in a time of too many options? Amazon recommended what to read. Netflix told us what to watch. Thanks to Twitter, we learned to follow the crowd, but the signals are still mixed. Should we click on the most viewed, the most emailed, or the most liked?

Authenticity was a vexing problem on the internet until Facebook gave us the ability to gather all our favorite people, those we know and trust, in one convenient place. We also made new friends thanks to old friends' recommendations. Our networks expanded and Facebook didn't let us hide behind pseudonyms or avatars. We were challenged to put our history, our education, even our religious beliefs out in the open. Such authenticity felt exhilarating until Facebook started exploiting our friends' recommendations, turning our trust into commerce.

This book explores the problems generated by abundance, the promises offered by algorithms, and our ongoing search for authenticity. Social media is such a relatively new phenomenon that we've barely had time to consider how it is redefining community. We have plugged into our smartphones without a sense of how they affect our relationships to family, friends, and even the Almighty.

Who Should Read This Book?

We vacillate between feeling empowered by and powerless in the wake of the iGods' influence. Digital natives have all the tools in hand but may benefit from some perspective. Parents, teachers, and pastors wonder how to compete with the electronic distractions. The ease of access, the pace of acceleration, and the division of attention show no signs of abating. We are all rats who seem to have signed up for the same race—acquiring more bits and bytes than we can possibly process.

For those who already feel overwhelmed by too much information, this book will include tales from an accelerated culture. The mobiquity of smartphones (adopted by ever younger users) guarantees that the next generation will have more access to more information at earlier ages. In an era of too much information, the need for discernment and wisdom will be greater than ever.

Consider this book an active resistance to a thoughtless embrace. I want to awaken our senses, to make room for thought, for contemplation, for beauty, for God. How might Christians recover these ancient and timeless virtues in a wired era?

This book is for parents, teachers, and pastors. As a parent of two digital natives, I wrestle with questions of what is appropriate and when. We used to worry about the age of accountability. Now, we measure rites of passage according to when they get their first cell phone. And should it be just a phone? What about the ability to text? Is internet access a problem, making a phone too smart? Once the phone enters the teenager's (or child's) life, what are the times and limits? Should it be used only for emergencies? Pulled out of a backpack only during lunch and between classes? What about using the phone in a bedroom? Should it be turned off at night?

Educators too wrestle with how to teach children who enter their classroom with a phone in tow. Assignments and pedagogy must change to accommodate a generation that has all the basic answers at their fingertips. Innovators like Sal Khan aim to replace higher education altogether (or at least to make it affordable to all). As technology disrupted the newspaper business and the music industry, could the Khan Academy (an online library of educational lectures) undermine colleges and universities? We must figure out how to incorporate smartphones and tablets into our educational process. And, surprisingly, less may turn out to be more.

Finally, how should pastors respond to parishioners who make their primary connections via Facebook? Youth ministers are already engaged in online ministry. As virtual communities continue to flourish, faith communities are still figuring out how to respond. Surveys have found that the larger the church, the broader their embrace of new technologies. To organize a crowd, they turn to electronic mail and social networks. To underscore a pastor's sermon, they rely on video screens and stage lighting. Churches often buy the latest gear out of instinct rather than theology. This book is an effort to hit pause, to challenge us to consider how technology shapes worship, before we consider how our worship should shape a congregation. Hopefully, this book will answer such practical questions in a thoughtful and theological way.

While I acknowledge the pastoral and parental concerns, I am primarily interested in the theological shifts accompanying technological upheaval. I see most of us buying phones for our children without pausing to consider the changes that will happen in their thoughts and practices. Students are awakened by their cell phones in the morning and say goodnight on Facebook and Twitter. While this book is informed by know-how, I want us to know *why*. It is primarily a theology of technology. We will consider the history and the philosophy of technology in light of spiritual implications. We will study wildly successful companies in an effort to uncover our enduring questions. I am hopeful that the results will be worthwhile for students and teachers, pastors and parents. Questions at the end of each chapter are designed to provoke face-to-face group discussions.

The Goal

British economist E. F. Schumacher wrote in his prescient 1973 book *Small Is Beautiful*, "Wisdom demands a new orientation of science and technology towards the organic, the gentle, the non-violent, the elegant and beautiful."[27]

Many books have been written about how millions of dollars were made (and lost) during the dot-com bubble. These books profile the people who rose so quickly from obscurity to infamy. Plenty of how-to manuals discuss launching a company and capitalizing on social media. This book will include some history, some descriptions, but mostly analysis—not just how these companies came to be but what these technologies are doing to us and through us. This book is an effort to grasp how technology alters our hearts and minds. We need to understand how Google works but also what Google does to our understanding of who we are and whose we are. I want us to consider what that smartphone in our pocket can and can't accomplish. I hope readers will be challenged to move beyond data and information gathering toward understanding and wisdom. The goals of system analyzers and technologists mirror those of professors and priests. We want to shift people from data to wisdom.[28]

The Bible holds up wisdom as a rare and precious goal. It is worth striving for, setting aside distractions for, doing everything we can to obtain. The Proverbs of Solomon are collected "for gaining wisdom and instruction; for understanding words of insight; for receiving instruction in prudent behavior; doing what is right and just and fair."[29] Augustine called it faith seeking understanding. Yes, we have the information provided by the Bible. We have the knowledge to understand how it all fits together, to see the big picture of biblical history, but do we have the wisdom to apply ancient truths to today's situation? G. K. Chesterton famously declared theology as that part of religion that requires brains. It can feel ponderous or off-putting, an academic study of God, but that is not the whole of our calling. We must translate that theology into meaningful action. Wisdom involves acting on our convictions, applying the Word of God in a thoughtful and appropriate manner.

If science is an accurate description of how the world works, technology is putting fundamental truths of biology, chemistry, and physics into action. We may not grasp all scientific truths, but we welcome the results that bless our lives via better technologies. Theology can seem lofty, abstract, or remote. Like science, it can sound intimidating. Yet, our beliefs invariably drive our decision making. The goal is to turn our beliefs into practices. Our head, our heart, and our hands should be aligned in purposeful actions. If technology is applied science, then faith is applied theology. Karl Barth allegedly encouraged young theologians to live with the Bible in one hand and the newspaper in the other.[30] Both those texts are now gathered in a single device. We are challenged to unlock the Bible contained within our smartphone. This captivating device, tied to all of human knowledge, could lead us to folly or wisdom.

Technology has been largely a nerdy boys' world, full of pissing contests and monopolizing egos. The press cast Bill Gates and Microsoft as the techno-villain, trying to control all. Windows was painted as the evil, unimaginative operating system. Jobs and Apple got plenty of mileage playing the underdog. In countless Mac-vs.-PC ads, Apple juxtaposed the drab, boring bean counter in a suit with the hip, relaxed Apple user with his shirttail out. Under his wife Melinda's positive influence, Gates turned into the most generous, global-minded technologist of our era. Through the Giving Pledge, the Bill and Melinda Gates Foundation has dared fellow billionaires toward benevolence. Rather than following the single-minded empire building of Jobs, Mark Zuckerberg has joined the Gates Foundation by vowing to give away the billions generated by Facebook. It is interesting that wisdom is personified as a woman throughout the book of Proverbs: "Do not forsake wisdom, and she will protect you; love her, and she will watch over you."[31] The entire tech world could benefit from more female influence. Executives like Marissa Meyer at Yahoo! and Sheryl Sandberg of Facebook are making headlines, challenging the next generation to lean in.[32] The next wave of iGods may be remembered for their generous hearts and transformative practices—sustaining wisdom.

Next Steps

German philosopher Martin Heidegger defined technology as a "challenging revealing." I am studying technology as a potential source of divine revelation. God was the first technologist who put a tool in our hands and challenged us to till the earth. We've been (re)producing ever since. In examining why particular companies have come to dominate our culture, I hope to uncover the deeper longings that they unlocked. The success of the iGods is intoxicating. The promises of technology are alluring. The temptation to become iGods of our own making is ever present. What can we learn from their best practices without being blinded by their wealth, fame, and utopian ideals?

A master craftsman is entirely at home with his medium, having full knowledge of its possibilities. The ancient Greeks associated *technē* with *episteme*, since both were forms of knowing. In an artist's hands, a block of wood could be transformed into a shoe, a pipe, or a musical instrument. Michelangelo could see the sculpture contained in the marble, waiting to be revealed. Wind, water, and oil were ever present. But it took millennia before we recognized their energizing power. Technology reveals the potential contained in our physical world. What powers have today's technologists tapped into and how might God be working through them?

Chapter 1 will attempt to define technology. Our relationship with technology alters our understanding of our world and of God. What we believe is shaped by the technologies that surround us. I want us to consider the nature of technology itself—is it a lifesaving gift a la Noah's Ark or a form of folly like the tower of Babel? The short answer is "yes."

Chapter 2 explores why Steve Jobs should be celebrated for creating (with Steve Wozniak) the revolutionary Macintosh computer. The press subsequently hyped each new rollout of an Apple product with rapturous headlines and cover stories. *Newsweek* declared, "iPod, therefore iAM." *Gizmodo* (the gadget guide) announced, "The Jesus Phone is finally here." For the iPad, Jobs climbed down from Cupertino to deliver tablets from on high. The glowing tributes that followed his death elevated him to a hallowed position reserved for few American entrepreneurs. He had become an iGod, both the creator and the redeemer within the cult of Mac.

Chapter 3 is a brief history of the internet, how the invention of the world wide web paved the way for ecommerce. Chapters 4 and 5 explain why the creators of Amazon and Google have also been celebrated for their ability to spawn billion-dollar businesses. They tapped into algorithmic authority to simplify our shopping and solve our searches. I spell out what people of faith can learn from these inventors. And I also explore what aspects of their groundbreaking technology we would be wise to resist.

After a brief history of social networking in chapter 6, I delve into an examination of our favorite frenemy, Facebook. In chapter 7, I discuss why so many of us have surrendered personal information in order to connect with friends. I also consider the ways in which Facebook potentially undermines our friendships, making us lonely and jealous.

Chapter 8 will address the demigods, angling for the iGods' place. YouTube, Twitter, and Instagram have all captured a significant audience. These delivery systems invite us to participate by broadcasting our talents, our passions, and our whereabouts. Their primary attributes are convenience and speed. They allow us to communicate quickly, efficiently, and broadly.

Finally, my conclusion will consider the *telos* of technology—where is the drive for smaller, faster, and smarter gadgets taking us? Cyber-optimists have profound faith in technology's ability to solve global problems. While Christians turn to the book of Revelation to envision the future, technologists build their eschatology around the noosphere (a collective mind) and the Singularity (a technological superintelligence). We will consider where their faith is misplaced and suggest how we can adopt a proper perspective on technology to build God's vision of a heavenly city. We need an embodied, incarnational faith amidst a digitized era.

Discuss

1. What technologies are you grateful for? How have they improved or complicated your life?
2. In what ways are you tethered to technology? Is it serving you or enslaving you?

Defining Technology

Jesus was more than a carpenter; he was a techie. The Greek word describing Jesus's trade in the Gospel texts is *tektōn* (τέκτων).[2] Strong's Greek lexicon defines a *tektōn* as a worker in wood, a carpenter, joiner, or builder. It may include a ship's carpenter or any craftsman or workman. A *tektōn* may also refer to those accomplished in the art of poetry, a maker of songs, or an author. He may be a planner, a contriver, or a plotter.[3] When the crowd refers to Jesus with the derogative question, "Isn't this the *tektōn*?" or "Is not this the son of the *tektōn*?" most translations refer to Jesus as a carpenter's son. It was intended as a cut-down, a way to mock Jesus's presumption. How can an unskilled laborer presume to position himself as a prophet? My esteemed provost at Pepperdine University, Darryl Tippens, pointed out to me the potential double entendre embedded in the question, "Isn't this the artisan, the maker of things?" It could also have been read after the fact as "Is not this the son of the Artisan, the Maker of (all) Things?"[4]

In his book *Pilgrim Heart*, Tippens calls Jesus the Great Artist, the model for how we are to respond to beauty. He writes,

> If God is the Master Builder, then Christ is the supervising architect and agent of Creation: "for in him all things in heaven and on earth were created, things

visible and invisible . . . all things have been created through him and for him. He himself is before all things, and in him all things hold together" (Col. 1:15–17). Given this original cosmic assignment, it seems appropriate that in his earthly life in Nazareth, Jesus was a craftsman by trade. Having built the universe, it seems fitting that, as a human being, he would turn to building houses or furniture.[5]

In his effort to determine Jesus's occupation, New Testament scholar Ken M. Campbell focuses on Jesus's teaching. Campbell found that Jesus makes far more references to construction and finance than agricultural allusions. Israel is a land of ample stone but comparatively few trees. Perhaps it is wise to think of Jesus more as a mason than a carpenter. Campbell notes that Jesus makes almost no reference to the carpenter's craft but does refer to the importance of selecting a cornerstone (Matt. 21:42–44) and the decoration of tombs (Matt. 23:27–28), the importance of building on a firm foundation (Matt. 7:24–27), and the need to conduct careful cost analysis prior to construction (Luke 14:28–30). Campbell surmises, "In light of all this knowledge of the building trade it is hard to resist the conclusion that Jesus was involved in construction."[6] He may have specialized, but given the technology of the time, it is easy to imagine Jesus being well acquainted with winepresses, millstones, olive press stones, tombstones, cisterns, farm terraces, vineyards, and watchtowers. We might call such a builder a tinkerer or a jack-of-all-trades.

We may call upon a *tektōn* to construct a mansion or to fix our roof. They may carry a wrench and be handy with a hammer. In the entertainment industry (and many churches), a *tektōn* is comparable to a techie. They may be involved in lighting or set construction. These stagehands may be called upon to fly in a set or place props between scenes. Techies are always equipped with a flashlight. They wear headsets, carry walkie-talkies, and are comfortable behind a board. Techies keep up with the latest gadgets and gear. They can assemble homemade computers from component parts (a Hackintosh!) that run on open source software like Linux. They dress in black so they can go about their business backstage so quietly and surreptitiously that we only focus on the show. If problems arise, they can usually patch it up with a piece of electrical gaffer's tape. Techies are invariably overworked and underpaid. They may be derided as geeks or take pride in running with the nerd herd. Often, they are barely noticed. Was Jesus a carpenter, a builder, or a mason? Perhaps he was a techie, an artisan content to make others look good.

Technology Is an Art

While we like to think that our theology shapes our understanding of the world, our understanding of the world often shapes our theology. The central metaphors of an era will often shift our notions of God. When Benedictine monks introduced the mechanical clock, we became far more aware of time. As we studied the gears of the clock, it became much easier to imagine God as the great Watchmaker in the sky, setting the planets in motion. What if the earth revolved around the sun, rather than the planets encircling us? The Copernican revolution altered our theology. Church leaders viewed advances in astronomy brought about by Galileo and his telescope as a threat. Eventually, we spoke more about the heavens than heaven. Our defining technologies tend to define us (and our beliefs).

If we need a fresh understanding of Jesus's trade, perhaps we also need a broader definition of technology. We tend to think of technology as something shiny and new, what Alan Kay describes as "anything that was invented after you were born."[7] The roots of technology, however, are ancient, embedded in the primeval prologue of the Bible. From the beginning, God was bringing order to chaos, trying to get things under control.

The word *technology* stems from the ancient Greek *technikon*, which belongs to the concept of *technē*. Philosopher Martin Heidegger describes *technē* as "the name not only for the activity and skills of the craftsman, but also for the arts of the mind and the fine arts."[8] We tend to think of technology as more science than art, but we often use the term "state-of-the-art technology." It reminds us that technology is more art than science, or at least an applied science dependent on art. (Could this be a key for holding arts and sciences together?) Heidegger links *technē* to a bringing forth, to the notion of *poiesis*. It is something *poietic*, akin to the original understanding of poetry. At its best, technology is a creative act, merging thought with matter and time. Creation can be seen as God's poetry, the realization of word and image, ideas made manifest.

Can we see computer code as equally poetic and potentially beautiful? Technologist Kevin Kelly suggests, "If a thousand lines of letters in UNIX qualifies as a technology, . . . then a thousand lines of letters in English (*Hamlet*) must qualify as well. They both can change our behavior, alter the course of events, or enable future inventions. A Shakespeare sonnet and a Bach fugue, then, are in the same category as Google's search engine and the iPod. They are something useful produced by a mind."[9] Perhaps we need to recover the art of technology.

Technology Is Not Neutral

Those who've felt the roar of a tank, breathed the gas in chemical warfare, or experienced the fallout from a nuclear meltdown find it difficult to call technology neutral. In the wrong hands, it appears deadly and malicious. Technology reflects human complexity, both our remarkable potential for beauty and our frightening power to destroy. We can bless our neighbors with lifesaving therapies or exact vengeance in a flash of blinding light. The same technologies that our National Security Agency uses to monitor our calls and online activities can intercept a terrorists' plot or snoop on our private lives.

The brilliant Catholic Canadian media theorist Marshall McLuhan also insisted that technology is never neutral. In *The Gutenberg Galaxy* (1962), he pointed out that "any technology tends to create a new human environment. . . . Technological environments are not merely passive containers of people but are active processes that reshape people and other technologies alike."[10] He spoke in terms of media ecology, noting how technology alters our senses. His writing was an effort to describe the technology we were swimming in. McLuhan cut through the first flush of electronic media, giving us an initial handle on how to define technology before it redefined us. McLuhan invited us to step outside our electronic inputs long enough to gain some perspective, to consider the delivery systems as the shaping story. We may have faith in technology, but it should never be blind.

Technology as Applied Science

We enjoy the benefits of technology without understanding almost any of the science behind it. We rarely ask how an app works; we download it and go. In his 1984 study of technology and the character of contemporary life, philosopher Albert Borgmann draws important distinctions between science and technology. Science defines and explains how the world works. Technology involves a determination to act transformatively on these possibilities.[11] Science uncovers real-world principles (like gravity). Technologists figure out how to apply or overcome them (with rocket ships). American schoolchildren may lag behind China in scientific test scores while still enthusiastically embracing each new update of the iPhone. We can be completely ignorant about how or why something works and yet still relish the results.

Scientist Ursula Franklin sees technology as a process, how something is done. As a metallurgist, she understands it as a way of doing things, a practice handed down.[12] The prehistoric bronze bells and urns contained in the Shanghai Museum reveal remarkable sophistication. The *Bronze Bo with Four Tigers* from 771 BC merges art and craft, science and technology to form an enduring musical instrument. The craftsmen may not have understood the chemistry behind why bronze could be molded when heated, but their artistic results speak volumes about their humanity. Franklin distinguishes between holistic processes (like the craft of sewing) and the prescriptive processes that arose in the industrial revolution. Production is a system formed by a mind-set. Standards like "bigger is better" elevate unchecked growth to the highest good. Technology transformed sewing from a handcrafted art into a machine-driven industry.

Technology Is More Than a Product

We rarely pause to consider the origins of the products or devices we hold (and that hold us). Borgmann derides the device paradigm that dissolves our old ways of approaching the world by how things work. In our electronic gadgets, the machinery is concealed; the circuit board is often beyond our understanding. The complexity of the device itself pushes us toward consumption rather than comprehension. We are cut off from context, both how it works and how it was made.[13] Think about big-box stores like Best Buy, Walmart, and Costco. We have no idea how the goods are made or how they get there. Reports of suicidal workers assembling iPhones in China fall on deaf ears.[14] We have no relationship to the people selling the goods either; it is all anonymous.

Since we don't know how things are made, we also don't know how to fix them. Borgmann remarks that "devices make things disposable. We don't know how microprocessors are made or how they are fixed. So we just toss out old phones. Care, repair, bodily engagement are removed from our understanding of the device. So we can only consume it. We can't care for it, nurture it, repair it."[15] Old recording and playback devices form a toxic trail behind us. DVRs replaced VCRs. The Walkman gave way to the iPod. The Blackberry was displaced by the iPhone. Today's technology will likely be tomorrow's landfill.

Technology Can Bring Us Together

Technology is the new tie that binds us, that brings us together. From chat rooms to social networks, we have formed countless virtual communities. For professionals, technology is how we get LinkedIn. Children congregate at Club Penguin. Teens prefer the self-destructing messages of Snapchat. Tech companies appoint evangelists to spread the word about their products. Newspapers and magazines position for the privilege to report on the new iWhatever. We line up outside the Apple store, hoping to catch a glimpse or even touch the hem of the iPhone's garment. We are so eager for connection that we willingly bind ourselves to long-term cell phone contracts. We set countless alerts and updates that interrupt our day. It is not unusual to abandon a task for a trip through Facebook's looking glass. Few things capture our attention more completely.

What is a person who wants to follow Jesus and Twitter supposed to do? Are we in a situation similar to the one that Jesus warned against: "No one can serve two masters"?[16] Would he insist that you cannot serve both God and Google? The former editor of *Wired*, Kevin Kelly, sees technology stepping into the gap formed by the decline of religion's influence. He suggests, "Because values and meaning are scarce today, technology will make our decisions for us. We'll listen to technology because our modern ears listen to little else. In the absence of other firm beliefs, we'll let technology steer. No other force is as powerful in shaping our destiny. By imagining what technology wants, we can imagine the course of our culture."[17] As noted in the introduction, technology has become a new religion, a way to make sense of the world.

Technology Is Not a Panacea

In ancient Greece, Panacea was the goddess of universal remedies; we have faith in technologies to solve our problems. Jonas Salk saved millions of lives

with the polio vaccine that he gave away for free. I am grateful for the che-
motherapies that healed my wife of Hodgkin's lymphoma. Simple technology like a mosquito net can guard against malaria. Efforts to distribute One
Laptop Per Child were hailed as an educational breakthrough, yet four years
after the program was launched in Peru, test scores in mathematics and science remain the same.[18] The Global Alliance for Clean Cookstoves aimed
to reduce respiratory ailments and enhance air quality in India. A study of
15,000 homes over five years determined that after the initial year, few of the
stoves were maintained or still in use. Controversy continues to swirl around
Monsanto's genetically modified corn. We often don't recognize the downside
of new technologies until after they're introduced.

Our fastest growing churches are largely embracing electronic technology—
but often without adequate theological reflection. A *Faith Communities Today*
survey found that the embrace of technology corresponded to the size of the
congregation. The bigger and wealthier the church, the more likely they were
to incorporate technologies, from stage lights to podcasts. Congregations with
major tech use (electronic instruments, projection screens) also demonstrate
a greater clarity of vision and purpose and more active recruiting among its
members. Pastors must not conclude that technology is a panacea for a dwin-
dling congregation. Scott Thumma of the Hartford Institute for Religious
Research insists, "It is not a matter of having a webpage, a Facebook account
or projection screens, but of using these to enhance and expand the activities
and communal life of the congregation."[19] We cannot place our faith in technology as the solution to our congregational ills. We need a robust theology
of technology to precede our adoption of lights, cameras, and action. Bigger,
louder, and faster don't necessarily create deeper disciples.

Technology Can Be a Temptation and a Tyrant

Before cell phones, we had pagers. They were given to traveling salesmen as a
way to track their whereabouts. A pager offered a not-too-subtle way for the
boss to insist, "Call me now." When I was in film school, working for a commercial production company, I remember my manager referring to his pager
as a digital leash. While the production staff and interns went away for the
weekend, completely out of reach, the manager was on call, answerable to his
boss and his clients. He experienced technology as a tyrant.

Now, we struggle to respond to the always-on demands of text and Twitter. We don't want to miss out on news or opportunities. So we are always available, ever reachable. The updates are so constant that we don't know how to turn them off, when to shut down. We wake up to email alerts and say goodnight on Facebook. We feel more fragmented and harried than ever. Technology designed to manage our schedules, our relationships, and our environment has left us feeling out of control.

Devices designed to organize our schedules have made us busier than ever. Families have fragmented along technological lines. Nights that used to be spent gathered around the fire gave way to the radio and television, before splintering into individualized screens. We inhabit the same space but follow our own feeds. We have an iPhone in our hand and buds in our ears. How can we hear God (or each other) amid the din?

Researchers at the Barna Group have found that Christians increasingly see technology as a temptation.[20] When asked what tempts us, many Americans list the ancient sins of gluttony (eating too much), avarice (spending too much money), envy (gossiping and jealousy), and lust (viewing pornography). Yet, 44 percent of people listed "spending too much time on media" as a gnawing temptation, and 11 percent tried to resist "going off on someone via text or email." It is easier to flame someone when they're not in front of us. Comments on Facebook and Twitter can be riddled with ridicule and scorn. We love our devices and loathe what they do to us.

Technology Is about Control

Borgmann defines technology as the systematic process of trying to get everything under control.[21] From massive projects like paving a road or building a dam to smaller projects like cleaning our house or coordinating our calendars, we are forever attempting to control our environment. Perhaps we are merely following God, the original technologist. The first creative act was bringing order to chaos. In the beginning, the earth was formless and empty. In Genesis 1, God brought shalom to a volatile situation. *Elohim* separated light from darkness, day from night, earth from sky, land from sea. God set the stage for humanity, providing a space to inhabit and plants and animals to provide for our needs. The results were good, even very good.

God blesses humanity and issues instructions: "Be fruitful and increase in number; fill the earth and subdue it. Rule over the fish in the sea and the birds in the sky and over every living creature that moves on the ground."[22] Fruitfulness and filling sound like fun. The King James Version challenges us to "replenish the earth." It implies we must pour into or even replace whatever we harvest. If we cut down a tree, we should plant a new one. However, problems arise from our understanding of subdue and rule—in Hebrew, *kvsh* and *rdh*. Subdue has echoes of a power move when we demand that others submit to our authority or serve as a subjugated peoples. Does God want us to strong-arm the earth? Lexicons translate the verb *rdh* as "have dominion, rule, dominate."[23] Images of conquering armies or bulldozers spring to mind. Does Genesis sanction domination, treading on and trampling the earth? This could create biblical justification to kill as many animals, to knock down as many forests, to siphon as much ore and oil from the earth as can be found.

Lynn White traced "The Historical Roots of Our Ecological Crisis" back to Genesis 1:26–28. The study provided biblical justification from whence all manner of unsustainable technology sprang. White wrote, "Christianity, in absolute contrast to ancient paganism and Asia's religions . . . not only established a dualism of man and nature but also insisted that it is God's will that man exploit nature for his proper ends."[24] The engines of the industrial revolution churn from these verses.

The results have been deadly and dangerous. Martin Heidegger suggested, "Contemporary man's inveterate drive to master whatever confronts him is plain for all to see. Technology treats itself with 'objectivity.' The modern technologist is regularly expected, and expects himself, to be able to impose order on all data, to 'process' every sort of entity, nonhuman and human alike, and to devise solutions for every kind of problem. He is forever getting things under control."[25] Why is technology such a driven business? Why do we desperately want to master nature and exert control? When we treat the earth as an object, we dehumanize ourselves.

Thankfully, theologians like Sallie McFague and faith-fueled activists like Bill McKibben have helped us see another side to Scripture. The Hebrew words *kvsh* and *rdh* can sanction conquering and control, but consider what kind of control God demonstrated. Creation arose from holding back chaos. In our calling to be like God, we are commanded to subdue the earth in similar ways. It is closer in spirit to beating down a path or forging a footpath.

Perhaps we should conjure images of keeping the weeds, the rodents, and the insects under control. What kind of rule are we supposed to enact? In Genesis 1, God modeled creativity and benevolence, pouring out blessings on humanity. Throughout the Bible, good kings are contrasted with evil rulers. Just leaders practice shalom, demonstrating particular concern for the poor and needy, the widows and the orphans.[26] Godly dominion is marked by care and concern for the least of these. It is rooted in interdependence rather than personal gain. What a far cry from greedy or tyrannical despots. McFague notes the contrast between these competing visions of our calling in Genesis: "The first model sees the planet as a corporation or syndicate, as a collection of human beings drawn together to benefit its members by optimal use of natural resources. The second model sees the planet more like an organism or community that survives and prospers through the interrelationship and interdependence of its many parts, both human and nonhuman."[27] Genesis 1:28 is a call to responsible rule. While God rests from creating, our job is to keep chaos at bay.

Technology Should Be about Creating and Cultivating

In Genesis 2, we get a more detailed take on our calling. Man now has a name, "Adam," and his first job is to name things, to makes sense of all of God's generative activity. Adam engages in sorting, filing, labeling. Maybe not according to genus and species but certainly a broad separation between birds, livestock, fish. Humanity is called to distinguish among living creatures, to pay attention to our surroundings, to notice the differences, to celebrate the diversity. This process of observing our world, assigning names, developing categories is at the root of our endless information gathering. Many, many centuries before Google, we were involved in organizing things, cataloging, giving each and every thing an identifiable (and eventually searchable) name. Like Adam, woman gets a particular name, Eve. Before hunting and gathering came labeling. We were born to organize.

God places humanity in the garden for a dual purpose: "to tend and to keep it."[28] Tend is a translation of the Hebrew verb *abd*, which means "to work or serve." How do we serve a garden? Some translations insert the agricultural terms "till" or "cultivate." The King James Version opts for "dress." It implies an active adornment, embellishment, or even improvement. When we tend a garden, it should yield far more than when we started. "To keep," from the Hebrew word *shmr*, means "to exercise great care over." Adam and Eve are given a responsibility to watch over the garden like a loving caretaker. We are called to make something more out of what we've been given. Our calling is to care and to cultivate, to create culture in all its myriad forms—from agriculture to the arts.

It is our job to nurture the earth, to replant what we harvest, to protect the fish supply, to guard the rain forest. Technology can yield solar power, more robust crops, and longer life. Thanks to breakthroughs in science, we have eradicated so many life-threatening diseases. Technology has allowed us to thrive. It is a God-given blessing, making our world much more habitable.

We have two very different views of technology, of how we are to live in this world. Genesis 1 could be construed as all-consuming domination, but Genesis 2 is clearly about cultivation and caretaking. Perhaps these are the two competing poles of technology—to make us more efficient consumers or to make us more thoughtful creators. Technology can be used to exploit and devalue the earth or it can be a boon and blessing to all. How we define technology may determine what we do with it.

How Technologies Define Us

Technologies reflect our culture and our values. In his prescient 1999 book, *God and the Chip*, William Stahl observes how "it has become common to define our species as *Homo faber*, 'man the tool-maker,' and to identify cultures with their technology—neolithic, Stone Age, Bronze Age, Space Age. . . . We increasingly come to identify who we are by and through the machines we use."[29] J. David Bolter studied "defining technologies" across history. Bolter points to the spindle and the potter's wheel as the central, defining technologies in ancient Greece.[30] Their mythologies are recorded on gorgeous pots, celebrated by poet John Keats in his "Ode on a Grecian Urn." Keats celebrates the timelessness captured in the beauty of the vase: "Thou foster-child of silence and slow time." For Keats and the Greeks, the images encased in the pottery have a transcendent power and an eternal appeal.

We see why the apostle Paul standing in the Greek Areopagus would announce, "People of Athens! I see that in every way you are very religious. For as I walked around and looked carefully at your objects of worship, I

even found an altar with this inscription: TO AN UNKNOWN GOD."[31] He studied their art, their public space, their technology and then connected it to
God's creation of the world. Paul drew upon Greek poetry, "For in him we
live and move and have our being," incorporating it into his sermon. But
after saluting their handiwork and praising their poets, he challenged them
to move past idolatry: "Therefore since we are God's offspring, we should
not think that the divine being is like gold or silver or stone—an image made
by human design and skill. In the past God overlooked such ignorance, but
now he commands all people everywhere to repent."[32] Saint Paul respected
the Greeks' *technē* but challenged them not to be blinded or bound by it. He
challenged the iGods of his era.

We often don't realize the ways in which our technologies reflect and affect
us. Medieval monks seeking to regulate their prayers and work invented the
mechanical clock. Their theology (prayer is good, work is better than idleness)
offered a rationale for technological advance. Historian Ernest Benz pointed
out how frequently medieval iconography showed God as a master mason,
measuring out the universe with a compass and a T square.[33] "God as the Architect of the Universe" steadies the universe with one hand while measuring
it with a compass with the other.

In his *Summa Theologica*, Thomas Aquinas wrote, "God, Who is the first
principle of all things, may be compared to things created as the architect is to
things designed."[34] While the Benedictines sought to define sacred time, they
also inadvertently ushered in the ability to isolate and evaluate it. We began
to view God as the ultimate watchmaker, setting the wheels of the universe
in motion.

In studying the mechanics of winepresses in the Rhine Valley, Johannes
Gutenberg eventually invented the printing press. He could not have anticipated the Protestant Reformation that followed. Yet, the ability to print and
distribute Bibles and pamphlets and maps on a massive scale altered church
history. Instead of people thinking more alike, gathered around a single text, it
sparked the individualism and denominationalism that continue to divide the
church into smaller and more personalized communities.[35] In the sixteenth century of Francis Bacon, "inventors and mechanics had increasingly invoked the
image of God as craftsman and architect in order, by analogy, to lend prestige
to their own activities: in their humble arts, they were imitating God and hence
reflecting his glory."[36] To be a technologist was to be like God, but we were
beginning to shift the emphasis from the glory of God to the marvels of man.

Samuel F. B. Morse grasped the enormity of his invention, the telegraph. His first instantaneous message, sent from Washington to Baltimore in 1844, was taken from the Bible. Annie Ellsworth, the daughter of the United States Commissioner of Patents, suggested Numbers 23:23.[37] This is a defense of the people of Israel against a conspiring Moab. Morse transmitted, "What hath God wrought." While Morse and his witnesses in Washington couldn't have anticipated all the revolutionary changes that flowed from their collapsing of time and distance, the Bible verse suggests many did understand the enormity of the implications. They gave the creative credit to God, even as the postmaster general failed to authorize the purchase of the patent for a paltry $100,000.[38] Not everybody recognizes the potential of what God hath wrought.

Combine the monks' clocks with Gutenberg's Bible and we get the Protestant work ethic. Notions of time equaling money culminated in industrial workers punching the clock. Frederick W. Taylor published the holy book for American industry, *Principles of Scientific Management*, in 1911. Taylor announced a significant shift: "In the past, the man has been first; in the future the system must be first."[39] Taylor's emphasis on efficiency placed technical calculation above human judgment, reason over feelings, objectivity over subjectivity, and scientific measurement as the rule.[40] As machines made us more productive, it was difficult for managers to trace the shifts in supply and demand. Captains of industry needed up-to-date calculations to make decisions about where to deliver goods and services. We needed smart machines to give us spreadsheets that spelled out the productivity of our physical machines. The success of the industrial era led to the rise of the information age. Now, machines do most of the thinking for us, and efficiency drives nearly all decision making today.

In the twentieth century, our aspirations grew bigger and smaller. Skyscrapers reached for the sky, and scientists split atoms. The triumph of World War II was tempered by the stark photos and harrowing clean-up that followed. How could the Nazis have been so evil to target an entire people for extermination? The barbarism of the Holocaust made us question the notion of human progress. Robert Oppenheimer had named his atomic bomb project Trinity. Upon the explosion of the first bomb, he quoted the *Bhagavad Gita*: "I am become death, destroyer of worlds."[41] Horrific images from Hiroshima and Nagasaki made us question our war machine. Public resistance and suspicion regarding technology followed. During the Cold War, we looked to the stars with fear and wonder. The race to dominate space commenced, but an early techno-enthusiast like Lewis Mumford switched sides, writing *The Myth of the Machine: The Pentagon of Power* in 1970. Warnings of environmental disaster and nuclear nightmares included Rachel Carson's *Silent Spring* (1962), Barry Commoner's *Science and Survival* (1966), and Jonathan Schell's *The Fate of the Earth* (1982).[42] Collectively, these eco-activists asked, "What hath man wrought?"

Theologians added to the introspection not just with a loss of faith but by asking, "Is God dead?" Perhaps the only thing that died was our faith in bureaucracy and institutions to save us. We saw what we were capable of—and our evil was frightening. Philosopher Jean-Luc Marion sees this as a positive development; the death of God is the end of our idolized concept of God, as something or someone controllable, containable, capable of serving our side.[43] Idolatry brings God near, putting power within our grasp. Life was revealed as far more fragile, volatile, and explosive than we imagined. But what if the death (or least the absence) of God in the face of nuclear holocaust was a withdrawal from our idolatry? Such a withdrawal could be a form of revelation. The absence of God could make room for renewed presence. Only when we start with what we don't know or cannot control, do we begin to approach wisdom.

From Counterculture to Computer Culture

Founded in 1968, the *Whole Earth Catalog* arose as an alternative to the system. The first issue promised "access to tools" and featured a photo of the earth taken by astronauts from space. The catalog encouraged responsibility for our fragile planet and aimed to reduce our dependence on corporations for agriculture, for oil, for entertainment. Stanford-educated biologist Stewart Brand offered a back-to-nature plan comparable to the Amish, which took people off the power and manufacturing grid.[44] Hippies in San Francisco formed a counterculture in opposition to the Vietnam war, racial injustice, and the overall technocratic society.[45] The seminal sixties film *Easy Rider* begins when Captain America removes his watch. He will tour the back roads with no concern for schedules, deadlines, or financial responsibilities. He dropped out of the system that the industrial revolution and the military industrial complex had created.[46]

For the California counterculture, small was beautiful.[47] Individuals learned to live off the land. The *Whole Earth Catalog* allowed readers to swap recommendations of useful tools for gardening, carpentry, welding, and pottery. It was a *tektōn*'s dream. Writers like Wendell Berry challenged readers to "think little." Berry described the practical ethos: "A person who is growing a garden, if he is growing it organically, is improving a piece of the world. He is producing something to eat, which makes him somewhat independent of the grocery business, but he is also enlarging, for himself, the meaning of food and the pleasure of eating."[48] But instead of positioning themselves as new Adams and Eves trying to get back to the garden of Eden, the followers of the *Whole Earth Catalog* seemed content to farm on their own, beyond God-given parameters. The do-it-yourself attitude of the Whole Earth movement included a specific theological point of view. Brand wrote,

> We are as gods and might as well get good at it. So far, remotely done power and glory—as via government, big business, formal education, church—has succeeded to the point where gross defects obscure actual gains. In response to this dilemma and to these gains a realm of intimate, personal power is developing—power of the individual to conduct his own education, find his own inspiration, shape his own environment, and share his adventure with whoever is interested. Tools that aid this process are sought and promoted by the WHOLE EARTH CATALOG.[49]

Note the emphasis on personal power and the ability to shape our own environments. This sounds like humanity after the fall—cast out, but determined to forge a future. The emphasis falls on practical knowledge, useful tools, and technology. While Berry's ecological focus sprang from his abiding Christian faith, Brand placed his faith firmly in us. For the Whole Earth movement, we may be interdependent for information, but we consider our fate as residing in our hands, independent of divine guidance or blessing.

Brand's alma mater, Stanford University, unleashed the engineers that gave us the first personal computer. Bill Hewlett and Dave Packard founded their company in a Palo Alto garage. Hewlett-Packard released the world's first marketed and mass-produced personal computer in 1968. The Hewlett-Packard 9100A was called a "desktop calculator" but sold for the rather prohibitive price of $5,000. The greatest technological achievement of our era may be the single chip microprocessor, first made commercially available by Intel in 1971. It has made all of our increasingly complex and intelligent machines possible. A microprocessor is essentially a minicomputer most of us rarely see and barely understand. They make our gadgets smaller, faster, and smarter. The Intel 4004 crammed all the elements that make a computer think (input and output controls, memory, and a central processing unit) onto a single silicon chip. Microprocessors are the brains of the computer that allow data to be processed and delivered quickly. It simulates and stimulates quick thinking—the transmission of data and information at light-speeds. It could be pictures from our vacation or the purchase of a book on Amazon. Thanks to microprocessors, things are being delivered to us or broadcast by us almost instantaneously. Following the trajectory of Intel cofounder Gordon Moore's Law (that the number of transistors on integrated circuits doubles every two years), microprocessors have gotten smaller and smarter and faster each and every year. Silicon Valley—founded on transistors, expanded by microprocessors, and enriched by personal computers—became the locus for our defining technologies. Advanced technology met countercultural idealism.

The *Whole Earth Catalog* was only published regularly for four years, but its back-to-nature, small-is-beautiful, do-it-yourself influence has been immense, especially in the information age. Brand explains the unique position occupied by his movement:

> At a time when the New Left was calling for grassroots political (i.e., referred) power, Whole Earth eschewed politics and pushed grassroots direct power—tools and skills. At a time when New Age hippies were deploring the intellectual world of arid abstractions, Whole Earth pushed science, intellectual endeavor, and new technology as well as old. As a result, when the most empowering tool of the century came along—personal computers (resisted by the New Left and despised by the New Age)—Whole Earth was in the thick of the development from the beginning.[50]

In 1985, the creative energy gathered around the catalog shifted to the internet with Brand and Larry Brilliant hosting one of the first virtual communities, the Whole Earth 'Lectronic Link, aka The WELL. It took the conversation regarding self-sufficiency and effective tools online. Kevin Kelly explains, "The hippies of the previous generation did not remain in their Amish-like mode because as satisfying and attractive as the work in those communities was, the siren call of choices was more attractive. The hippies left the farm for the same reason the young have always left: The possibilities leveraged by technology beckon all night and day."[51] The internet facilitated the sharing of sustainable principles and alternative lifestyle tips far better than a magazine like the *Whole Earth Catalog* ever could. Brand reached out to the emerging generation of computer hackers who shared the same core values: access to computers should be unlimited, information should be free, authorities were not to be trusted, formal age and education doesn't matter (just programming ability), and computers can create art and beauty and change lives for the better.[52] This is the faith of technologists.

Today, the ethos of the Whole Earth community is infused across Silicon Valley. At Stanford University's 2005 commencement, Steve Jobs called the catalog "one of the Bibles of my generation . . . like Google in paperback form."[53] Consider the creativity it unleashed in the Bay Area. Steve Wozniak and Jobs brought a do-it-yourself attitude to their Apple II computer. George Lucas felt no need to settle in Southern California with his profits from *Star Wars*. His special effects house, Industrial Light & Magic, stayed closer to the burgeoning computer industry by settling in Marin County, California. When a young animator named John Lasseter felt rejected by the Walt Disney Company, he found like-minded people in the Bay Area. Pixar was started with backing from Lucas and expanded after the investment of Jobs. By merging computing power and compelling characters, Pixar usurped Disney's hallowed tradition (and earned a $7 billion purchase price). Lasseter became president of Disney Animation while guiding it from Pixar's Northern California office. Stanford University alums have founded or cofounded Hewlett-Packard, Yahoo!, PayPal, Electronic Arts, Google, Firefox, LinkedIn, Netflix, and Instagram.[54]

These Silicon Valley start-ups follow a similar trajectory: "eureka moment, simultaneity of invention, formation of a development team, acquisition of funding, acquisition of momentum, and transfer of management from inventor-entrepreneurs to management entrepreneurs."[55] Silicon Valley companies are characterized by informality (like Jobs's famous uniform of blue jeans and black turtleneck) and are committed to a flat hierarchy. The walls in Pixar's Emeryville offices are glass, with animators free to design their own workspaces. Jobs famously insisted that the restrooms be placed in the middle of the building so that employees were more likely to interact with others on their way to the restroom. Casual, idea-laden exchanges may arise over cereal in the mornings or gourmet pizza at noon. Thomas Hunter describes the organizational culture of Silicon Valley as "information sharing, collective in learning, informal in communication, fast moving, flexible in adjustments, entrepreneurial, start-up inclined, and thoroughly networked."[56] This is almost a direct echo of the *Whole Earth Catalog*'s purpose statement. When the TED conference gathers around "Ideas Worth Sharing," they transform the ethos of The WELL into videos shared enthusiastically around the world. They are evangelists disseminating their dreams of technological progress and the end of world hunger via the internet. It is an admirable, inspiring, alternative religion.

Our theology once shaped our understanding of technology, but now we wonder how technology may alter our theology. From each tech company profiled in this book, we can deduce a creation narrative. They follow a similar path, from humble beginnings, when the founders were seen as foolhardy, to the early test launch when a few more believers came on board (as additional investors). Many continue to scoff at a small band of outsiders taking on an established system (think of young entrepreneur Elon Musk's chutzpah expressed in his move from PayPal to Tesla Motors or his SpaceX program). How could they dare to take on such hierarchy and dominance? The narrative shifts when the scoffers are ultimately defeated by those they previously dismissed (think Apple versus Microsoft). The scrappy outsiders become esteemed insiders, establishing a new standard. They liberate the public from a life of dull servitude into greater clarity, purpose, and practice. Whole Earthers that tried to drop out of the system now run the system, with so many of us directing our MacBooks toward Google's searches and Facebook's newsfeeds.

Some will recognize the similarities to the biblical narrative, where a creator God aligns with a marginalized people to take on established kingdoms and principalities. Jesus undercuts the established practices of his time with an upside-down ethic that supports the poor, the marginalized, and the oppressed. Such a countercultural power rearrangement was bound to create resistance, but despite the appearance of defeat, Jesus and his band of devoted followers rise and overturn the dominant people and paradigm. The outsiders become the insiders, the powerless are given access and authority. It becomes easy to see how faith in technology becomes an alternative religion, a way to reverse the curse of the fall, to provide comfort to hurting people, to offer us a glimpse of eternity. American optimism has morphed into faith in technology. The only problem—technology cannot save us.

Technology's Faith

While the Japanese invented the Walkman and Israelis created instant messaging, the computer age has essentially been an American revolution. Thomas Friedman and Michael Mandelbaum of the *New York Times* note, "The IT Revolution was started in the United States. The transistor, communications satellites, the personal computer, the cell phone, and the Internet, not to mention the PalmPilot, the iPad, the iPhone, and the Kindle were all invented in the United States and then were brought to the world market by American-based companies."[57] Our innovations are fueled by American faith, optimism, and ingenuity. We have much to be proud of but plenty to be wary of. Our strengths can also be our weaknesses. I can agree with much of the Whole Earth ethos that encourages the sharing of resources, caring for the environment, and the practical benefits of technology.

Unfortunately, these countercultural values haven't always accompanied the rise of the information era. The massive wealth generated in Silicon Valley hasn't been shared. Despite the efforts of the TED conference, the tendency to hoard continues to vex us. Technology cannot free us from the grip of personal and collective sin. Theologian Marcus Borg insists, "The dominant values of American life—affluence, achievement, appearance, power, competition, consumption, individualism—are vastly different from anything recognizably Christian. As individuals and as a culture . . . our existence has become massively idolatrous."[58] When we place efficiency before humanity, we can quickly lose perspective. The speed that accompanies smaller, faster, smarter can keep us from perceiving things clearly. Technologies meant to empower us can also blind us.

The computer has become our metaphorical truth.[59] Consider how we describe ourselves. When we're slow to recall a fact, we might talk about "having trouble retrieving that file." A long conversation or an intense lecture or sermon might be called "a massive download." After a particularly draining day at the office, we might say our hard drives are full. Throughout, we are likely to think of ourselves as information gatherers, struggling to process all the data we've picked up on a given day. Historian David Noble notes how the thinking machine "reflected a new form of divine worship, an exultation of the essential endowment of mankind, that unique faculty which man shared with God, because of its link to God, not to man. The thinking machine was not, then, an embodiment of what was specifically human, but of what was specifically divine about humans—the immortal mind."[60] The only problem with that thinking is that we are more than our minds. We have bodies that need to be fed, nurtured, cared for.

Technology can make us more efficient farmers, better laborers, more productive workers. It can save us time and money. It can give us more free time but still enslave us. As our devices have gotten smaller, our vices remain just as vexing. We still buy more than we need and waste as much as we consume. We get things more quickly, but our tempers and patience have grown shorter. We're likely to blow up over tiny inconveniences. The same weapons that we claim keep the peace can also wipe out entire cities in a single blast. Hiroshima and Nagasaki show how deadly technology can be. Medicine may prolong our lives, but it cannot offer eternity.

In the information age, technology categorizes, itemizes, and atomizes. It maximizes profits with disregard for people. It bases decisions on data, and sometimes the facts can be quite cold. Much of the iGods' dehumanizing power is hidden. We don't know why our loan was rejected or our refund denied. We press "4" to erase or "7" to save, but the odds of speaking to an operator dwindle. Technology turns everything in its path to 1's and 0's, but we are more than pixels and bigger than our brains. For some reason, God gave us bodies and dared to walk among us. The incarnation of Jesus is an affront to technologists who view the body as "meatspace" and only cherish the brain. The earth is worth tilling and cultivating (as the Whole Earth Catalogers know), but why? The Christian community believes heaven is coming to earth, but we don't need to build platforms to the sky. Jesus and the New Jerusalem are descending to us in an act of majesty and wonder.

We are just starting to grasp the theological implications of our technological shifts. When it comes to religion, Stahl suggested in 1999, "The One True Faith is technological mysticism: faith in the universal efficacy of technology. It is a system of beliefs uniting communists and capitalists, tycoons and unionists, the rich and those who would be rich. At the moment its most potent icon is the computer."[61] In the decade since, our all-in-one calculator and communicator and broadcaster—the smartphone—has usurped the computer. It is the magic box in our pocket, a computer on the go. Now, the symbol of power is an iPhone and the most valuable company on the planet (for the moment) is Apple. The products will evolve, and the most powerful companies may change (from IBM to Microsoft to Apple), but the central truth remains: our economy is fueled and our faith is renewed by technology. We will study the leading technology companies as a means of determining what theological shifts are occurring. We will measure these general revelations against the special revelation of Scripture to figure out whether they need to be embraced and encouraged or resisted and reframed.

Discuss

1. How would you define technology? In what ways does technology define you?
2. How do you picture Jesus? What do you imagine his relationship to technology would be?

Apple

Aesthetics First

Man as a tool maker has the ability to make a tool to amplify the inherent ability that he has and that's exactly what we're doing here. We're making bicycles.

—Steve Jobs, 1980[1]

The only computers I've ever owned have been Macs. I still recall the thrill of lining up at the University of Southern California in 1992 to pick up the computer we'd ordered. It was a bit like Christmas Day, particularly because of the cool wrapping that surrounded the Mac. The packaging was as sleek as the computer inside. The Macintosh LC was long and thin, nothing like the blocky computers we'd come to expect from their competitors. It was shaped like a pizza box, something that college students knew and loved. We didn't realize that "LC" stood for "low cost"; the quality of materials felt more like "loving care." From the beginning, Apple understood that your experience of the computer began on the outside before you turned it on. How it looked said as much about the hardware and software contained therein. Aesthetics matter.

And, oh, what software! No special commands or knowledge were necessary to navigate a Mac. It was strictly plug in and play. The screen was simple and uncluttered, exactly what one didn't expect from a computer. And the mouse allowed you to browse across the screen. You couldn't get lost; a simple click was enough to get a result. And everything could be personalized, from the names of your files, to your favorite colors for highlighting, to your preferred fonts for writing. Apple encouraged creativity and choice. The Mac was a warm and humane alternative to cold and impersonal PCs.

Apple challenged the assumptions contained within the average computer. The Mac raised core questions about who we are and who we are intended to be. Are we calculators geared toward efficiency? Or do we also operate via feelings and intuition, leading with the right side of our brain as well as the left? On a Mac, we became creative forces, overflowing with fruitfulness. Apple launched the personal computer revolution by embracing innovation and encouraging rebellion. It communicated California countercultural cool. But after competitors like IBM and Microsoft entered the fray, Apple struggled, and their founders were forced out.

Apple climbed back on top via the "reality distortion field" generated by a visionary leader and/or megalomaniac named Steve Jobs. His commitment to immaculate design and dogged pursuit of perfection resulted in products that irrevocably altered the music business, telecommunications, and the publishing industry. The best of Apple approximates humankind's original calling to create. Mac computers unleashed self-publishing, garage bands, and film editing—all on a laptop. But Jobs was so focused on dominating his company and the PC market that he created a walled garden hostile to all challengers. Walter Isaacson's authorized biography summarized Jobs's contradictions: "Driven by demons, Jobs could drive those around him to fury and despair. But his personality and products were interrelated, just as Apple's hardware and software tended to be, as if part of an integrated system. His tale is instructive and cautionary, filled with lessons about innovation, character, leadership, and values."[2] The Apple story is both a tribute to our calling in Genesis and a cautionary tale about the lure of hubris.

Genesis

Apple's origins are more garage band than multinational company. Steve Wozniak ("Woz") built the first Apple computer by hand in Jobs's parents' garage. The scene harkens back to depictions of the nativity, where proud parents huddled around their glowing child. Inspired by what Woz gave birth to, they sold their modest possessions (Woz's scientific calculator, Jobs's VW Microbus) to raise $1300 to pay for circuit boards for their nascent computers.

A local Bay Area computer store, The Byte Shop, ordered fifty. The first Apple I computers were released on April Fool's Day, 1976. An initial ad said, "Byte into an Apple," a creative merging of technical terms with Adam, Eve, and the garden of Eden. The initial price was an apocalyptic $666.66. Woz and Jobs later claimed they weren't making any theological statement with the name or the cost. The first round of Apple I computers sold out.

The Steves took on new investors to launch the Apple II. Rob Janoff, an art director for the Regis McKenna advertising agency, was hired to design a new logo. He incorporated Jobs's fruitarian habits with the colors of a rainbow. It distinguished Apple in the marketplace for years to come. Former Apple executive Jean-Louis Gassée recalled, "One of the deep mysteries to me is our logo, the symbol of lust and knowledge, bitten into, all crossed with the colors of the rainbow in the wrong order. You couldn't dream a more appropriate logo: lust, knowledge, hope and anarchy."[3] Janoff also acknowledged the strong influence of hippie culture: "Both Steve and I came from that place, but the real solid reason for the stripes was that the Apple II was the first home or personal computer that could reproduce images on the monitor in color. So it represents color bars on the screen. Also, it was an attempt to make the logo very accessible to everyone, especially to young people so that Steve could get them into schools."[4] But when asked if he was influenced by the origin stories in Genesis, Janoff said, "Well, I'm probably the least religious person, so Adam and Eve didn't have anything to do with it. The bite of knowledge sounds fabulous, but that's not it. . . . I designed it with a bite for scale, so people get that it was an apple not a cherry. Also it was kind of iconic about taking a bite out of an apple. . . . It was after I designed it, that my creative director told me: 'Well you know, there is a computer term called byte.' . . . So, it was like perfect."[5]

A year later, the Apple II, designed and built by Wozniak, was released. While most of their competitors sold kits, the Apple II came fully assembled. It came with clear, concise instruction manuals. Woz brought the engineering know-how, and Jobs brought the marketing mind, believing that people would want a personal computer. He took on the role of educator-in-chief, teaching consumers what a computer could do. A two-page ad in *Scientific American* explained, "You don't even need to know a RAM from a ROM to use and enjoy Apple II." The ad promised, "As you master Apple BASIC, you'll be able to organize, index, and store data on household finance, income tax, recipes, and record collections."[6] They created a brand-new market for a brand-new product. Woz and Jobs made a dynamic (and profitable) duo. *Time* magazine reported, "In 1976 the company had no employees other than the two founders and $200,000 in sales; by 1978 the payroll was up to 150 and sales totaled $17.5 million. This year (1979) the company, which is privately held but admits to pretax earnings equal to about 20% of sales, expects to be doing $75 million in business with 400 employees."[7]

Apple banked on creativity. A 1980 advertisement featured Benjamin Franklin, with his kite beside him, pondering an Apple computer. The ad poses the question, "What kind of man owns his own computer?" The answer, "Rather revolutionary, the whole idea of owning a personal computer? Not if you're a diplomat, printer, scientist, inventor . . . or a kite designer. Today, there's Apple Computer. It's designed to be a personal computer. To uncomplicate your life and make you more effective." The tagline insisted, "It's a Wise Man Who Owns an Apple." Plenty agreed. They sold 4.6 million shares of Apple at $22 per share within minutes of the initial public offering in December 1980. It was the most capital generated by an IPO since Ford Motor Company in 1956, and it created 300 instant Apple millionaires—more than any company in history up to that point. The Apple computers and stock kept selling. In the PBS special *Triumph of the Nerds*, Jobs recalled, "I was worth over a million dollars when I was twenty-three, and over ten million dollars when I was twenty-four, and over a hundred million dollars when I was twenty-five. . . . And it wasn't that important because I never did it for the money."[8]

Apple was celebrated for unleashing a wave of innovation. A 1981 ad claimed, "Edison had over 1,800 patents in his name, but you can be just as inventive with an Apple." The Apple origin story merged Thomas Edison's shop with the psychedelic sounds of rock. Jobs's and Wozniak's San Francisco roots coincided with the hippie vibe, all long hair and beards. Early press coverage emphasized Jobs's youth, his humble origins as a college dropout and self-made engineer, and his unusual lifestyle and amazing financial success. *Time* recognized Wozniak as "the true technological genius" but portrayed Jobs as a religious visionary. They rhapsodized about Jobs "possessing a smooth sales pitch and a blind faith that would have been the envy of the early Christian martyrs, he is 'positively hypnotic when he takes the computer gospel to the young.'"[9] When IBM finally unveiled their first personal computer in 1981, Apple took out a cheeky ad in the *Wall Street Journal* welcoming them to the market—late. The implication was clear: IBM was old, East Coast, establishment; Apple was hip, West Coast, and happening. The cult of Mac was forming.

After a near fatal, self-piloted plane crash in 1981, Wozniak stepped back from day-to-day life at Apple. He got married and went back to Berkeley to finish his college degree. Woz confirmed the collision of rock and Apple by sponsoring the US Festival, a fusion of the Woodstock era with emerging technologies. It featured new wave pioneers like The Clash as well as heavy metal acts like Van Halen. Apple profits weren't going to go to stuffy endeavors, but loud, extravagant, and ultimately unwieldy rock shows. With Woz in the background, Jobs graced the cover of the newly launched *Inc.* magazine claiming, "This Man Has Changed Business Forever," and *Time* celebrated him for "Striking It Rich" and representing "America's Risk Takers."

In coming decades, Woz nearly got written out of the origin story, his engineering expertise steamrolled by the forceful personality and marketing skills of Jobs. Jobs's philosophy would be chronicled by his chosen biographer, Walter Isaacson, and portrayed on film by Ashton Kutcher in *Jobs*. These populist origin stories burnished the legend of the brilliant and demanding soul of Apple. Jobs's legend wouldn't have solidified without a dramatic arc, a fall and rise, a corporate death and resurrection. Jobs became a legendary techno-savior after being fired, cast into the wilderness. His loss and influence at Apple was felt palpably by a series of substitutes who proved unworthy of the title. Only after a dramatic defeat and comeback did Jobs become the iGod by whom all subsequent contenders will be measured. The resurrection of Apple via the iMac, the iPod, and the iPhone secured Jobs's place atop the tech pantheon.

Beauty

Apple made computers human, or at least humane. The Lisa computer of 1983 (named after Jobs's illegitimate, initially unclaimed daughter) emphasized aesthetics over what had previously been only efficiency. Beyond the bits and bytes, Jobs worried about presentation. Graphic representations of "trash" and "folders" were introduced. The interface, developed at Xerox's PARC laboratories, felt like something we wanted to spend time with, to look at, maybe even admire. It came with a premium price of nearly $10,000. But the innovations were to be rolled into the much more affordable Macintosh project. Jobs brought Bill Gates down to Cupertino to discuss an exclusive partnership combining Xerox's interface with Microsoft's software code into the Macintosh computer. But the two titans ultimately split when the Macintosh took longer than expected to arrive, and Gates hurdled forward with Windows. Isaacson recounts the passionate fight, where Gates announced, "We're doing Windows," and Jobs countered, "You're ripping us off! I trusted you, and now you're stealing from us!" Isaacson chronicles how "Gates just sat there coolly, looking Steve in the eye, before hurling back, in his squeaky voice, what became a classic zinger. 'Well, Steve, I think there's more than one way of looking at it. I think it's more like we both had this rich neighbor named Xerox and I broke into his house to steal the TV set and found out that you had already stolen it.'"[10] This was the beginning of the Mac-vs.-PC tension that played out decades later in a series of commercials. Apple asked us to imagine if IBM or UNIX had ultimately won the computer wars. How ugly would our world be if it was ruled strictly by a PC? Apple took the long view, opposing computationalism.

God also began with beauty. The creation story in Genesis begins with forging order out of chaos, separating night from day, light from darkness, earth from water. The resulting world is pronounced "good." Catholic theologian Hans Urs von Balthasar points out that ethics flows out of beauty. In the garden, humanity could see how things were supposed to be. The beautiful was good, the ugly was bad. Aesthetics preceded ethics. But we often invert the order, talking about "truth, goodness, and beauty," in that order. Balthasar points us back to God's theological method that put beauty before goodness and truth. How quickly we forget that the Ten Commandments arrived long after creation. How shortsighted to start with objective truth claims, preach about good behavior, and yet rarely make time for beauty. Balthasar discusses the consequences of a life without beauty:

> We no longer dare to believe in beauty and we make of it a mere appearance in order the more easily to dispose of it. Our situation today shows that beauty demands for itself at least as much courage and decision as do truth and goodness, and she will not allow herself to be separated and banned from her two sisters without taking them along with herself in an act of mysterious vengeance. We can be sure that whoever sneers at her name as if she were the ornament of a bourgeois past—whether he admits it or not—can no longer pray and soon will no longer be able to love.[11]

Beauty is never a shortcut. It is a long play, with an eye toward posterity. Beauty is among the first things to get tossed in almost any process. When budget cuts arrive, art and music are always first on the block. Athletics linger in the schedule long after aesthetics have been banished. So God bless Jobs's font-loving heart. Because he couldn't handle normal classes and a prescribed curriculum, Jobs dropped out of Reed College and dropped into a class that covered calligraphy. In his famous 2005 commencement speech at Stanford, Jobs talked about what he discovered at Reed:

> The minute I dropped out I could stop taking the required classes that didn't interest me, and begin dropping in on the ones that looked interesting . . . and much of what I stumbled into by following my curiosity and intuition turned out to be priceless later on. Reed College at that time offered perhaps the best calligraphy instruction in the country. . . . I learned all about serif and sans serif typefaces, about varying the amount of space between different letter combinations, about what makes great typography great. It was beautiful, historical, artistically subtle in a way that science can't capture and I found it fascinating.
>
> None of this had even a hope of any practical application in my life. But ten years later, when we were designing the first Macintosh computer, it all came back to me. And we designed it all into the Mac. It was the first computer with beautiful typography. If I had never dropped in on that single course in college, the Mac would have never had multiple typefaces or proportionally spaced fonts. And since Windows just copied the Mac, it's likely that no personal computer would have them. If I had never dropped out, I would have never dropped in on this calligraphy class, and personal computers might not have the wonderful typography that they do.[12]

Apple became the most valuable company on the planet by investing in design. Prior to Apple, nobody would have talked about the notion of "Beautiful Code." But Jobs never disguised his disdain for competitors like Gates and Microsoft. "The only problem with Microsoft is they just have no taste," Jobs chided. "They have absolutely no taste. And I don't mean that in a small way, I mean that in a big way, in the sense that they don't think of original ideas, and they don't bring much culture into their products."[13] Apple's commitment to excellence suggested that software can promote beauty and simplicity rather than just functionality. Software can be written that approximates poetry, with patterns and consistency and order. Comments can be included in the code with space, lines, and indentations that offer room for pause and reflection. Elegant code has encapsulation; it models what it is trying to achieve. Form and function meet in a glorious synergy. Erich Gamma rhapsodized about design patterns in 1994, Joshua Kerievsky advocated refactoring to patterns in 2004, and Andy Oram and Greg Wilson unveiled how the leading programmers think in beautiful code (2007).[14] None of these notions would likely have surfaced without the modeling and success provided by Apple.

The care poured into the design of the early Apple products attracted creative types who shared their attention to detail, like British-born designer (and now senior vice president of industrial design at Apple) Jonathan "Jony" Ive. He recalls,

> I went through college having a real problem with computers. I was convinced that I was technically inept, which was frustrating as I wanted to use computers to help me with various aspects of my design. Right at the end of my time at college I discovered the Mac. I remember being astounded at just how much better it was than anything else I had tried to use. I was struck by the care taken with the whole user experience. I had a sense of connection via the object with the designers. I started to learn more about the company, how it had been founded, its values and its structure. The more I learnt about this cheeky almost rebellious company the more it appealed to me, as it unapologetically pointed to an alternative in a complacent and creatively bankrupt industry. Apple stood for something and had a reason for being that wasn't just about making money.[15]

In the early days, Apple was an outsider company, a David battling for market share against the PC Goliath, IBM (run on Microsoft's Windows). Apple cemented the "blows against the empire" idea with the acclaimed 1984 Super Bowl commercial overseen by Lee Clow, creative director for the Chiat/Day ad agency. Clow was a surfer, schooled in Southern California cool. He had long hair, offices in Venice, and advocated the sixties' ideals shared by Jobs. For the 1984 campaign, Clow hired acclaimed director Ridley Scott, who extended the creepy, futuristic vibe he brought to the groundbreaking films *Alien* (1979) and *Blade Runner* (1982). The spot only aired once. And I caught it, live. It arrived in the third quarter when the Oakland Raiders were handily defeating the Washington Redskins.

While it is easy to look back and say, "Ah yes, such a clear and brilliant piece," in the context of the time, it was strange and mystifying. MTV was barely begun, and this ad captured the look and feel of a Duran Duran video, equal parts slick and scary. The blonde heroine wears a white shirt and red shorts, identifying with the running craze that was sweeping the nation. So Apple was associated with the young, the healthy, the progressive. It can also be read as sunny California taking on the cold East Coast establishment. The Big Brother character quotes from George Orwell's *1984*: "For today we celebrate the first, glorious anniversary of the Information Purification Directive! We have created, for the first time in all history, a garden of pure ideology. Where each worker may bloom secure from the pests purveying contradictory truths. Our Unification of Thoughts is more powerful a weapon than any fleet or army on earth."[16] It is a corporate clampdown on creativity. Apple's revolutionary runner tosses a hammer at the fuzzy, blue image of Big Brother, projected on a screen. Luminescent light flows across the previously lifeless masses. The closing text read, "On January 24th, Apple Computer will introduce Macintosh. And you'll see why 1984 won't be like 1984." Apple (and its computers) are white knights while Big Blue/IBM are cast as the thought police, pushing conformity. The commercial was iconoclastic, literally smashing those who control our thoughts (and our computers). Jobs took on the technocrats of IBM with an evangelistic fervor.

At the subsequent rollout for the Mac, Jobs quoted from Bob Dylan's "The Times They Are A-Changin,'" challenging the press not to speak too soon: "For the loser now / Will be later to win / For the times they are a-changin'."[17] The pirates at Apple were waging war, empowering people, creating computers for the masses that were user-friendly, built more by artists than by engineers. The spot seemed more designed to send a message to the competition at IBM than the millions of home viewers munching on chips and salsa. But perhaps Apple slipped into our subconscious in a haunting manner. They were the little guys, the rebels, armed like David with a single shot, taking on a corporate Goliath. The overall message was clear: "Owning a Mac was a subversive act." And to a generation weaned on punk rock and rap, that was the song we desperately wanted to sing.

The Apple Macintosh of 1984 distinguished itself with the graphical user interface and the use of a mouse. There were no secret code words necessary to unlock a Mac. Everything was drag and drop, from one folder to the next. And each folder could be labeled to describe its contents in fun ways. This was computing as entertainment, rather than drudgery. Maybe the Mac couldn't do spreadsheets, but it made writing papers feel like a joyous adventure. Desktop publishing at home became a liberating possibility. With Aldus PageMaker software and a LaserWriter printer, anybody could be a publisher. The Mac attracted the creative class, those who wanted to write and design and paint with computers. Apple unleashed a collective creative spirit. The bite-size columns we've come to expect from bloggers stem from the Mac. And the endlessly entertaining infographics and data visualization we love with our news arose from the Mac.

Apple prospered by engaging in a bit of theological anthropology. They identified both our problem and our potential. Classical Christian theology would label our problem as sin, ignoring God's directives and placing ourselves in the center of the garden. Apple's advertising suggested our problem is inefficiency, not living up to our potential. Who are we intended to be? Apple saw us as born to be creative. Born to paint, to draw, to design. Not too far from the biblical calling to be fruitful and multiply. Such creativity might look like rebellion, taking on the status quo, not being satisfied with how things are, but hungering for something deeper, smarter, more pleasing to the ear and the eye. Creativity is a rebellious act, challenging those who would seek to box us in. We were expected and encouraged to push the boundaries.

The irony of Apple's outsider status is that they were also insistent about making people conform to their standards. Apple became the most valuable company on the planet by building a walled garden. The Mac didn't interface with other computers. In the early days of software and programming, this proved costly. People wondered about the weird kid in the corner of the PC store who didn't mix with others. It may have been the most beautiful garden in the computer-verse, but it was private. Users had to comply with the established rules. Apple fended off clones, preferring to maintain control in exchange for a smaller market share.

Apple was the first tech company with a "technology evangelist" anointed to woo software developers away from PCs. The first Apple evangelist, Mike Boich, was soon joined by a raft of dedicated followers, who praised the perks of the Macintosh with missionary zeal. They demonstrated the power of their product, selling both computer users and code writers on the joy of inhabiting Apple's exclusive kingdom. The rigor of Apple's exacting standards inspired devotion among Mac users. The cult of Mac expanded through evangelism.

Jobs got rich by being a benevolent dictator—dispensing blessings to his followers, but ruthlessly demanding adherence to his prescribed program. Tales of his bad behavior abounded in Silicon Valley: "He parks his Mercedes in handicapped spaces, he reduces subordinates to tears, and fires employees in angry tantrums. Yet, many of his top deputies at Apple have worked with him for years, and even some of those who have departed say that although it is often brutal and Jobs hogs the credit, they've never done better work."[18]

For a Buddhist, he was awfully acerbic and short-fused. Steve's way or the highway worked when profits were flowing into the now publicly held company. Shareholders may not ask questions as long as profit projections were met. Yet, Jobs seemed to care more about perfection than profits (or people).

Snakes in the Garden

Jobs was fired by the Pepsi executive he recruited to run his burgeoning computer company. John Sculley embodied all the things Apple opposed: old money, East Coast, Ivy League, Wall Street. But with Apple now a highly profitable public company, Jobs felt the need to bring Sculley's business acumen to the mix. Jobs famously wooed him with the pitch, "Do you want to sell sugar water for the rest of your life or do you want to come with me and change the world?" Does that make Jobs the smooth-talking snake, tempting Sculley, or did Sculley's arrival tilt the balance of power in destabilizing ways? Who was the snake in Apple's garden? Sculley hated the "1984" commercial and had no love for Chiat/Day, the ad agency behind it. After three tumultuous years of trying to work with (or around) each other, Jobs and Sculley faced off for control of the company.[19] In his memoir, *Odyssey*, Sculley likened Jobs to Russian revolutionary Leon Trotsky, calling him "a zealot, his vision so pure that he couldn't accommodate that vision to the imperfections of the world."[20] Jobs told the Stanford commencement audience, "How can you get fired from a company you started? Well, as Apple grew, we hired someone who I thought was very talented to run the company with me, and for the first year or so things went well. But then our visions of the future began to diverge and eventually, we fell out. When we did, our board of directors sided with him. So at 30 I was out. And very publicly out. What had been the focus of my entire adult life was gone, and it was devastating."[21] In 1985, Jobs was removed as Apple's chairman. Shortly thereafter, Chiat/Day was dropped as Apple's advertising agency. Both the visionary founder and the public image-maker of Apple were gone.

Apple began to wobble in the marketplace when they let other manufacturers into their garden, licensing out their technology and interface to upstarts like Power Competing and UMAX. In retrospect, it is tough to imagine Apple agreeing to be cloned. Didn't duplication and copying fly in the face of every core Apple principle of individuality and creative expression? Perhaps those were the snakes who tempted Apple with promises of riches and quick fixes to their bottom line. While Jobs created a new computer company aptly named NeXT, Apple jacked up its prices and Macs suddenly stopped selling. The product line proliferated without focus, confusing customers and blurring the image Jobs had cultivated so carefully.

Sculley gambled on a costly new product, a personal data assistant (PDA). He correctly anticipated the rise of an entirely new type of computer. The Blackberry and smartphones that eventually followed incorporated many of his notions. But when the Newton finally appeared in 1993, its sales and performance were both dismal. Sculley was ousted.[22]

Designer Jonathan Ive recalls the malaise that fell over Apple: "When I joined Apple the company was in decline. It seemed to have lost what had once been a very clear sense of identity and purpose. Apple had started trying to compete to an agenda set by an industry that had never shared its goals."[23]

In the meantime, cast into the technological wilderness, Jobs had bought the computer graphics division of LucasFilm Ltd. and launched Pixar Animation Studio. By 1995, Pixar had its first massive hit with *Toy Story*. While Apple floundered, Jobs told the Stanford graduating class, "I didn't see it then, but it turned out that getting fired from Apple was the best thing that could have ever happened to me. The heaviness of being successful was replaced by the lightness of being a beginner again, less sure about everything. It freed me to enter one of the most creative periods of my life." He also learned how to be a better businessman. In 1997, Apple bought NeXT for access to Jobs's software. They also brought him back as interim CEO. It was a triumphant return. Ive noted the immediate shift: "By re-establishing the core values he had established at the beginning, Apple again pursued a direction which was clear and different from any other companies. Design and innovation formed an important part of this new direction."[24] Jobs cut back the product lines from fifteen items to four. Had he mellowed? In *The Second Coming of Steve Jobs*, Alan Deutschman describes Jobs's shake-up of Apple employees as a "reign of terror" epitomized by public humiliations.[25] He was just as "driven, obsessive, relentless, controlling, stubborn, messianic."[26]

Jobs spearheaded the development of the iMac, a new line of affordable home desktops, called "a computer with soul." Under his guidance, Apple quickly returned to profitability, and by the end of 1998, it boasted sales of $5.9 billion. Against the odds, Jobs pulled the company he founded and loved back from financial crisis. He had resurrected the company like a techno-Messiah.

Jobs's legend grew by engineering the most triumphant comeback in American business history. Having once dressed as Jesus for a company Halloween party, he now took on the mantle of techno-savior. Marketing professor Russell Belk noted the blind faith of Mac's dedicated acolytes:

> The Mac and its fans constitute the equivalent of a religion. This religion is based on an origin myth for Apple Computer, heroic and savior legends surrounding its cofounder and current CEO Steve Jobs, the devout faith of its follower congregation, their belief in the righteousness of the Macintosh, the existence of one or more Satanic opponents, Mac believers proselytizing and converting nonbelievers, and the hope among cult members that salvation can be achieved by transcending corporate capitalism.[27]

The stage was set for Jobs to elevate Apple to a higher plane.

Think Different

During his exile from Apple, Jobs learned the multiplying power of disciples who are equally driven, exacting, and inspired. Among his key partners in Apple's resurgence: ad man Lee Clow of Chiat/Day and the lead designer for Apple, Jonathan Ive. They returned Apple to its core mission—delivering beautiful, uncompromising products at a premium price to discerning consumers.

Apple regained its mojo when it retained control of its brand and image. The rainbow logo was simplified into a monochromatic white on white background that conveyed a certain sleekness. Some might call it stark, but in a busy world, the familiar sight of the Mac logo became a source of comfort and a mark of quality. Jobs and company added it to as many surfaces of their products as possible, starting with the Bondi blue iMac.

Jobs brought Apple back to prominence by rehiring Chiat/Day as their lead agency. In August 1997, Clow proposed a two-word campaign, "Think Different." While plenty questioned why not the more grammatically proper "Think Differently," Jobs was attracted to the use of "different" as a noun, comparable to "think victory" or "think beauty."[28] And while Clow suggested using DreamWorks animators in the ads, Jobs suggested great thinkers in simple black-and-white photographs like the portrait of Albert Einstein that decorated his home. Clow's creative team was given only seventeen days to complete the campaign. Jennifer Golub directed the television commercial with daily input via satellite links with Jobs. The commercial was created on Apple computers. Chiat/Day copywriter Craig Tanimoto composed the free verse that actor Richard Dreyfuss narrated:

> Here's to the crazy ones. The misfits. The rebels. The troublemakers. The round pegs in the square holes. The ones who see things differently. They're not fond of rules, and they have no respect for the status quo. You can quote them, disagree with them, glorify or vilify them. About the only thing you can't do is ignore them. Because they change things. They push the human race forward. And while some may see them as the crazy ones, we see genius. Because the people who are crazy enough to think they can change the world—are the ones who do.[29]

This simple manifesto reestablished Apple's mojo. While this description certainly fit historical figures like Alexander the Great, Jesus, or Napoleon, the television commercial was limited to those twentieth-century figures captured on film or video. The sixty-second ad included scientific pioneers like Thomas Edison, Albert Einstein, and Buckminster Fuller juxtaposed with political visionaries like Martin Luther King Jr. and Mahatma Gandhi. Painters like Picasso, architects like Frank Lloyd Wright, and dancers like Martha Graham were also cited as crazy. Muhammad Ali brought artistry and innovation to the boxing ring. Singers like Bob Dylan, John Lennon, and Maria Callas; directors like Alfred Hitchcock; and puppeteers like Jim Henson were labeled geniuses. Aviator Amelia Earhart was seen as a forebear to adventurer/entrepreneurs like Richard Branson and Ted Turner. The only thing missing from the "Think Different" campaign was a computer. Apple didn't show or discuss its products. But the implication was clear. Apple computers were made for creative people who did not conform to the status quo. They spark innovation and maybe even revolution.

Who are we intended to be? In the biblical book of Genesis, we are called to create, to plant and to harvest, to be fruitful and multiply. We are made in the image of our Creator. God demonstrates plenty of faith—giving us dominion over nature. Some might call such freedom "madness." We could easily abuse our calling through neglect or greed. We've seen the fruits of our foolhardy efforts to kill the buffalo, to cut down trees, to bend streams. Sometimes it was a matter of survival. But mostly, it was an effort to dominate rather than tend. We might build skyscrapers to heaven as a tribute to our genius. Or we might turn our attention to better yields, to creating tasty combinations. It often involves experimentation, trial and error. We may graft together previously separate elements, like merging a plum and an apricot to create a glorious new fruit, the pluot, or introducing genetically desirable traits into animals (or humans). Such creativity might look like rebellion, playing God. It suggests a certain dissatisfaction with how things are. But hungering for something deeper, smarter, and more pleasing to the ear and the eye is well within our original mandate. We are called to be fruitful—from pluots to people.

Did Apple overreach in its celebration of human potential? Genesis tells us we are created by God to be like God, to reflect the Creator's care for the earth and its habitants. We should live in harmony with our environment, tending to the garden we've been entrusted with. That allows room for experiments, for combining crops, for better yields, for medical advances. The psalmist describes humanity as a little lower than angels, crowned with glory and honor.[30] According to Saint Peter, God's divine power has given us everything we need for a godly life; we are expected to participate in the divine nature.[31] Apple appealed to our most creative side to distinguish themselves in the marketplace. They appealed to our better angels and saw their market share increase.

Orthodox Christian theology also recognizes our tendency toward dominating each other. We like power. We long to rule over our neighbors, our children, our spouses. Treating others as an object or an end is the root of so much inequality, the source of so many personal and public wars. Apple's declaration of creativity, "Think Different," could have masked a declaration of war. We had seen how grandiose a battle Jobs envisioned in Apple's infamous commercial for the Super Bowl, "1984." Ennobled athletes who challenge Big Brother stood in for Apple. Now, Apple aligned itself with celebrated forces for justice like Gandhi and King. But perhaps Apple was more like Branson and Turner, business innovators pursuing a bigger share of the market. Would Jobs overreach, succumbing to Nimrod's temptation to build a tower in tribute to himself? Could he become so single-minded in his quest to be best that he succumbed to Big Brother's totalizing tendencies?

The Cult of Good Design

The iMac, which Jobs designed in 1998, revolutionized Apple, which was close to bankruptcy at the time. The iPod, in 2001, went even further and transformed the record industry. The iPhone had a similar effect on the mobile phone business when it was launched in 2007. And the iPad, which debuted in 2010, is leading the way in a whole new category of computing.[32] What do all these revolutionary products have in common? They were all designed by Jonathan Ive. How did Jobs bring Apple back? By returning to the core principles of design and innovation at a premium price. By offering Apple's devoted users a more satisfying computing experience. By empowering and haranguing Ive and his team into designing the most satisfying consumer products possible.

After a decade of dominance by PCs, Apple made computing something beautiful again. Ive recalls, "In the 1970s, Apple talked about being at the intersection of technology and the arts. . . . The defining qualities are about use: ease and simplicity."[33] Consider Ive's design for the iPod, iPhone, and iPad that made these new products instantly comprehensible; people could pick them up and start playing immediately. Dieter Rams, a famous designer of consumer products who heavily influenced Ive, wrote "10 Principles of Good Design:"[34]

- Good design is innovative.
- Good design makes a product useful.
- Good design is aesthetic.
- Good design helps us to understand a product.
- Good design is unobtrusive.
- Good design is honest.
- Good design is durable.
- Good design is thorough down to the last detail.
- Good design is concerned with the environment.
- Good design is as little design as possible.

In these principles, we hear the echoes of our original creation in Genesis: It was certainly innovative and an aesthetic triumph, marked by remarkable diversity. It was understandable, capable of being distinguished and named. Creation was made to last, "thorough down to the last detail." We still marvel at the earth's ability to provide and sustain. Humanity was called to care for creation, to be concerned with the environment. We were told to make ourselves useful. We fell short on the honesty. It seems, then, that good design springs from the original Designer.

A sense of wonder and "fascination with the what-if questions" flows throughout Apple's design team, from idea to prototype, particularly when Apple is designing products (like the iPod) that have few predecessors. Ive notes,

> The nature of having ideas and creativity is incredibly inspiring. There is an idea which is solitary, fragile and tentative and doesn't have form. What we've found here is that it then becomes a conversation, although remains very fragile. When you see the most dramatic shift is when you transition from an abstract idea to a slightly more material conversation. But when you make a 3D model, however crude, you bring form to a nebulous idea, and everything changes—the entire process shifts. It galvanises and brings focus from a broad group of people. It's a remarkable process.[35]

Sounds almost like creation *ex nihilo*—out of nothing.

But these products were not willed into existence by a single word. A key to Apple's success has been the collaborative process. While companies would traditionally hand off a new product from the designers to the engineers, at Apple, the departments work together. Steven Johnson notes,

> Apple's development cycle looks more like a coffeehouse than an assembly line. . . . All the groups—design, manufacturing, engineering, sales—meet continuously through the product-development cycle, brainstorming, trading ideas and solutions, strategizing over the most pressing issues, and generally keeping the conversation open to a diverse group of perspectives. The process is noisy and involves far more open-ended and contentious meetings than traditional production cycles—and far more dialogue between people versed in different disciplines, with all the translation difficulties that creates. But the results speak for themselves.[36]

Ive notes how fluid the positions and roles become in the Apple process: "As we're sitting together to develop a product you would struggle to identify who the electrical engineer was, who's the mechanical engineer, who's the industrial designer."[37] By keeping the same creative team together for over fifteen years, Ive and his colleagues experimented, failed, and succeeded together. Ive describes their overlapping spaces:

> We have assembled a heavenly design team. By keeping the core team small and investing significantly in tools and process we can work with a level of collaboration that seems particularly rare. Our physical environment reflects and

enables that collaborative approach. The large open studio and massive sound system support a number of communal design areas. We have little exclusively personal space. In fact, the memory of how we work will endure beyond the products of our work.[38]

The process aligns with the product. Shared values infuse both.

What can our faith communities learn from this type of collaborative design process that leads to innovation? Could we structure our church governance to be more collaborative? Or, if our church already has open-ended governance, then why don't we see more innovation? Perhaps the creative chaos that is necessary to forge something new is scary and therefore gets smoothed out in the name of building consensus. Or our best ideas get squashed in committee. Or perhaps we consider our product already refined, in no need of creative adjustments.

The commitment to polish and perfect a product translates into passionate followers (like me!). Ive reflects, "As consumers we are incredibly discerning, we sense where there has been great care in the design, and when there is cynicism and greed."[39] Can God's people renew our ancient commitment to aesthetics?

Magic Boxes

Before the iPod, there had been portable music players. In the fifties, it was the transistor radio. Sony's Walkman started a craze in the 1980s. The Diamond Rio MP3 player entered the marketplace in 1998. Even iTunes wasn't an original Apple invention but a perfection of the SoundJam MP3 technology it purchased in 2000. Yet, despite all of these predecessors, in 2001, the iPod still felt revolutionary. Ive recalls, "With the iPod, the MP3 phenomenon gave us an opportunity to develop an entirely new product and one which could carry 4,000 songs. The big wrestle was trying to develop something that was new, that felt new and that had a meaning relevant to what it was."[40] The iPod was an immediate hit. It made dialing up a song so easy, so elegant. The shuffle function allowed the iPod to play DJ. The playlists approximated mix tapes of yore but offered so many more options. The iPod crossed over into iconic and essential status almost instantly. Author Steven Levy called it "the perfect thing."[41]

Stephen Moss raved in *The Guardian*, "If the Three Wise Men were buying gifts today, it would have to be an iPod. Preferably 40 gigabytes. . . . At the moment, there is only room for one religion—and can it really be a coincidence that iPod rhymes with God?"[42]

With the arrival of the iPod and the launching of the iTunes store in 2003, Apple almost singlehandedly saved the record industry. Napster had made file sharing of music so tempting. A wave of illegal downloading had almost swamped the music business. Apple proved that (some) consumers were willing to pay 99 cents for a digital download, especially when the process felt so cool and convenient. Unfortunately, iTunes also hastened the demise of record stores. Who would want to buy a compact disc when ten thousand songs could be crammed onto an iPod? But the iPod turned out to be far more than a music player. Podcasts arose, providing a new format and outlet for pundits, professors, and preachers. Jobs unveiled the fourth generation of the iPod on the cover of *Newsweek* with the headline, "iPod, Therefore i Am." In the article, Jobs spells out how the iPod could also be used to back up a computer, to store photos, to call up addresses. Jobs was still educating consumers about what his pocket computer could do.

iPod changed how we listen to music, making our entire music collection portable. It could accompany us during workouts, in the car, in our dorm, even on vacation. We were never separated from the soundtrack of our lives. iTunes also tracked our listening habits, forming our "Top 25 Most Played" list. It made us more self-conscious music listeners. We could see which songs seeped into our subconscious. We might find our tastes embarrassing, leading to thoughts of "What should I be listening to?" Burgeoning adults couldn't erase their earlier devotion to teen idols like Britney Spears or Justin Bieber; iTunes remembered. The only way to alter our Top 25 was by listening more to other songs and artists. Everything about the iPod and iTunes pushed us toward more. A few artists and music aficionados complained about the sound quality of MP3. The high trebles and low bass were cut off to compress the sound into small files. But most consumers embraced the quantity over quality. Apple eventually altered their compression rates, offering larger files and richer sounds (for a higher price!). New iterations of the iPod meant more room for more songs.

The revolution that arrived with the iPod turned out to be merely the warm-up for the iPhone. Jobs's goals for the iPhone appeared rather modest: "You know, everybody has a cell phone, but I don't know one person who likes their cell phone. I want to make a phone that people love." Consumer demand reached a fever pitch prior to the iPhone's 2007 release, with Apple acolytes camping out to get theirs. Giddy tech analysts declared, "Much like the Western calendar marks time from before and after Jesus Christ . . . I am certain that the mobile telecoms world will count its time in two Eras. The Era BI: time Before the iPhone, and the ERA AI: time After the iPhone."[43] Communication professors Heidi Campbell and Antonio C. La Pastina of Texas A&M tracked, "How the iPhone became divine."[44] *Gizmodo* blogger Brian Lam mocked a Christmas speech by Pope Benedict XVI that asked, "Is a Savior needed?" Lam answered, "Of course we still need a Savior. Hopefully, our shepherd, Steve Jobs, will unveil Apple-Cellphone-Thingy, the true Jesus Phone—or jPhone—in two weeks, at the Macworld Keynote. It shall lift the hunger and disease you speak of from the land, as it will cure the rabid state of mind infecting Mac fanboys like yours truly."[45] The term *Jesus phone* caught on, becoming both a term of enthusiasm and derision, with the Canadian National Post mocking American gullibility: "The iPhone cometh . . . the day the mute will talk, the deaf will hear and the lame will walk."[46]

Rather than shying away from the religious connotations, Apple embraced the spiritual hype in an ad for the iPhone that echoed Michelangelo's Sistine Chapel, where the touch of God brings life to Adam. A hand reaches out to the phone screen. Light emanates from the phone, piercing the darkness. The tagline declares, "Touching is believing."

Why did we embrace the iPhone with such fervent enthusiasm? Ive and the Apple design team tapped into our yearning for aesthetics. How a phone looked proved as important as how a phone worked. Ive's innovative designs merged humanity and technology in pleasurable ways. With an infinite number of applications, backdrops, and accessories, our iPhones could be modified to suit our every mood. The Apple experience was all about personal expression. Apple went from making the computer accessible (with the Apple II, Macintosh, and iMac) to making it common, everyday, something in our pocket. Even those who didn't want to break their current cell phone contract could get close to the greatness with an iPod Touch (all the features of an iPhone without the phone).

The iPhone also pulled together the public and private aspects of our lives that had long been separated. We could attend our children's school performances and still check in with work. Such power in the palm of our hands means that we can instantly share an idea that occurs to us or get our questions answered as soon as we ask them. In addition, the array of technologies available in the App store turned the iPhone into a stock market ticker, a menu planner, a musical instrument, and even a light saber (complete with sounds and vibrations).

Pop culture was repackaged with the iPhone in mind. Our news, information, and video feeds were reformatted to Apple's specifications. In a *Wired* cover story, Nancy Miller dubbed the resulting shift as "snack culture." She described the endless buffet of "music, television, games, movies, fashion: We now devour our pop culture the same way we enjoy candy and chips—in conveniently packaged bite-size nuggets made to be munched easily with increased frequency and maximum speed. This is snack culture—and boy, is it tasty (not to mention addictive)."[47] We are all grazers, sampling from a wide array of apps and inputs. Professor S. Craig Watkins notes how we are consuming less of more. Thanks to the iPhone, "we have evolved from a culture of instant gratification to one of constant gratification."[48]

The iPhone is always on, always wired, always with us. It wakes us up, putting a song in our hearts. It delivers text messages and email from friends and family throughout the day. It accompanies us when we travel, offering directions and restaurant recommendations. It can almost feed us—or at least get food delivered to our door. We check in with it at night before we close our eyes. The iPhone orders our lives in comparable ways to praying the hours in the ancient church.

There is the constant temptation to relate to the iPhone rather than our world. It is a convenient filter for screening calls, keeping colleagues at a manageable distance. It provides a safe place to hide when we're anxious in a crowd. We avoid awkward moments by fading into our phone. It prompts us to look down rather than up, to ask Siri for answers rather than our friends, our parents, or our God. The iPhone is our most valuable possession and our closest companion. It records our lives, broadcasts our photos and thoughts, and serves as our traveling studio and electronic megaphone. It lives up to its hype.

The Power to Unplug

Unfortunately, all that power in our pocket has proved irresistible. We can't imagine living without it. We are always on, always available. And with so many entertainment options, "the one sure way for young people to use all of the media and technology they own is to use it simultaneously. . . . Communication scholars call it media multi-tasking."[49] While most of us consider texting harmless, we've seen disasters that can arise with multitasking. In Los Angeles, twenty-five people were killed when a Metrolink commuter train crashed into an oncoming Union Pacific freight train in 2008. The investigation afterward revealed that the Metrolink engineer was sending and receiving text messages seconds before the crash. Keeping his eyes on his smartphone rather than the train tracks turned into a deadly mistake. Dr. Rene Marois from the Human Information Processing Laboratory at Vanderbilt University has found that the brain fails at dual task trials. He wrote in the medical journal *Neuron*, "Our brains, it turns out, are not wired to process dual information simultaneously."[50]

The most common form of multitasking occurs around the house, where teens might text and tweet while studying on their laptop with the television and/or music on in the background. I've been known to play music while live sporting events play on the television. And if a phone call came in, I probably wouldn't turn either off. Now we feel the need to see and hear it all, to take in as much information as possible. Communication technology consultant Linda Stone says we multitask to save time: "We are motivated by a desire to be more productive and more efficient." Unfortunately, our brain creates "an artificial sense of constant crisis," which, in our "24/7, always-on world," makes us feel overwhelmed, overstimulated, and unfulfilled.[51] I have seen that sense of anxiety in my students and experienced it in my own sweaty, cell-phone-clutching hands.

Have we developed too much dependence on our iPhone? We sense that our smartphones are a source of distraction. But we feel powerless to resist them. We even carry them into the bathroom at the risk of dropping our devices in the toilet, shower, or sink. In the *New York Times*, Lizzie Skurnick proposed a new word to describe us: "Fidgital."[52] In his research with twenty-somethings, Watkins found, "If there are any regrettable aspects related to their engagement with social and mobile media, they consistently point to one factor: the difficulty in turning it off when they need to focus on school or work." The lure of instant updates is constant. Yet, Watkins concluded, "It is clear that they are looking for a place of refuge from the deluge of content accessible through their computers. They are also looking for a place to simply stop, disconnect, and think."[53] Can parents, educators, and pastors offer the permission students seek?

For a class experiment, I have our communication and media majors unplug for a day. No electronic devices allowed. They are fine with giving up email or laptops, maybe even the car stereo, but the thought of separating from their mobile devices is devastating. They bargain and cajole, insisting that their parents will panic. I hold my ground. No electronics and no cell phones. The results are revelatory. Students find the day unfolds slower than imagined. A lengthy to-do list turns into too much time on their hands. Drama between friends that felt like a crisis diminishes when they can no longer follow it on Facebook. They can't take sides when they can't text. Instead, the day may be spent hiking in the mountains, walking on the beach, sleeping in a dorm. My students consistently enter the exercise stressed out and exit feeling remarkably renewed. This is the power of perspective, the gift of Sabbath. Surely, if God took a break from work, we can follow that example. Can we shut off the cell phone long enough to recover the original purpose of Sabbath rest? Perhaps small groups or congregations could attempt cell-phone-free Sundays.

Or we could follow the example of Tiffany Shlain, director of the documentary *Connected*. As founder of the Webby Awards, Shlain thrived amid San Francisco's tech industry. Yet, she and her family honor her Jewish roots with a "technology Shabbat." Shlain writes,

> Every Friday, we all unplug from all our technologies and don't turn them on again until Saturday Evening. Unplugging for a day makes time slow down and makes me feel very present with my family. I not only appreciate this quality time with my family, but it has also made me appreciate technology in a whole new way. By Saturday night we can't wait to plug back in and act on every single thought I have.[54]

This high-tech maven acknowledges, "The idea of taking one day a week off from responsibilities and work is a very, very, very old idea. I think today with all the potential of the internet we also need to know when to 'not' be online. And that our minds and souls also need to unplug."[55] Spouses and families may be brought closer together by getting everyone's head looking up rather than down (at a smartphone).

Shlain and her colleagues at The Sabbath Manifesto have taken their movement nationwide. This collective of Jewish artists, playfully named "Reboot," launched a National Day of Unplugging in 2010. The group includes harried creatives, like the founder of Razorfish, the producer of *Six Feet Under*, and the creator of Showtime's *Weeds*. While acknowledging that they are not particularly religious, they begin in Genesis, "Way back when, God said, 'On the seventh day thou shalt rest.' The meaning behind it was simple: Take a break. Call a timeout. Find some balance. Recharge. Somewhere along the line, however, this mantra for living faded from modern consciousness. The idea of unplugging every seventh day now feels tragically close to impossible. Who has time to take time off? We need eight days a week to get tasks accomplished, not six."[56] Inspired by back-to-basics efforts like the Slow Food movement, the manifesto explains, "We have adapted our ancestors' rituals by carving out one day per week to unwind, unplug, relax, reflect, get outdoors, and get with loved ones."[57] Their ten principles are simple, basic, and quite doable:

1. Avoid technology.
2. Connect with loved ones.
3. Nurture your health.
4. Get outside.
5. Avoid commerce.
6. Light candles.
7. Drink wine.
8. Eat bread.
9. Find silence.
10. Give back.

What a refreshing weekend plan, whether started on Friday night in the Jewish tradition or observed from Saturday night to Sunday in Christian practice. Perhaps those furthest down the technology trail are best equipped to invite us to embrace an ancient alternative. We are called to cultivate the earth, to be creative with our tools. But we are also commanded to rest.

Parting Gift

Apple culled the best of the iPod and the iPhone together into Jobs's final gift to the world, the iPad. While I initially dismissed it as a "big iPod touch," others received the tablet as a new form of computing (or at least the fulfillment of John Sculley's long-forgotten aspirations for the Newton). Russell Belk noted how Apple's devoted followers ignored criticism, lining up outside Apple stores to buy the iPad: "That sort of loyalty and devotion would suggest that there's something more than an objective appraisal going on, and it's the same sort of faith and loyalty that we see in religions oftentimes."[58]

The iPad could undermine Apple's laptop business, but it also freed us from the desktop. We could now write or paint or draw from any room or setting we preferred. Tablets made the computer completely mobile—a constant companion in every setting. Creativity could occur whenever or wherever the inspiration struck.

The iPad also solidified Apple's hold on our pocketbooks. With the iPad, Apple loaded in all software, games, movies, books, and shows through the iTunes and App stores. It also locked out those developers and companies who refused to conform to Apple's standards. Those who had crossed Jobs were banished from Apple's garden. No Adobe Flash apps or media play on the iPad. *Forbes* magazine suggested that such tyrannical behavior made Apple more like Big Brother. Jobs was described as *The Simpsons'* Mr. Burns in a turtleneck.[59] Could the demands surrounding this parting innovation tarnish his legacy?

In death, Jobs was celebrated as a remarkable entrepreneur and innovator who changed how we relate to technology and one another. His biography was read around the world. Hollywood created multiple movies to celebrate his legacy. Jobs revolutionized computers, animation, cell phones, and music. But some still questioned why he was never known as a philanthropist. His perfectionism resulted in amazing products but very little outside of his amazingly profitable company. Was his life an inspiration or a cautionary tale—more angel or devil? A posthumous cover story in *Wired* magazine asked, "Do you *really* want to be like Steve Jobs?"[60] The question will be answered by the aspiring iGods that follow. The fluctuations in Apple's stock price since his death suggest that no one may be able to replace Jobs's marketing acumen.

While my children love the portability of the iPad, I was ultimately turned off by Jobs's parting gift. Was I too tethered to traditional desktop computing to appreciate the shift? The iPad seemed more like an effort to drive us toward the Apple Store than a creative revolution. Could the man who taught us what a computer could unleash have been satisfied to build a better store? Was the end goal of Apple to keep us inside their glowing confines? By putting their wares on the table, the Apple Store has become the most profitable retail experience per square foot. Employees, called "geniuses," find you. They answer your questions. An attitude of service, of informing, of bringing people along slowly pervades the store. Their products seemingly do not need to be pushed. They sell themselves. So the only questions revolve around makes and models. How big a screen do you need? What color do you want? How much memory and processing speed?

To create such a consistent experience in Apple Stores around the globe requires a rigorous regimen. *The Wall Street Journal* found that the stores demanded "full loyalty, no negativity." Thick training manuals for employees resulted in "intensive control of how employees interact with customers, scripted training for on-site tech support and consideration of every store detail down to the pre-loaded photos and music on demo devices."[61] From Shanghai to Manhattan, the Apple Store experience is remarkably consistent—a gleaming cathedral of consumption.[62]

Apple showed us how much we could do to and through a computer. Innovations in fonts and design enabled us to become desktop publishers, garage band musicians, or Final Cut pros. So why did the creative revolution begun with the Apple II and the Macintosh ultimately evolve into better ways to buy music and movies? Did Apple unleash so much creativity that we're desperate for containers to hold it? We've rewarded the rigorous creativity of Ive and his design team. We've paid a premium for the cachet associated with the Apple brand. Their products could unlock creativity in us or keep our consumption contained within their system. After Apple gave us amazing new ways to publish and edit and paint, I worry that the iPad is more about us paying Apple to be creative for us. It is a sleek new way to tap into old forms of media; but is the iPad a new way of relating to the world? It enables us to broadcast and podcast from anywhere on the planet. If it mostly drives me back to the Apple Store, then we've simply purchased a convenient way to consume more media. Apple may be offering new packaging of old media, beautiful products designed to keep us occupied inside their garden.

What is the application for people of faith? I am encouraged by how we've recovered our creativity. Aesthetics are returning to our worship settings and practices. I hope we are not merely creating better products to consume. Unlike the iPad, our churches should never be walled. They may have walls, but their doors are open. On the great cathedrals of Europe, the magnificent medieval steeples served as a clarion call to the entire community. Groundbreaking technology like bells ordered the day, telling neighbors what time it was, what activities might be most appropriate. The church served as a center for key rituals—baptisms, weddings, funerals. And while collections were taken up, churches were ultimately open-source, adopting Jesus's ethic expressed in the Gospel of Matthew, "Freely you have received; freely give."[63] Church should be a place you want to be (like we are attracted to the aesthetics and beauty of Apple). In those medieval cathedrals, the greatest architects and designers built a beacon of hope, a massive tribute to the most important thing in their lives—their faith. Artisans poured over minute details of statuary, masonry, doors, and stained glass. The finest workmanship went into the ground-shaking organs that communicated awe and wonder. Their values were invoked in every aspect of the experience, from the bells calling you to worship, to the doors inviting you into a sacred space, to the smells setting it apart as holy, to the music lifting your spirits, to the Gothic heights of the heavenly vision on the ceiling. Worship should feel so transporting, such a foretaste of glory divine, that you want to linger, to bask in the glory of the sights and sounds of the eternal story. It should feel better inside the walls than outside the walls. As with Apple, we know there is a significant difference simply because of the care put into each aspect of the design. But what is that transporting experience inside the garden—inside the cathedral, inside the Apple store—designed to inspire?

I wonder about that iPhone in our pockets. Will it make us better people, more awake and engaged with the world around us? Can we learn to think of it as a paintbrush used to paint God's glory? Can those apps become a call to God and a practical beacon of hope for our neighbors? The Apple experience may make my computing more creative, my photos and music organized with more access and aesthetics, but the test resides in my response—what have I done with the beauty to extend it to others? How do my words and images and actions bless the wider world after I've been inside the garden? We are called to be creative, to tend and plan and plow. They shall know us by our fruit.

Discuss

1. How has technology encouraged your creativity and enhanced your appreciation of beauty and design? Has it also encouraged you to consume more media and information?
2. What is the longest you've been unplugged from your devices? How did you feel?

A Brief History
of the Internet

Never memorize what you can look up in books.
—Albert Einstein

Once upon a time the internet had no advertising. It began as a government project, a backup system for the military housed at select universities. As primarily a network for academic research, the internet did not engage in business. When those restrictions began to lift in 1992, a flood of economic investment and possibilities followed. Business could be conducted via email, goods could be sold over the internet, and advertisers could sponsor webpages.[1] People rushed to get online. But how would those outside of academic circles gain access? Who could make sense of the arcane computer code that made email and websites possible? We didn't know who or what was online. And how to find what you're looking for amid an uncharted maze of possibilities? Seeking was easy, but finding proved elusive.

Like libraries of old, the internet was initially available only to the intelligentsia. Only academics and government researchers had electronic mail. It was used to exchange information about their projects with colleagues around the world. But the early days of the internet were messy, disorganized, and chaotic. How to create a web of connection to make it navigable?

A British computer scientist working at CERN (the particle physics lab in Switzerland) was frustrated by how much research was being done in physics that wasn't readily retrievable. He knew that breakthroughs are often built on prior discoveries, so the pooling of information is tremendously important for researchers. In 1990, this computer scientist, Tim Berners-Lee, built the first web browser, the first web server, and the first webpages that described his project—the world wide web. He recalls,

> Creating the web was really an act of desperation, because the situation without it was very difficult when I was working at CERN later. Most of the technology involved in the web, like the hypertext, like the Internet, multi-font text objects, had all been designed already. I just had to put them together. It was a step of generalizing, going to a higher level of abstraction, thinking about all the documentation systems out there as being possibly part of a larger imaginary documentation system.[2]

Working on a NeXT computer (from Steve Jobs's company!), Berners-Lee introduced the elements that have become web standards—uniform resources locators (URLs), hypertext transfer protocol (http), and hypertext markup language (HTML). His world wide web offered a unifying language, a way to organize and follow the pockets of research happening among scholars across the globe. Think of hyperlinks as academic footnotes, a way to track who said what, where, and when. (This metaphorical understanding would eventually launch Google.) Berners-Lee employed technical programming code to solve a communication problem. He reminds us, "The web, of course, is not a network of computers. The web is a network of people. The web is humanity interconnected."[3] Mathematician Ralph Abraham went even further in his enthusiasm, declaring,

> The WWW is miraculous. It is theological creativity in action. If you look at the Web, there are all these different pieces of software without which it couldn't run. These pieces were created by volunteers, people who were responding to a kind of divine guidance. They were being pushed toward creative synthesis. The miraculous way the parts go together can't be a coincidence. There were too many different inventions in totally different labs.[4]

For technologists (and many users), the world wide web was a miracle that brought us together in unprecedented ways. But what if I couldn't afford a NeXT computer? Or didn't have access to electronic mail?

In his "A Brief History of Cyberspace," circa 1995, Mark Pesce said, "There are two ages of the Internet—before Mosaic, and after. The combination of Tim Berners-Lee's Web protocols, which provided connectivity, and Marc Andreessen's browser, which provided a great interface, proved explosive. In twenty-four months, the Web has gone from being unknown to absolutely ubiquitous."[5] While Berners-Lee provided the standards for the world wide web, the average computer user was still a long way from knowing how to navigate it. The web was great for finding academic papers, but what about images to go with those texts? In 1993, the National Center for Supercomputing Applications (NCSA) at the University of Illinois launched a browser named Mosaic. The graphical user interface was user-friendly, incorporating both text and images. The creators of Mosaic, Andreessen and Eric J. Bina, emerged as early icons of the internet. (But like Jobs and Woz, Andreessen made the magazine covers while Bina faded into the background). Mosaic made the web truly multimedia.

After graduation from Illinois, Andreessen moved to Silicon Valley. The Mosaic browser was reimagined as the product Netscape Navigator for the for-profit venture Netscape Communications Corporation. Netscape Navigator quickly became *the way* to navigate the web. Unfortunately, Netscape Communications did not have the deep pockets to hold off challenges from software titans like Gates and Microsoft. The NCSA had licensed their Mosaic code to a for-profit subsidiary, Spyglass, Inc. Later Mosaic formed the basis for Microsoft's Internet Explorer. Who would win the internet browser war—the upstart Netscape Communications or the Goliath-like Microsoft? Given the discrepancy in financial resources (Microsoft made more on interest than Netscape Communications earned in a year), it was never a fair fight. Netscape Communications charged for their browser while Microsoft could afford to give theirs away. When Microsoft bundled their browser with Windows, almost all of us became Internet Explorers. Microsoft won the first internet war—over browsers.

The second big internet fight was over access. How would people outside of academic communities get online? America Online (AOL), CompuServe, and EarthLink provided dial-up access to the internet for an affordable price. I vividly recall researching internet access for a Danish production company in Hollywood that was eager to get online. When I compared these pioneering internet service providers, I discovered that AOL was mostly interested in keeping their customers inside their friendly confines; people who dialed into

AOL did not realize that they weren't ever getting to the world wide web. They were roaming around AOL's channels, carefully curated to offer all sorts of accessible information. AOL was a glossy, walled garden that blended broad newspaper categories and the ethos of television channels with early online games. Their chat rooms became a popular way to meet people online. While the Danish production company chose EarthLink over the more tech-heavy CompuServe, most people opted to pop in the compact discs from AOL that blanketed magazines, newsstands, and mailboxes. It seemed so quick and easy. AOL's enthusiastic greeting, "You've got mail," provided a warm, human feel to electronic mail. AOL made millions providing the easiest on ramp to the information superhighway. And their customers rarely realized that they were spending all their online time at AOL's gas, food, and lodging.

The race was on to become the most popular internet portal. The questions shifted from who provides our internet access to who would centralize services—email, news, search. Who could make sense of the internet?

With the expansion of the world wide web, we suddenly had a vast database to comb through. But it lacked a Dewey decimal system. It was easy to get lost online or not even know what we might be missing. I bought a copy of *MacWorld* magazine simply because it included a huge fold-out map of cyberspace. It grouped pioneering websites under broad categories, like education, entertainment, and sports. We were constantly surprised by how many islands of information had already been established. Pioneers were staking out domain names, planting digital flags, founding websites like "The Church of Tarantino." We bookmarked favorite sites, planning to return. But we weren't sure if we would ever find the same corner of cyberspace. How to navigate this jumble of pages, profiles, and links?

Two students working on their doctorates at Stanford University inadvertently stumbled across a solution. One was born outside the United States, immigrating to America as a child. Both were in search of a dissertation topic that would sustain their interest. They didn't recognize the financial upside of their research. Interest spread via word of mouth among their fellow grad students. They could barely keep up with the traffic generated by their project. The Stanford servers were taxed and tested by their rapid success. They needed to move their operation off campus. But to do this, they needed money. They tried to sell their project to many existing Silicon Valley companies, but nobody wanted to buy it. So they backed into a business plan in order to attract investors. Their start-up grew so rapidly that they never returned to Stanford to complete their PhDs. Becoming billionaires before they were thirty ensured that they left without regrets. This is the story of Larry Page and Sergey Brin, cofounders of Google. (We'll return to their story in chapter 5.) But this is also the narrative of Jerry Yang and David Filo, creators of Yahoo!.

In 1993, Jerry Yang started making lists of all the interesting sites he found on the world wide web. His fellow Stanford grad student, David Filo, wrote a software program to automate Jerry's lists, called "Jerry and David's Guide to the World Wide Web." It debuted in late 1994. Global demand for their directory exploded. John Battelle, editor of *Wired*, noted, "Within the first thirty days, the site had logged visitors from thirty countries, a fact that still astounds Yahoo!'s founders."[6] In search of a more memorable name, Yang and Filo turned to the dictionary, and started with "YA," a computer science acronym for "Yet Another," and decided on "Yahoo." The word operated on multiple levels—as a reference to a country hick (Filo was from Louisiana), as a playful shout (and thus the addition of an exclamation point to the company's name), and as an acronym for "Yet Another Hierarchical Officious Oracle."[7] Yahoo! sorted their links into broad categories like arts, science, business, and so on. To create a hierarchy of categories and subcategories required a fair amount of editing. Yahoo! served as a curator of the early world wide web, identifying what existed and determining what deserved the most attention. Their power was concentrated in directories; their focus was on quality. It was a labor-intensive process. Like the ancient oracles, Yang and Filo (and their rapidly expanding staff) became the font of wisdom, the high priests of unchartered territory. To those wandering into cyberspace without a guide, Yahoo! offered a smart and fun way to navigate the web.

What Yahoo! and many, many others failed to anticipate was the sheer growth of the world wide web. Like the Dewey decimal system, the Yahoo! model organized sites according to categories and interests. It put like-minded sites and subjects together. But what if my questions were more specific? What if we didn't want to know where to look but just needed a simple answer? Yahoo! editor-in-chief Srinija Srinivasan reflects, "The shift from exploration and discovery to the intent-based search of today was inconceivable. Now we go online expecting everything we want to find will be there. That's a major shift."[8] While Yahoo! was battling AOL, Excite, and Microsoft to become the biggest web portal, all of them overlooked the burgeoning problem of too much information.

Today's Deals   Gift Cards   Sell   Help

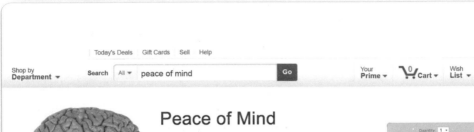

Shop by
Department ▾   Search   All ▾   peace of mind   Go   Your
Prime ▾   0 **Cart** ▾   Wish
List ▾

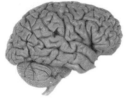

Peace of Mind

★★★★★ ☑ (1,000,000,000 customer reviews)

$999.99 & eligible for free shipping

Out of stock.

Order now and we'll deliver when available. We'll e-mail you with an estimated
delivery date as soon as we have more information. Your account will only be
charged when we ship the item.

Quantity: 1 ▾

Add to Cart

or

Sign in to turn on 1-Click ordering.

Add to Wish List

Amazon

Personalized Abundance

In some ways the Web is the most important book in the world.
—Jeff Bezos[1]

What is your favorite book? It may be a childhood classic that transports you back to your childhood, curled up in bed, comforted by your parent's voice, as vibrant images flip past. *Peter Rabbit. Pat the Bunny. The Cat in the Hat. The Very Hungry Caterpillar. Goodnight Moon.* The look, the feel, the smell of books awakens our senses, conjuring up all kinds of vibrant associations. We may recall a golden summer of reading at the beach when Harry, Hermione, and Ron felt like our new best friends; Hogwarts was the one school we never wanted to leave. We may remember the sensation of riding the subway, matching the pace of a page-turning thriller by Stephen King or Patricia Cornwell. Books are mental trips that we associate with the world around us. I can remember where I was when the truth of Ralph Ellison's *Invisible Man* bore into my psyche. I cherish my first soul-stirring encounter with *The Brothers Karamazov* on a train in Japan. Stories have the power to move us to laughter and tears, to shift our paradigms, to alter our behavior.

For Jeff Bezos and Amazon.com, it was never about books. It could have been cereal or shoes or screwdrivers. The ecommerce revolution was about how things are bought and sold, not what is bought and sold. Books were merely a pawn in a much bigger retailing chess game. For book lovers, that is a hard truth to accept.

Authors, publishers, and bookstores took Amazon's disruption of their industry so personally. How could a well-heeled, long-established business like book publishing be upended by a virtual store? How could a warehouse in Seattle dictate the terms to editors in New York? How could a delivery service undercut the comfort of a well-lit bookstore and a warm cup of coffee? The combination of low prices, fast service, and endless choice brought stores like Borders to their knees.

Nevertheless, there are more books being published than ever, almost 200,000 new titles per year in the United States. Martin Luther observed in 1569, "The multitude of books is a great evil. There is no measure of limit to this fever for writing; every one must be an author; some out of vanity, to acquire celebrity and raise up a name; others for the sake of mere gain."[2] In Amazon's world, anybody can be an author. Self-publishing has never been easier. No more waiting for editors or publishers to approve a manuscript. We don't need the permission or approval of a New York publishing house. With the Kindle, Amazon promises higher royalty rates, and "publishing takes less than five minutes and your book usually appears on the Kindle Store within a day."[3] We can fulfill God's calling to be fruitful by sending our stories around the world in one click.

Unfortunately, capturing someone's attention and collecting their cash is tougher than ever. Amazon expanded our choices but added to the clutter. Publishers and editors used to sort through the stacks of submissions for us, plumbing for gold amid the dross. Now, the onus is on us. Clay Shirky notes how technology expands freedom but undercuts quality. He suggests, "Before Gutenberg, the average book was a masterpiece. After Gutenberg, people got throwaway erotic novels, dull travelogues, and hagiographies of the landed gentry, of interest to no one today but a handful of historians. The great tension in media has always been that freedom and quality are conflicting goals."[4] Let the author and buyer beware.

As a writer, I was initially pleased to see Amazon offer sales updates in something close to real time. When people ask how a book is doing, I used to have almost no way of knowing. Or at least not until a quarterly sales report arrived. But Amazon tracks how a book is selling even before it is released. Of course, the downside is seeing your sales slow and maybe even plummet.

Amazon can be the bearer of bad news when your book is selling for a penny (plus shipping and handling). It is humbling to see that your words become remarkably close to worthless.

Amazon also democratized reviews. Authors still covet a blurb in *Publisher's Weekly* or a review in the *New York Times*. But in the meantime, Aunt Tilly's recommendation on Amazon might spark a spike in sales. Professors could assign an entire class to post a review. It turns out you need a thick skin to publish in Amazon's world because you also must endure the slings of the public such as, "Derweiller's insights in his INTO THE DARK fall short on both the theological and artistic levels." (I can handle the criticism, but at least spell my name correctly.)

Amazon is even tougher for publishing companies with thin profit margins. Publishers know what they need to make their economic model work. And yet, Amazon upsets that shopping cart by undercutting list prices with narrow margins. This downward spiral has been most troubling for bookstores. Borders buried local bookstores with their bigger inventories. But they did not understand the size or scope of ecommerce. In 2001, they outsourced their online business to Amazon. In 2011, they filed for Chapter 11 bankruptcy. They were put out of business by a virtual store that had no walls, low overhead, and an endless supply that scaled up to meet demand almost in real time.

The most galling aspect of Amazon to writers, publishers, and booksellers: it was never really about books. Or rather, it was always about more than books; it was a new way to sell stuff, built on a culture of metrics that tapped into customers' preferences and demands. Amazon got rich by being the customer's best friend (and the traditional, brick-and-mortar retailer's worse nightmare). It brought an abundance of options to the widest audience possible in the most convenient matter imaginable: from desire to doorstep in days. As TechCrunch declared, "We now see that Amazon's ultimate, bold vision is to credibly offer any*thing*, any*where*, any*time*—to everyone."[5]

This chapter will study the long view adopted by Jeff Bezos to dominate online retail. From an initial impetus to "get big fast," Amazon has made incremental shifts in their interface and delivery systems that allowed it to scale up during the initial internet bubble and survive when in popped. A relentless commitment to convenience, from 1-click ordering to "Free Super Saver Shipping," separated Amazon from their competitors. By personalizing the shopping experience through recommendations, Amazon replaced the local bookstore. While Steve Jobs was making headlines for Apple, Bezos was slowly studying metrics for Amazon. He wasn't creating devices but building loyalty. Amazon now owns the store, the mall, and the customer. What can Amazon's practices tell us about abundance, about how to respond to the stuff that surrounds us? And how can we recover a connection to the things we buy, to the people who created them?

No Regrets

Like Jobs, Bezos never knew his biological father. His seventeen-year-old mother, Jackie Gise, eventually married eighteen-year-old Mike Bezos, who had fled Castro's Cuba in the early 1960s. Mike legally adopted Jeff, raising him as if he were Jeff's natural father. Jeff didn't learn his full origin story until age ten, but he told *Wired*, "I'm not embarrassed by it."[6] Mike Bezos became a petroleum engineer for Exxon. Jeff's maternal grandfather, Pop Gise, worked on space technology and missile defense systems before supervising 26,000 employees at the Atomic Energy Commission's Albuquerque office.

Bezos was always fascinated by space, by technology, and he loved tinkering. His mother, Jackie, recalled countless trips to Radio Shack. Bezos graduated as valedictorian of his Miami high school and enrolled at Princeton as a physics major. When he discovered that the competition to be the best was fiercer than expected, he "settled" for majoring in computer science. His analytical skills were a great fit for Wall Street. By age thirty, he was a senior vice president for D. E. Shaw, an investment management firm, making seven figures managing their hedge funds. Bezos could easily have followed the comfortable trail blazed by countless Princeton grads who made millions on Wall Street. But he couldn't ignore the numbers. When Al Gore sponsored the Information Infrastructure and Technology Act of 1992, it opened up the government-sponsored project to commercial interests, paving the way for the information superhighway to be monetized. Shortly thereafter, the National Science Foundation privatized the internet domain registry, and ".com" became truly commercial. By 1994, the internet was growing by 2,300 percent annually. Bezos put those numbers into his personal "regret minimization framework." He asked himself, "When I'm 80, am I going to regret leaving Wall Street? No. Will I regret missing the beginning of the Internet? Yes."[7]

How did a Wall Street broker decide to become a bookseller? Bezos analyzed the top twenty mail-order businesses and determined which one could be conducted more efficiently over the internet.[8] Books were the only commodity with too many items to print in a catalog. The two largest book distributors, Ingram and Baker & Taylor, had massive electronic lists that they shared with bookstores. They stocked warehouses full of titles that even the largest bookstores couldn't keep on hand. The bookstores filed the customers' requests, and the distributors filled them. There was a lag between what we might be searching for and the system that delivered it.

Bezos stepped into that breach, enabling us to find what we were searching for. He understood that the internet loved massive, dynamic databases. What if he could fill in the gap between customers' requests and the distributors' electronic lists? Amazon was born out of the problem of too many books and not enough space, or as Bezos put it, "Real estate doesn't obey Moore's law." (Moore's law says that the number of transistors that can fit on an integrated circuit doubles every two years; in other words, computers have taken up less space over time. Not so with books.) Bezos could afford to do on the internet what a physical bookstore could never do—offer easy access to three million different books. So, why did Amazon end up in Washington state? Seattle was located just six hours from Roseburg, Oregon, home of the Ingram book warehouse. Such proximity meant Amazon could fill requests faster than most bookstores. Washington was also a sparsely populated state, unlike Silicon Valley in California. Amazon would have to pay sales tax on only a small percentage of its orders—those originating from within Washington. A third reason to choose Seattle was the large talent pool associated with Microsoft.[9] Bezos wanted to build the company around the best and the brightest.

Like all good internet creation narratives, the Amazon story begins in the modest garage of the home that Jeff and his wife, MacKenzie, rented in Bellevue, Washington. The first employee was Shel Kaphan, a programmer who moved up from Santa Cruz, California. Kaphan was a product of the sixties who had worked on the *Whole Earth Catalog*. He liked the mission of Amazon, "which was basically providing information to people in far-flung places that would have a hard time getting access to it otherwise."[10] They were joined by a University of Washington computer whiz, Paul Davis. Jeff set up three Sun SPARCstations on tables made out of doors (bought at Home Depot).[11] While Kaphan and Davis handled the programming, Bezos refined the business plan. The potbelly stove and space heaters in the garage weren't enough to keep them comfortable through the winter, so they often retreated to the Starbucks inside Barnes & Noble for strategy sessions. What irony—traditional booksellers offered comfortable space for the start-up that would undo them. "Amazon" was chosen as the company's name because as the world's largest river, it connoted size and selection. And it started with the letter *A*, a competitive advantage in an era when the first directories of cool websites were being created. It was good to be at the top of the list.[12]

On July 16, 1995, Amazon went live on the web. Bezos told his three hundred friends who had served as beta testers to spread the word. In the first thirty days, Amazon sold books in all fifty states and forty-five foreign countries with no press or advertisements, just word of mouth. By September, sales were topping $20,000 per week.[13] Many may assume that Amazon was the first online bookseller, but books.com, clbooks.com, and wordsworth.com had already beaten them to the marketplace. How would Amazon climb to the top of the ecommerce ladder? By following Bezos's directive to "get big fast."[14]

The Long View

Adam and Eve didn't need to shop. They were surrounded by abundance in the garden of Eden. They also didn't have anybody to compare themselves to—no need for status symbols. But envy drove a wedge between their sons, Cain and Abel. In Genesis 4, Cain is described as a farmer while Abel worked as a shepherd. When it came time to honor God with sacrifices, Cain put forth the fruits of his crop while Abel drew from his flock. The Bible doesn't spell out why God looked with favor on Abel and his offering rather than Cain, but rage, jealousy, and murder resulted. We've been comparing ourselves to our siblings, parents, and neighbors ever since. We envy our neighbors' cars, homes, jobs, reputations, and businesses. We want bigger, better, brighter, shinier, and newer. Goods can be good. I admire a finely crafted jacket or shirt. I love the feel of Egyptian cotton and four-hundred-thread-count sheets. We can all tell the difference between the finest European chocolate and a cheap candy bar. Greed and jealousy have a way of capturing our hearts and obscuring our vision.

In the early days of the commercial internet, it didn't matter if a company was profitable. Bigger was better, irrespective of the cost. Amazon rode the first wave of web enthusiasm. Silicon Valley venture capitalists like Kleiner Perkins Caufield and Byers invested in Bezos's start-up. Amazon added employees every month, hurtling toward an initial public stock offering. The race was on to become the biggest brand names on the internet. Websites scrambled to dominate each sector of the marketplace, from drugstore.com to carsdirect. com. Pets.com became the largest online seller of pet supplies. They made a big, initial splash with investors even though the company lost $1.32 for every dollar of merchandise it sold![15]

Brand names and luxury goods became symbols of conspicuous consumption. Sociologist Sharon Zukin observes that since the nineties,

> Shopping has become our principal strategy for creating value. With the shift of the economy toward consumption and our weaker attachment to traditional forms, religions, and politics, shopping has come to define who we, as individuals, are and what we, as a society, want to become. . . . Low prices define our conception of democracy. Brand names represent our search for a better life. Designer boutiques embody the promise of an ever improving self.[16]

Amid the dot-com boom, Bezos's goal of becoming "Earth's Biggest Bookstore" made sense. When Amazon went public on May 15, 1997, the initial public offering raised $54 million, giving the company a market value of $438 million (even though they hadn't turned a profit).[17] By October, Amazon had become one of the top twenty-five most visited sites on the internet, and one million customers had entrusted Amazon with their names, addresses, phone numbers, and credit cards. One out of every hundred books purchased in the United States was now sold by Amazon.[18] What looks modest in retrospect was astounding at the time: a virtual store selling real goods.

Over the next two years, Amazon stock split frequently with the value rising 5,600 percent (that is not a misprint—five thousand six hundred percent in two years).[19] The gold rush was on—and speculation ran wild. Amazon turned their influx of cash into a buying spree, swapping stock for other start-ups. Bezos invested in e-tailers like pets.com, gear.com, drugstore.com, and homegrocer.com for far more than their real-world worth. Such growth during the dot-com boom proved costly. By 1999, Amazon was serving 14 million customers but lost $720 million for the year. Yet, *Time* magazine named Bezos their "Person of the Year."

At age thirty-five, the tech wunderkind was the youngest honoree since Martin Luther King Jr. in 1963. *Time* editor (and Steve Jobs biographer) Walter Isaacson explained their choice: "The fact that Amazon.com hasn't turned a profit and may be a bubble is part of the news and part of the story. He's a symbol of dotcom companies that don't turn a profit but have high market valuations."[20] In 2000, Amazon expanded their reach to 20 million customers, and their financial losses grew to $1.4 billion.[21]

So how did Amazon manage to survive when so many other companies perished? If Amazon's short-term goal was "get big fast," their long-term goal was more measured. Their first letter to shareholders in 1997 was titled, "It's all about the long term." Bezos reasoned,

> If everything you do needs to work on a three-year time horizon, then you're competing against a lot of people. But if you're willing to invest on a seven-year time horizon, you're now competing against a fraction of those people, because very few companies are willing to do that. Just by lengthening the time horizon, you can engage in endeavors that you could never otherwise pursue. At Amazon we like things to work in five to seven years. We're willing to plant seeds, let them grow—and we're very stubborn. We say we're stubborn on vision and flexible on details.[22]

"Get big fast" was chastened by another popular motto for Bezos: "It is always Day One at Amazon."[23] Amazon built infrastructure and scale, hiring wisely, learning as they grew. In 2001, they earned their first quarterly net profit, becoming one of the first profitable online businesses.

They made mistakes (like trying to take on eBay in the online auction business), but they adjusted. They purchased companies like cdnow.com and imdb.com (Internet Movie Database) that fit in with their core business of books, music, and video. Amazon proved to be a cyber-tortoise amid internet hares. Bezos seemed to operate with a wisdom that other dot-com speculators lacked.

At a TED talk in 2003, Bezos compared the early internet bubble to the California gold rush.[24] When the gold was mined, the rush was over. But he suggested that the internet is more like the rise of electricity. Ecommerce is a utility, something that powers our lives. And the appliances that arose from Edison's invention took years to be perfected. Bezos wasn't trying to win a quick sprint toward gold but a long race, composed of small steps (small margins and profits) en route to something larger—a relationship.

Personalization

My father sold used cars. Electronic commerce was utterly inconceivable to him because his business was based on trust. It was rooted in relationships—in looking a customer in the eye, negotiating a price, and shaking hands to seal the deal. Satisfied customers would return and even recommend him to friends and family. My Dad believed businesses are built on customer satisfaction and word of mouth. So he was skeptical of online transactions. My Dad wondered, "Why should I entrust my credit card numbers to a machine? How do I know if I will ever receive the goods I paid for? Who can I complain to if an internet company fails to deliver?" The notion of a used car salesman who doesn't trust the internet seems humorous, but prior to Amazon and eBay, nobody knew if people would take the risks inherent in online commerce. Amazon had to convince millions of people that they were not only trustworthy but preferable to brick-and-mortar stores. Almost twenty years later, Amazon regularly tops the University of Michigan's annual Customer Satisfaction Index, ranking higher than retailers like Target, Walmart, Costco, and even Apple.[25] How did Amazon.com build such loyalty and trust in a start-up brand?

Bezos spelled out his priorities: "Our vision is the world's most customer-centric company. The place where people come to find and discover anything they might want to buy online."[26] According to Bezos, Amazon has always focused on three things: the best selection, the lowest prices, and the cheapest and most convenient delivery. He doesn't expect those desires to change: "Ten years from now, customers will still want vast selection, low prices and fast, accurate delivery. In fact, it is impossible to imagine a world 10 years from now where customers will say, I love Amazon, but I just wish your prices would be higher."[27] While Apple appealed to customers willing to pay higher prices for the sleekest products, Amazon was content to take small slices of a much bigger pie. Bezos acknowledges the differences:

> There are two ways to build a successful company. One is to work very, very hard to convince customers to pay high margins. The other is to work very, very hard to be able to afford to offer customers low margins. They both work. We're firmly in the second camp. It's difficult—you have to eliminate defects and be very efficient. But it's also a point of view. We'd rather have a very large customer base and low margins than a smaller customer base and higher margins.[28]

Amazon may not have been perceived as cool or as sexy as Apple. Bezos didn't make as many magazine covers as an iGod like Steve Jobs. But the long, slow ascent to slim margins from the world's biggest bazaar proved equally profitable.

Amazon never had the lowest prices. Books.com sold their titles for less, yet customers preferred Amazon. What separated Amazon from their competitors? Amazon focused on customer satisfaction. Bezos understood the power of word of mouth on the internet—for profit or loss. In 1996, long before the rise of social networking, he noted, "If you make customers unhappy in the real world, they might each tell six friends. If you make customers unhappy on the Internet, they can each tell 6,000 friends."[29] Customers want products that are available (selection), affordable (price), and accessible (convenience). With constant updates to their interface, Amazon made the online shopping experience easy.

In 1999, Amazon was granted a patent for its "1-click ordering." A big initial barrier to electronic commerce was inputting data. Who wanted the hassle of taking out a credit card and entering their personal information for every purchase? Brand expert Nick Shore noted the distinction offered by 1-click ordering: "Amazon is saying, 'we're not a book brand, we're a convenience brand with books, music, auctions, video.' They are locking into a higher need state."[30] In a busy world of infinite choices, low prices are not necessarily enough. With 1-click ordering, Amazon became the king of convenience.

They also invested millions in regional warehouses and distribution centers to fulfill orders in an efficient manner. To cover the East, their second warehouse was built in Delaware, a state that has no sales tax. Another was built in Reno, Nevada, close enough to deliver to California but just outside California's substantial state taxes. Bar codes ensured that orders rose above human error. With the introduction of Super Saver Shipping in 2002, Amazon discovered that we will buy more in order to save on shipping costs. Margins lost on Super Saver Shipping were exceeded by the profits made on a second book or another CD or DVD. What Amazon delivers to our door is captured in the logo on the box—choices from A to Z, served with a smile. We never communicate with a human in the buying process, and yet we still feel like Amazon knows us. The company comes across as Santa Claus, offering stealthy delivery of our hearts' desires through our chimney.

Amazon tapped into core shifts in customer behavior. While we may like the sociability of shopping, the hassles of traffic and parking can make it a chore. And nothing is more frustrating than discovering that an item is out of stock. Amazon removes the pain of parking and the possibility of disappointment. It raises our level of efficiency. We have come to prefer the click to the brick—five satisfying minutes online rather than an afternoon at the mall.

Yet, all that time spent online is a step away from human contact. We are removed from a local store that might host a regional author, and we lose the personal connection from a clerk who offers us a recommendation or who says, "I *loved* that book." So does the convenience of Amazon undermine community? Online shopping may be tailored to our tastes, but it is a disembodied experience.

Products used to be created and distributed locally. We knew the cobbler, the tailor, the candlestick maker. Manufacturing went overseas in pursuit of lower labor costs, and big-box stores collected our dollars. Shopping became transactional and impersonal. The rise of Amazon was the logical extension. No (visible) people necessary. The smile is on the box rather than on a person.

Relational Shopping

Why do we prefer interacting with a computer more than a salesperson? Perhaps we have more faith in metrics than in local merchants. Amazon built customer loyalty through personalization—they built a relationship with each customer—and by educating their customers. Amazon welcomed customer reviews—both positive or negative. Professional critics for newspapers and magazines carried no more weight at Amazon than the average Joe. Amazon became a dynamic and democratic form of Consumer Reports, a place where everyone could have a voice and a vote. The risky move was upsetting to authors and book publishers and controversial to all kinds of consumer product companies. Bezos insisted that "inventing and pioneering requires a willingness to be misunderstood for long periods of time."[31] He remembers a befuddled letter that said, "You don't understand your business. You make money when you sell things. Why do you allow these negative customer reviews?" Bezos says, "When I read that letter, I thought, we don't make money when we sell things. We make money when we help customers make purchase decisions."[32] Amazon builds relationships with customers, not products, or perhaps more accurately, relationships between customers and products and products and products. Loyalty arises from offering the most helpful information and accurate recommendations.

Customer reviews became a valuable commodity when combined with purchasing patterns. Greg Linden designed and developed the recommendation algorithm at Amazon, distinguishing it as "item-to-item collaborative filtering." Linden and his colleagues explained the mathematical process: "Rather than matching the user to similar customers, item-to-item collaborative filtering matches each of the user's purchased and rated items to similar items, then combines those similar items into a recommendation list."[33] Unlike traditional algorithms that require a large database to be effective, the Amazon model could pinpoint and personalize recommendations after only two or three purchases. It required less than a second of processing time to generate online recommendations and could react immediately to changes in our buying or searching habits. The more we bought, the smarter Amazon's computers got.

"Customers who bought this item also bought . . ." became a powerful and profitable marketing mechanism. An early Amazon employee, James Marcus, recalls "the strange and dispiriting phenomenon: the religion of statistics." He served as a book editor, writing capsule descriptions and reviews; he describes Amazon's bean-counting cult: "Numbers were everything. A spreadsheet with its panoramic procession of figures, had the sort of clout once reserved for the Delphic oracle . . . we were able to track customer behavior like no other company in the history of retail."[34]

Amazon's metrics made recommendations that approached or even exceeded the old notion of the local merchant. Such personalization made a powerful imprint and instilled customer loyalty. Bezos explained, "It's just like in traditional retail. If a small-town merchant knew your tastes, he could tell you if something interesting came in and he suspected you might want it. That was very valuable. If there was another merchant who opened up next door and didn't have five years of experience with you, then you wouldn't have as good a shopping experience there, just because the person didn't know you as well."[35] The algorithm became a trusted authority. We bought more on impulse because the recommendations reflected our interests so accurately.

Evan Schwartz, author of *Webonomics*, suggests that companies like Amazon are primarily selling intangible relationships: "Amazon should not be compared to actual stores selling books. Rather . . . the value that Amazon adds is in the reviews, the recommendations, the advice, the information about new and upcoming releases, the user interface, the community interest around certain subjects. Yes, Amazon will arrange to deliver the book to your door, but you as a customer are really paying them for the information that led to your purchase."[36] Kevin Kelly concludes, "When you log on to Amazon you get a relationship generator, one that increasingly knows you better."[37] Netflix applied the same principles to home video. The more we watched, the better their prediction patterns got. We gravitated toward companies that anticipated our needs, recommended our wants. In a world of too much, we desperately needed a retailer who "knew us." The power of the iGods resides in their ability to reflect and refine our tastes. They provide a mirror forged in metrics.

Traditional retailers spent millions decorating their storefronts, trying to draw shoppers in off the street. In 1897, L. Frank Baum, author of *The Wizard of Oz*, began publishing a trade journal called *The Show Window* and a year later founded the National Association of Window Trimmers. He described the goal of any good store-display designer to "arouse in the observer the cupidity and longing to possess the goods."[38] Window shopping became a source of entertainment. But it was always a guessing game, trying to figure out what colors or styles would appeal to shoppers. What if they invested in brown when customers wanted black? Amazon's algorithms removed the guesswork. They now knew what we wanted even before we entered. They could send an email pegged to our previous purchases. They could remind us of things we searched for weeks ago that were newly arrived. Amazon personalized the storefront. They could tailor the store to reflect our wants, our desires, our passions. Shopping was more about us than ever before.

Church Shopping

What are the implications of personalized shopping for faith communities? We are so accustomed to Amazon catering to our interests that we began to evaluate congregations based upon what they could do for us. A fully programmed "family life center" became a standard feature for those hoping to attract young parents. Churchgoers became church shoppers, comparing Sunday school rooms, playgrounds, and sports facilities. What pastor would want to have their sermons rated online? Will the performative aspects of preaching become even more pronounced under such additional pressure? Yelp, a user review website, currently lists 2,322 churches in Los Angeles. Many of the reviews are quite enthusiastic and positive. They were written by "fans" who attend on a regular basis. Imagine how important the discipleship process may become: "satisfied" church members will retain the power to post glowing reviews online and in the local community. But there are also responses from first-time visitors and those looking for a wedding site. Comments refer to the appearance of the sanctuary or the ease of parking. There is praise and criticism directed at everyone from the greeters to the pastors.

While I can see the value of Yelp, particularly for a person new to a city who is trying to assess where to begin, it plays into the Amazon narrative—it makes everyone a potential critic and church just another experience waiting to be reviewed.

Dwight Friesen, professor at Mars Hill Graduate School in Seattle, sees church reviews as comparable to an "ecclesiastical bandstand" with people ranking places of worship as if it were an Olympic competition. The danger, according to Friesen, is that "it reduces church to a commodity to be consumed." Friesen offers a helpful caution: "The church, at the end of the day, is not a commodity—it's more like a family."[39]

We don't get to choose the families we're born into, but church shopping and church hopping continue to vex pastors. People come and go in search of a place that matches their needs and lines up with their convictions. Could people of faith be helped by an application that matched their beliefs to churches? What's the problem with that? Isn't that what denominations used to do? The problem with an Amazon- or Yelp-style system is that it puts the customer in charge. It aligns the church to our will when discipleship is rooted in conforming ourselves to God's will. Long-term commitment to the same church community is designed to shave off our self-destructive edges. Those who know us best may be best equipped to call us toward a higher plane, to inspire our better angels. The wisdom of Proverbs 27:17 says, "As iron sharpens iron, so one person sharpens another." But what if we're always on the move, looking for a better church or school or partner?

The church is one place where we could come together as a diverse community, but many churches will often divide people into smaller units of parents, seniors, youth, and schoolchildren. We plug people into prepackaged programs geared around one particular age group or interest. Scottish theologian John Drane worries about the "McDonaldization of the church."[40] In commodified religion, following God is reduced to a formula, salvation a one-time transaction. As with Amazon and McDonald's, efficiency, calculability, and predictability reign. We've seen the adverse effects of an unbalanced, supersized diet of spiritual junk food.

In an Amazon world, a plethora of choices is also accompanied by the expectation that our choices will be cheap and convenient. We expect things to be fast, easy, and painless. During World War II, Dietrich Bonhoeffer warned us of the dangers of cheap grace that sells the sacraments and the forgiveness of sins at cut-rate prices. Amid the horrific choices of Nazi-era Germany, Bonhoeffer wrote, "Cheap grace is the grace we bestow on ourselves. Cheap grace is the preaching of forgiveness without requiring repentance, baptism without church discipline, Communion without confession. . . . Cheap grace is grace without discipleship, grace without the cross, grace without Jesus Christ, living and incarnate."[41]

The Bible makes it clear that our ways are not God's ways. We are called to do justly, to love mercy, and to walk humbly with our God.[42] The danger arises when we've fashioned that God out of our own shopping list. Perhaps that is why our preaching and practices can feel so anemic. Having crafted a God measured upon our own hopes, we inevitably live within those modest parameters. Irish theologian Peter Rollins suggests, "The idea of God today preached within much of the church is nothing more than an impotent Idol. . . . God is treated as nothing more than a product, a product that promises certainty and satisfaction while delivering nothing but deception and dissatisfaction."[43] The more comfortable we become with personalized stores, the more pastors, churches, and parishioners may be tempted to offer an idol rather than the authentic, demanding Jesus that invites whoever wants to be his disciple to "deny themselves and take up their cross daily and follow me." Who else would recommend that "whoever wants to save their life will lose it, but whoever loses their life for me will save it"? It is an odd sales strategy to ask, "What good is it for someone to gain the whole world, and yet lose or forfeit their very self?"[44]

From Store to Landlord to Utility

What consumers considered a convenience—"ecommerce"—businesses considered a threat. Amazon beat brick-and-mortar stores on selection, convenience, and price. But instead of burying the competition, Bezos seemingly tossed them a lifeline, offering to make them "Associates." In a counterintuitive move, Bezos opened up the Amazon Marketplace to his competition. Was it folly to allow independent bookstores to sell their titles through Amazon's system or a brilliant, additional revenue stream? Sellers could gain access to Amazon's customers for a price (or rather a percentage). The fees vary with the products from 6 percent of the price for a high-ticket item, like a computer, to 15 percent for books and DVDs. For thousands of retailers, the lure of Amazon's web traffic proved irresistible. It tapped into Chris Anderson's notion of "the long tail."[45] The internet enables collectors to find the used and the obscure with relative ease. Anderson encouraged retailers to embrace the new economy based on massive choice. Stores could thrive by capturing a niche; selling less of more. Amazon seized the long tail, taking small slices of more transactions. In a market of multitudes, the aggregator got rich on the economy itself. Amazon was happy to serve as middleman, brokering relationships between their massive customer base and the most remote used bookstore or comics shop. Nothing was out of reach.

Amazon was now more than a store. It was comparable to the mall, charging everybody rent. Except that Amazon had far more power than a landlord: they owned the customer and the real estate. Just like retailers, they could charge a premium for shelf space. Placement on the front page was also for sale. Eli Pariser notes how Amazon began to blur the lines between advertising and recommendations. Pariser suggests, "Buying off algorithms is easy: Pay enough to Amazon and your book can be promoted as if by an 'objective' recommendation by Amazon's software. For most customers, it's impossible to tell which is which."[46] Our trusted internet retailer could easily abuse their power.

Sellers could also choose FBA—"Fulfillment by Amazon." As a benevolent landlord, Amazon was willing to handle picking, packaging, and shipping for a small fee. They would offer space in their warehouses, so a seller never needed to physically handle their inventory. Thanks to Amazon, everybody could be a retailer—for a price. Bezos envisioned a future where anonymous strip malls were no longer necessary. The new retail environment overseen by Amazon won't support "the sort of bad stores that people go to because they don't have any alternative."[47]

Rather than starting from scratch in ecommerce, many big brick-and-mortar businesses tapped into Amazon's expertise. Frustrated by their efforts to launch an online presence, Borders outsourced their ecommerce to Amazon in 2001 (before eventually going out of business). Stores like Toys "R" Us welcomed the chance to do business with, rather than merely against, Amazon. Even a seemingly cutting-edge retailer like Target found it easier to let Amazon run their online store. With the launch of Amazon Web Services (AWS) in 2006, Amazon was "trying to become a one-stop shop for your company's information technology needs—processing power, databases, and storage. Think of it as a digital utility company for businesses."[48]

All of Amazon's investment in infrastructure corresponds to our insatiable need for speed. As techno-lord, Bezos let the serfs farm on Amazon's digital kingdom. Tech companies powered by AWS include Netflix, Zynga, Pinterest, and Foursquare.com. Retail brands like Lamborghini, FC Barcelona, and Sega turned to Amazon for web hosting services. Researchers from Pfizer, Harvard Medical School, and Cal Berkeley who need high-performance computing tap into the AWS Cloud to analyze genome-sequencing data.[49] Even NASA's Jet Propulsion Laboratory uses Amazon's information technology to process the high-resolution satellite images that steer their robots. Companies can rent Amazon's supercomputers by the hour for special events or projects. Tech start-ups from Singapore to Germany have compared the costs of creating their own infrastructure and have opted to go with Amazon. It has now become clear that Bezos "doesn't just want to be the Wal-Mart of the Web; he wants to be its Con Edison, too."[50]

Of course, with great power comes great responsibility. When power outages cripple Amazon's grid and clients like Instagram, Airbnb, Reddit, and Flipboard go down, Amazon Web Services gets the blame.[51] God's clouds can still disable Amazon's cloud. Is it healthy for one company to serve as our largest online store and our largest online service provider? Electricity is regulated as a public utility; Amazon is not. Do we have faith that Amazon will pursue customers' best interests (and profit as a result)? Is Amazon prospering because they're prospering others?

From a Gadget to a Service to a Network

Alongside Amazon's investment in cloud computing came the 2007 release of the Kindle. The first edition, priced at $399, sold out in five and a half hours. Most of us saw it as a new gadget, designed to compete with companies like Apple. Rather than a music player, the Kindle was a book reader, able to hold a shelf full of titles in one handy portable device. What a great option for summer vacation. All the books a Mom, Dad, or child might not want to carry, loaded on a single device. And the profits on downloadable books for $9.99

definitely exceeded the profits on songs sold for 99 cents on iTunes. Amazon started to look like a store *and* an electronics company.

With the 2011 release of the Kindle Fire, Bezos aimed to change our perception again. It was an Android tablet aimed at undercutting Apple. For half the price of an iPad, the Kindle Fire could hold 80 applications and either 10 movies, 800 songs, or 6,000 books. As with Apple's iPad and iTunes, Amazon sold both the hardware (the Kindle) and the software (books, music, videos). But while Apple tried to make a premium on the front end by selling the iPad's sleek design, Amazon was content to lower the price of the device in exchange for a bigger slice of the back end. They sold Kindles at a loss, just to get more customers tapped into their content pipeline.

Bezos went to great lengths to distinguish the Kindle Fire as a "media service" rather than a device. Its proprietary browser, the AmazonSilk, synched to Amazon's cloud. Steven Levy of *Wired* noted, "When you pay $199 for Fire, you're not buying a gadget—you're filing citizen papers for the digital duchy of Amazonia." He elaborated on the differences between Apple and Amazon:

> Apple is fundamentally a hardware company—91 percent of its revenue comes from sales of its coveted machines, compared to just 6 percent from iTunes. . . . Amazon, on the other hand, is a content-focused company—almost half of its revenue comes from sales of media like books, music, TV shows, and movies— and the fire-sale-priced Fire is designed to be primarily a passport to the large amount of that content that's available digitally. The gadget comes preloaded with customers' Amazon account information, and anyone who signs up for Amazon Prime, the company's $79-a-year shipping service, will be able to access more than 12,000 (and counting) movies and TV shows on the Fire at no extra charge.[52]

Amazon Prime turned the Kindle Fire into more than an assault on the iPad. It showed that Bezos had his eye on Netflix and similar streaming services. The Kindle Fire turned out to be a Trojan horse, an over-the-top portal, ushering customers into Amazon's kingdom. The hardware had to work, but the much larger goal was to establish Amazon as the choice for all our electronic entertainment needs—one iGod to rule them all.

For an older generation of pop cultural junkies, we were raised to own our content. We wanted the comfort of our collections, to point to the LPs, then cassettes, then CDs in our living rooms. But digital natives have grown up with bits rather than its. I'm wedded to an Apple way of viewing the world—I want my stuff loaded onto my MacBook Pro. But my daughter has only owned Kindles. Sure, she still likes physical books, but she is not creeped out by the fact that she mostly owns digital experiences rather than physical content. For the next generation, access is more important than ownership. And acceleration, the ability to get what we want, when we want it, trumps all.

Amazon Prime became the long play, the beginnings of a new premium cable network. Pay your fee and get all the content you can consume. For Prime customers, the Kindle Lending Library makes 270,000 books available, including current *New York Times* bestsellers. Wouldn't such access cut into Amazon's sales? The numbers don't necessarily make sense. How can Amazon afford to offer their customers express shipping for $79 a year? Bezos admits it was initially scary: "The one thing you do know when you hold an all-you-can-eat buffet, the heavy eaters show up first." But over time, it worked because Amazon Prime customers tended to buy more than they would normally. We purchase more content in order to make our initial investment seem more valuable. We feel like we're saving money with every product we buy. The "generosity" of Amazon Prime proved profitable. Bezos acknowledges the counterintuitive nature of his business: "A lot of decisions around consumers are like that . . . when you do the math it's not clear what will happen."[53] Putting customers first has proved to be a wise decision. But is it making us all stuff ourselves with more content?

In the wake of Steve Jobs's death in 2011, *Harvard Business Review* passed the mantle of "Best-Performing CEO in the World" to Bezos.[54] Slow and steady had won the race. Unfortunately, his rise to iGod status has been costly to others. Amazon drove down prices for books, making $9.99 the top end for digital downloads. With the Amazon Price Check app, they've encouraged showrooming, where consumers scope out a product, like a phone or camera in a physical store, but buy it from Amazon. During the 2011 holiday shopping season, they offered a 5 percent discount to customers who used Amazon Price Check to order while in a rival's physical store. Retailers and even senators protested. Senator Olympia Snowe (R-Maine) called Amazon's promotion "anti-competitive" and "an attack on Main Street businesses that employ workers in our communities."[55] Amazon said they weren't antibusiness, just proconsumer.

When Amazon discovered that a digital version of a book had copyright issues, it vanished from users' Kindles without warning. When the book turned out to be *1984*, many found the parallels to Big Brother pulling levers behind the curtain frightening. We don't think about the fact that "when you read books on your Kindle, the data about which phrases you highlight, which pages you turn, and whether you read straight through or skip around are all fed back into Amazon's servers and can be used to indicate what books you might like next."[56] When such power is concentrated in the hands of one corporation, we can all end up paying for their collusion. We need vigilance in monitoring Amazon's pricing, packaging, and recommendation policies. Despite all this disruption, Bezos was still honored by the National Retail Federation with its 2012 Gold Medal Award: "Given to an individual who has served the industry with distinction and achieved a national reputation for excellence. . . . The recipient has also displayed creative genius and inspirational leadership and has won the respect of fellow merchants for devotion to the retail craft."[57] The competition honored their enemy who buried bookstores and siphoned off business from Walmart, Macy's, and Target. Perhaps it was retailers raising the white flag, admitting since they can't beat Bezos, they might as well honor him.

A Theology of Abundance

As the Sears catalog once revolutionized retail, so Bezos and Amazon fueled the internet era. From books to electronics to toys, Amazon became synonymous with convenience. We might browse through the actual products at a brick-and-mortar department store or big-box retailer, but when it came time to buy, we chose Amazon, delivered to our door. They kept everything in stock, selling us "the long tail of retail."

We got used to Amazon making recommendations for us. It is frightening to consider how much Amazon knows about our shopping habits, both individually and collectively. But what will happen in the new moment, where our friends' purchases have even more persuasive power? Can Amazon retain the comfort and familiarity of the general store? Or will they lose out to those who offer a chance to express our "Pinterests"? The recommendation economy puts the power with the consumer, rather than the marketer. User reviews matter more than ever. And our friends' experiences with a company or product will determine its viability. So the ancient community standards of word of mouth have been revived.

Why did the internet arise? To make shopping easier? To make consumers smarter? Those seem like modest goals. Yet, even the slightest bit of convenience attached to something we do almost every day is a huge innovation. Amazon got rich by focusing on a niche in which there were too many choices. We needed Amazon to tell us what books to buy, where to connect with our passions and interests. I used to keep a notebook of every film I ever watched. But there were just too many. So I took a ledger from Dad, but what happens when that ledger fills up? I needed a computer spreadsheet, and then I needed a dynamic database with room for new movies every year. Thankfully, the IMDb solved my problem; an online compendium of film history and storehouse for info on films still to come. Likewise, Amazon is the logical extension of too many books, songs, and videos to choose from. And Amazon Web Services is the solution to too many books, songs, and videos we own.

The cloud restrains our clutter. We can cram things into cyberspace rather than our apartments. We are all digital millionaires, gathering gigabytes of stories, terabytes of recordings, and exabytes of shows. Thankfully, we have Amazon willing to store and retrieve them for us—for a price.

Bezos has announced, "Our vision is every book, ever printed in any language, all available in less than 60 seconds."[58] A company built on long-term thinking is also profiting from unrivaled speed. Amazon's goal is anything, anywhere, anytime. They offer more stuff than we can ever contain in a single brick-and-mortar store. And there are more books and songs and shows than our devices can ever hold. So Amazon aspires to be king of the cloud—techno-lord of all. Just pay us to deliver stuff to your device. In fact, with Amazon Prime, prepay us to deliver stuff so you don't have to think about the cost (as much). They've seen our appetite for a bargain; we'll buy more when we think we're saving money on shipping. They make money off the product rather than the delivery. And there is such abundance that Amazon can make billions by taking just a little bit of everything—the world's biggest middleman.

Are they gambling on our gluttony, our insatiable appetite for more? Is our hunger for more stories delivered with more speed so boundless that there's no end to the Amazon empire? Can we ever get to the point where we say, "Enough. I am satisfied"? Or will a new product always beckon us to buy?

We inherently sense that the will to possess something or someone can overtake us. We can become possessed by our possessions. Any episode of "Hoarders" should serve as a sobering wake-up call. And yet, public storage continues to thrive as we store up for ourselves possessions under freeways where moth and rust destroy. Old Testament scholar Walter Brueggemann laments,

> We who are now the richest nation are today's main coveters. We never feel that we have enough; we have to have more and more, and this insatiable desire destroys us. Whether we are liberal or conservative Christians, we must confess that the central problem of our lives is that we are torn apart by the conflict between our attraction to the good news of God's abundance and the power of our belief in scarcity—a belief that makes us greedy, mean and unneighborly. We spend our lives trying to sort out that ambiguity.[59]

Are you caught between what you've been taught and what you still want to buy? I have heard countless sermons about being good stewards. We may know about our responsibility to give. Plenty of preachers tie giving into receiving. A prosperity gospel has emerged that suggests in tithing to the church, we will get rich (maybe even quick). But I am captivated by "the good news of abundance." That sounds more like appreciating what we've already been given, rather than obsessing over a God-sanctioned plan to get more.

The endless options on Amazon raise my interest in a theology of abundance. What is the proper attitude toward stuff? Can we develop a theology of shopping that affirms the goodness of goods, accepts our body's need to be refueled, and yet resists our compulsion to indulge? Can we consume without being consumed?

Brueggemann sees Genesis 1 as a celebration of abundance. There is so much abundance in the garden that humanity doesn't have to struggle to eat. The plants and trees yield so much that God can rest on his laurels. After six days of creativity, God is so overrun with fruitfulness that God says, "I've got to take a break from all this. I've got to get out of the office."[60] Our job is to be fruitful and multiply, tend the garden, and enjoy the harvest. That sounds like a sweet deal! Unfortunately, in our desire to possess all knowledge, we forfeited the free ride. Sweat became a precursor to rest. Tilling became more like toiling. Fruitfulness was replaced by fear. Scarcity took hold of our hearts.

Instead of serving as our brother's keeper, we became our brother's competitor. We joined the race to the top of the mountain or the mouth of the river. We wanted the best land for ourselves. Sharing was out of the question if there is not enough. And yet, time and time again, God demonstrated his ability to provide. On the run, in the desert, with no time to plant or to harvest, God's people were blessed with manna in Exodus. God dropped daily sustenance onto his refugees. The only provision was his provisions—the daily bread couldn't be stockpiled. Manna could not be warehoused. There is no day-old bread for God's people. It arrives new every morning.

You would think such a huge shaping story would be baked into the hearts of the Hebrews. But that tendency to fear, to worry, to scrap and scrape under the specter of scarcity invariably returns. For a forgetful people, Psalm 104 recapitulates Genesis 1, from God separating the waters to pouring it out for donkeys and birds to enjoy. The lions seek their food from God. Humanity enjoys wine, bread, and oil. "All creatures look to you to give them their food at the proper time."[61] Yet, Bruggemann notes how anxiety cuts across economic and political alignments. He suggests,

Wouldn't it be wonderful if liberal and conservative church people, who love to quarrel with each other, came to a common realization that the real issue confronting us is whether the news of God's abundance can be trusted in the face of the story of scarcity? What we know in the secret recesses of our hearts is that the story of scarcity is a tale of death. And the people of God counter this tale by witnessing to the manna. There is a more excellent bread than crass materialism. It is the bread of life and you don't have to bake it.[62]

Jesus revives the bread of life in his ministry to the multitudes. When confronted by the problem of hunger—"Where's lunch?"—he turns it back to his disciples for the answer. He challenges them to assess the resources at hand. Two fish and five loaves of bread hardly seem sufficient to feed the crowd. But it depends on whether you look at those resources as a problem of scarcity or an example of abundance. Where the disciples saw too little, Jesus saw more than enough. It just needed to be broken into smaller units for distribution. Brueggemann explains how Jesus's large-scale miracle challenges our thinking:

The market ideology wants us to believe that the world is profane—life consists of buying and selling, weighing, measuring and trading, and then finally sinking down into death and nothingness. But Jesus presents an entirely different kind of economy, one infused with the mystery of abundance and a cruciform kind of generosity. Five thousand are fed and twelve baskets of food are left over—one for every tribe of Israel. Jesus transforms the economy by blessing it and breaking it beyond self-interest. From broken Friday bread comes Sunday abundance.[63]

Given our propensity to forget, Jesus demonstrated his economy of more-than-enough more than once. And even though it was written down for us, we still don't believe it. Or if we believe he did it for them, we don't believe it applies to us. Somehow, a nation coming off a streak of such unprecedented abundance suddenly felt poor. After the economic collapse of 2007, we looked on the drop in our 401(k)s with lament. We never stopped to think about how many loaves and fish were still in our basket. And we didn't bother to ask, "Who's hungry?" We felt poor. And so we held on even tighter. Brueggemann says, "The power of the future is not in the hands of those who believe in scarcity and monopolize the world's resources; it is in the hands of those who trust God's abundance."[64]

So where is Bazos and Amazon amid all this abundance? Amazon continues to take a percentage of the top, allowing us to buy and sell and trade to our hearts' content (and their bigger bottom line). What does Bezos plan to do with all his money? He waited a long time to exercise his first stock options at Amazon. He has invested heavily in three personal projects. The first is Blue Origin, a private aerospace company (which transports him back to tinkering on his grandfather's ranch) that he is funding. What does he want from space? Perhaps he wants options since he worries that we may have too many eggs in this (earth) basket.

His second project seems counterintuitive: buying the *Washington Post*. Why would a new media entrepreneur invest in an old media industry like newspapers? Hasn't the Internet wiped out the profitability of printed news? Advertising rates and subscribers have plummeted for newspapers yet Bezos must foresee unexplored areas for innovation. How might an established company like the *Washington Post* deliver faster, more personalized news? Bezos will likely concentrate on what Amazon has done best: putting the customer first. Our hunger for news, books, and information hasn't subsided. It has simply accelerated. In a world of abundance, we have gravitated towards those who respond with the news we want, when and where we want it. Perhaps the depth of reporting and analysis associated with the *Post* can merge with the immediacy of the Internet. Or perhaps speed and insight are incompatible. His investment in old media could lead to a painful, public failure. For Steve Jobs, failure was the crucible for recovery and resurrection. If Bezos can save the newspaper business, he'll reach a new pantheon of power and influence. If not, he'll still have plenty of resources to invest in other arenas.

His third project is building a clock that will last ten thousand years; he has poured $42 million into this clock that is planted into the hills of his ranch in Texas. What a waste! Couldn't that money have gone toward something more useful, like feeding the hungry or housing the poor? Why do we need a ten-thousand-year clock? Bezos explains, "The clock is a symbol for long-term thinking."[65] Remember how long-term thinking separated Amazon from early internet also-rans? Bezos continues, "If we think long-term, we can accomplish things that we couldn't otherwise accomplish." Like what? As an example, Bezos "noted that asking someone to solve world hunger in five years might sound preposterous, but doing so in 100 years might not." So with the ten-thousand-year clock, "All we've done there is change the time horizon, we didn't change the challenge. Time horizons matter. They matter a lot."[66]

If you know the song, sing along: "When we've been there ten thousand years bright shining as the sun, we've no less days to sing God's praise, than when we've first begun."[67] Evidently, ten thousand years isn't much on God's timeline. It is good to sing. But it is also good to shop for a solution to world hunger. Bezos continues, "We humans are getting awfully sophisticated in technological ways and have a lot of potential to be very dangerous to ourselves, and it seems to me that we as a species will have to start thinking longer term. This is a symbol, I think symbols can be very powerful."[68] For people who never feel like they have enough time to enjoy all their stuff, ten thousand years might cover it. And for people looking for a symbol of what God is like, we could start with two loaves and five fish and twelve baskets left over. Both involve long-term thinking and an understanding of abundance.

Discuss

1. What prompts you to buy things? Do you save time or waste time shopping online?
2. How much is your time worth? What are some areas in which you could adopt long-term thinking and a more eternal perspective?

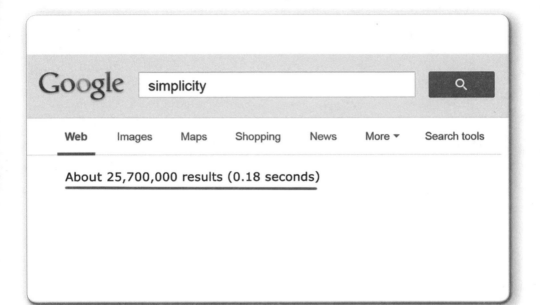

Google
Algorithmic Authority

Those who search will surely find me.
—Proverbs 8:17 NLT

I still haven't found what I'm looking for.
—U2

How do I love Google? Let me count the ways! First of all, Google News is my aggregator of articles. On one concise page, I can find headlines from across the journalistic spectrum. Next, Google Search and Google Scholar made research for this book so much easier; they allow me to touch the world's libraries and databases from any computer in the world. Then there's Google image search; I always start my work on a presentation with it. I am still amazed by how many charts, graphs, and photos are available almost instantaneously. And I adore Google Maps. Each click offers more details, better directions, smarter routes. And don't forget Google Earth; it shows us what our neighborhoods look like from outer space. We can zoom in on childhood homes or more than imagine places we wanted to visit. With Google's 3D technology, ancient monuments like the Roman Colosseum spring to vivid life. I am also enthralled by Google's Sky Maps. I can hold my smartphone up to the sky, and Google traces the constellations. It is an astronomy class field trip brought to life in any setting.

And there's more. When my ten-year-old wants to make a convincing argument, he often makes his case in Google docs. I've received presentations via Gmail on "How Samsung phones compare to Apple" and "Why we should get a dog." Also, Google translator comes in handy on homework assignments and in foreign travel situations. As an author, I wasn't fond of Google Books' campaign to digitally scan all kinds of books to create a giant online library, but I certainly use the service to preview various books online. Then, chastened by criticism, Google adopted a more cooperative approach to organizing the world's art, working with museums to document and post masterpieces in the Google Art Project. They offer an opportunity to zoom in for closer looks on collections ranging from the Art Institute of Chicago to Australian Rock Art. I relish the chance to revisit the works of contemporary Chinese artist Wu Guanzhong, which I saw in the Hong Kong Museum of Art, via Google. What do all these globetrotting services cost users? Nothing. They're free!

I vividly recall the day in 2004 when my invitation to Gmail arrived. Like many innovations in the internet era, it came from one of my college students, someone less than half my age. I felt honored to be invited to get a Gmail address. And how thoughtful of Google to offer free storage space! What had I done to deserve such generosity? Like most of us, I forget to read the fine print on the user's agreement. After initial embrace, many of us have developed conflicting feelings about our social contract with Google. They gave us free email, and we gave them access to all our electronic correspondence. Google knows our relationships; it charts our searches. Initially, Google charted searches in a macro way: What is trending? What are people searching for? But now they do it in a targeted way with smarter advertising linked to our search history and our stated interests. Web 3.0 could result in social blinders, in only listening to who and what we already know and agree with. And while Google may encourage *us* to share our information, *they* certainly hide their own proprietary technology. Their information appears free, but it is hidden and guarded with a ferocious vigilance.

Where did Google come from and where is it heading? This chapter will look at the meteoric rise of two Stanford grad students in computer science, Larry Page and Sergey Brin. They continued the work of Tim Berners-Lee, founder of the world wide web, and improved the groundbreaking directory of Jerry Yang and David Filo of Yahoo!. All of these revolutionary innovations arose within an academic context, where research was well funded and risks were encouraged. The wealth generated by their projects does not undercut the fundamental desire to connect people, to chart intentions, to make the web a more navigable place.

So what are the theological implications of Google's innovations? Will the desire to organize all knowledge tempt us to make a Faustian bargain, trading our privacy to gain this power? Or will the scale of their undertaking potentially make us appreciate the majesty of creation, the omniscience required to stand above such glory? Google can be seen as an extension of Nimrod's ill-fated project to build a tower to the heavens. Or it can be embraced as a beneficent gift, distributing divine wisdom to the masses. This chapter will explore the enduring lure of seeking and the eternal benefits of finding.

TMI

With the arrival of the world wide web, so many sites emerged that we soon had an unprecedented problem: How do we navigate a world of too much information? The wave of new webpages swamped us with such ferocity that we never had time to consider what the tsunami of information might produce. In the seventies, Alvin Toffler popularized the term "information overload" in his book *Future Shock*. We had plenty of time to prepare, but we were so busy gobbling up data that we rarely reflected on its purpose. As the world wide web was being launched, Neil Postman questioned our pursuit: "To the question, 'What problem does the information solve?' the answer is usually, 'How to generate, store and distribute more information, more conveniently, at greater speeds than ever before.'"[1] He criticized the values of the emerging world: "In Technopoly, we are driven to fill our lives with the quest to 'access' information. For what purpose or with what limitations, it is not for us to ask; and we are not accustomed to asking, since the problem is unprecedented. The world never before has been confronted with information glut and has hardly had time to reflect on its consequences."[2] In Web 2.0, the emphasis shifted from portals to search engines. Google rose to the top of the technological heap by tackling the challenge of the era—too much information. While Postman fretted about the implications, Page and Brin were busy solving the problem.

Brin and Page met on a tour for prospective Stanford grad students in the summer of 1995. The gregarious Brin served as a tour guide for a day in San Francisco. Page had been accepted to Stanford's computer science program but hadn't decided to enroll yet. Eventually, they bonded so closely that they were referred to as a collective, "LarryandSergey." Page's father was a computer scientist at Michigan State. His parents divorced when he was young, but his mother also had a computer science degree. Brin was born in Russia and emigrated to the United States as a boy with a NASA scientist for a mother and a math professor for a father. In elementary school, Brin and Page both attended Montessori schools where they were encouraged to follow their bliss. Google executive (and future Yahoo! CEO) Marissa Mayer noted how the self-directed education shaped them: "Their attitude is just like, 'We're Montessori kids. We've been trained and programmed to question authority.'"[3] Although Brin was ahead of him in the PhD program, Page settled more quickly on a dissertation subject—the world wide web—particularly the structure that resembled a massive graph full of indexes primed for analysis.

The chaotic nature of a new medium like the web raised questions of authority. Who should we pay attention to; what sources can we trust? Esteemed newspapers and established television networks had interpreted the news for us, but the internet moment decentralized authority, potentially making anybody an expert.

Page took a distinctive innovation created to navigate the web—the hyperlink text—and used it as a vehicle for assessing quality. He found that following the links from one webpage to another proved inconsequential, but tracing the links back to their source might yield more intriguing results. The world wide web had already become a bit of a popularity contest with companies like Yahoo! jockeying for web traffic. As the son of a professor, Brin understood that popularity was not equivalent to influence. The academic game was about peer review, getting colleagues to read your work and comment on it. Citing another's work in your paper was a form of respect, a way of giving credit where it was due. Scholars could also dispute another scholar's work in their paper. Citations (footnotes) acknowledge influence and comment on it in concise and constructive ways. The more significant and influential the scholarship, then, the more often it will be cited. Professors and researchers look back (to previous research) as a means of moving forward. They stand on (or sometimes trample on) the shoulders of those who came before them. Page thought that tracing who was linking back to whom (that is, who was being cited the most) was a much more valid way to measure power on the world wide web. It accounted for *authority*. In other words, Google was built on the importance of footnotes.

Page told John Battelle of *Wired*, "In a sense, the Web is this: anyone can annotate anything very easily by linking to it. But the early versions of hypertext had a tragic flaw—you couldn't follow links in the other direction."[4] That is, by looking at a webpage you couldn't tell how many other pages had cited it (had linked to it). His program, Backrub, was about reversing that. It gathered links on the web and traced them back to their source, enabling him to determine which pages were the most authoritative. Page could have tested his concept on a limited number of pages, but he audaciously set his sights on the entire world wide web. Backrub would count the links to the originating page, but it also needed to count the subsequent links from those links. Page needed the mathematical expertise of Brin to create a viable formula; "The result was PageRank, the original algorithm that made Google into the behemoth that it is today."[5] It created a new way of ascribing value on the internet beyond page views. Brin and Page's algorithm calculated and weighed who was pointing to whom. They found a way to recognize the sources and pages that informed what was popular. Respect and origins suddenly carried more weight than self-promotion.

Page and Brin pushed past interest by rewarding *influence*. By placing the substantive above the obvious, they sought to make our searches deeper and more rewarding. Established search engines like AltaVista and Excite focused on key words so a spammer could load their site with oft-searched terms like *cars* or *America* or *sex* to rise in the search results. PageRank outfoxed the spammers by analyzing links across the world wide web. Users wouldn't link to lousy or exploitative sites. Page and Brin noticed that their search results were far more relevant and helpful than AltaVista or Excite.[6] Eli Pariser of Upworthy.com suggests, "What Brin and Page had really figured out was this: the key to relevance, the solution to sorting the mass of data on the Web was . . . more data."[7] More importantly, in removing human editing from their equation, PageRank could actually grow with the web. The bigger the web became, the better their search engine.[8] Thus was born *algorithmic authority*.

They renamed their project "Google," a play on the mathematical term *googol*, the number 1 followed by 100 zeroes. It was released in August 1996 at google.stanford.edu.[9] It included the rather modest goal: "To make it easier to find high quality information on the web."[10] Encouraged by Page's academic advisor, they published a paper describing their research titled, "The Anatomy of a Large-Scale Hypertextual Web Search Engine."[11] They described the high cost of Yahoo!'s editorial approach to creating a web directory. The explosive growth in pages on the world wide web demonstrated how costly and impractical it would be to continue such human-generated practices. They noted how three of the four major search engines failed to find themselves. In contrast, PageRank was an objective measure that brought order to the web. They described it as "a model of user behavior." They even dared to reveal the algorithm that fueled their search engine. Their paper became "the most widely cited search-related publication in the world."[12] PageRank affirmed the power of their proposal.

Brin and Page also included an addendum that outlined ethical dilemmas that muddle our feelings about advertising and search engines and Google to this day. They asserted, "The predominant business model for commercial search engines is advertising." But they also acknowledged, "The goals of the advertising business model do not always correspond to providing quality search to users."[13] In a query for cell phones, PageRank returned a study titled, "The Effect of Cellular Phone on Driver Attention." They noted that no cell phone manufacturer or advertiser would want to see such a critical study alongside their product. Brin and Page wrote, "We expect that advertising funded search engines will be inherently biased towards the advertisers and away from the needs of the consumers." They called search engine bias "insidious," and concluded, "We believe the issue of advertising causes enough mixed incentives that it is crucial to have a competitive search engine that is transparent and in the academic realm."[14] How long could Google afford to remain transparent and academic?

The volume of searches coming into Google overwhelmed Stanford's computer network. Page and Brin needed to find a solution—off campus, beyond Brin's dorm room. So many well-funded companies already dominated the search engine market that Page and Brin sought to license their technology to someone like Yahoo!, Excite, AltaVista, or Infoseek. They found no takers. These companies wanted to drive people toward their portals, not away via web search.[15] When the founder of Sun Microsystems, Andy Bechtolsheim, wrote them a check for $100,000, they had the resources to move out—and into a friend's garage. To attract more significant funding, they expanded to seven employees, overwhelming Susan Wojcicki's Menlo Park garage. In 1999, two major venture capital firms in Silicon Valley, Sequoia Capital and Kleiner

Perkins Caufield & Byers, came onboard with a $25 million investment.[16] Page and Brin cleared out their offices on campus. They were now running a start-up, not engaging in a grad project. Their first press release outlined their grander ambitions in the now-famous mission statement: "to organize the world's information and make it universally accessible and useful."[17] They only lacked one thing—a viable business model.

Targeted Advertising

In an age of TMI, the engineers at Google solved a daunting problem (and were handsomely rewarded for it). Adoption and embrace was meteoric. Millions of pages were indexed, and a billion dollars of investment flowed into their initial public stock offering. A trillion pages of indexing later, the rest is (recent) history. In assigning value to a new commodity (digital information), Google became highly valued. Their metrics made them invaluable. While it is tempting to focus solely on the wealth generated by Google, Page and Brin did not set out to become billionaires. They resisted advertising altogether, not wanting to clutter their site with banner ads. So how would they satisfy their equity investors?

They adopted the principles established by web pioneer Bill Gross. He tackled the problem of spam, trying to distinguish between good web traffic—people genuinely interested in your site—and bad traffic—those lured by false promises, insidious links, and poor search results. Web portals may generate lots of traffic, but what is the point if people don't want to be there, if users don't translate their presence into meaningful (and commercial) actions? Battelle celebrates, "Gross's core insight, the one that now drives the entire search economy, is that the search term, as typed into a search box by an Internet user, is inherently valuable—it can be *priced*."[18] Giant portals like AOL and Yahoo! adopted an advertising model similar to television and radio. Companies paid for the privilege of buying space on their portal, especially in the form of banner ads. They were charged by CPM—cost per thousand of page views (with M representing the Roman numeral for one thousand).[19] As with traditional media, the results were indirect and left up to the advertiser to discern. But Gross leaned into the power and intention of a click. He recalls, "The more I thought about it, the more I realized that the true value of the Internet was its accountability. Performance guarantee had to be the model for paying for media."[20] Advertisers would pay his new website, GoTo.com, only when users' clicks translated into sales and loyal customers. If the results were effective, Gross reasoned that he could charge far more than a standard rate. In fact, he could auction off such access to the highest bidder. GoTo blurred the lines between search and advertising in ways that Page and Brin had warned about. But the arrangement was so transparent that few could be offended. Gross changed the name of the company to Overture, reflecting their mission: "making paid introductions (overtures) between visitors to its client Web sites and the company's vast network of advertisers."[21]

In 2001, Gross recognized the growing power of Google as a rival search engine but also knew they were not yet profitable. He proposed a merger to Brin and Page, who ultimately bristled at his mix of paid search. Shortly after their merger talks stalled, Google introduced AdWords. In popular perception, Google was credited with introducing a pay-per-click model. And they eventually adopted Gross's auction model, selling paid links to the highest bidders. Google also factored in an ad's popularity, its clickthrough rate, into its placement on the search results. But Gross and Overture still sued Google for copyright infringement. An out-of-court settlement allowed Google's IPO to proceed without incident.

Google also rose to the top of the advertising heap with AdSense. It was a passive source of revenue for webmasters around the globe. AdSense crawled across sites, delivering relevant ads that generated income when users clicked on them. Bloggers could potentially receive a check from Google simply by making space available for their links. Google did all the work—connecting the dots between content, users, and advertisers. They were using their algorithms to build links between our searches and companies' products. It approximated the church's gift of matching resources to need. Clicks signal our interests and intentions. AdSense matches advertisers to relevant content. Google served as a highly paid matchmaker.

To this day, Google's revenue comes primarily from advertising. Unlike websites that depend on banners and videos, Google ads are comparatively no-frills links. Their list of paid hyperlinks is nestled on the side of their search page, or even sometimes at the bottom. It is unobtrusive, neither distinguished nor disguised. Google is selling information, not persuasion.

This is an intriguing shift, especially for pastors and educators schooled in the art of rhetoric. Google may rank the relevance of an ad in relation to our search, but they never directly comment on the content. They allow their users to decide what appears helpful or interesting. They exhibit faith in their search engine and in their seekers. For those used to offering arguments and apologetics on behalf of the faith, the Google model offers a sharp corrective. If your information is dialed into the hearts and minds of the seeker, then it does not need extra garnish. The Bible is loaded with confidence in the search process, from Proverbs to Jesus's affirmation of those who ask, seek, and knock. God is responsive to our intent, rewarding our intentions. Google demonstrates a similar level of faith and confidence in their active seekers. While their competitors often focus on content, Google proceeds with faith in information.

Work and Play

A mystique has arisen around the Googleplex in Mountain View, California. Located in the former offices of Silicon Graphics, Google's corporate head-quarters have retained the ethos of a college dorm, a place where colleagues can engage in spirited dialogue, rigorous study, and ferocious play. Photos by Eros Hoagland in *Time* magazine showed Googlers shooting pool, playing volleyball, and swimming on the campus. Brin famously scooted around Stanford on Rollerblades. The Googleplex is populated with scooters and Segways. Marissa Mayer cited the Montessori ethos as essential to understanding Google's corporate culture: "In Montessori school you go paint because you have something to express or you just want to do it that afternoon, not because the teacher said so. This is really baked into how Larry and Sergey approach problems. They're always asking, 'Why should it be like that?' It's the way their brains were programmed early on."[22] Steven Levy writes of life in the plex, "The high holy day of Google culture is April 1, when imaginations already encouraged to run wild are channeled into elaborate pranks requiring months of work."[23] Googlers gather each Friday afternoon at 4:30 for a meeting dubbed TGIF. While mostly an occasion for announcements, there is also a greeting for Nooglers, new employees who wear beanies with propellers on top (echoes of fraternity pledges and hazing). The session concludes with a frank Q and A where Page and Brin tackle the toughest questions (ranked via online voting) with no offense taken.[24]

   The benefits for Googlers are legendary, starting with free food. Levy notes, "The centerpiece and symbol of their view of the ideal work experience was free and abundant healthful food in an atmosphere that forged employee bonding and the sharing of innovative approaches to work. When new Googlers gathered for their orientation welcome session, the human resources person would explain that Google begins with the stomach."[25] At $17 per employee per workday, the tab for free food was estimated at $80 million annually, a pittance against their bottom line. But the perks extended into all kinds of services. Googler Kim Malone said, "It's sort of like the corporation as housewife. Google cooks for you, picks up and delivers your dry cleaning, takes care of your lube jobs, washes your car, gives you massages, organizes your work-outs. In fact, between the massages and the gym, you'll be naked at work at least three times a week."[26] The benefits extend even after death. If an employee perishes, benefits are extended to surviving family members for a decade.[27] Google has repeatedly topped a Forbes survey of the most desirable places to work.

So how does one become a Googler? Their hiring process is notoriously rigorous. Grades matter. SAT scores count. A PhD is a plus. (Owen Wilson and Vince Vaughn were woefully underqualified in their comedic efforts to secure *The Internship* at Google). Those applying for a technical position must take the challenging Google Labs Aptitude Test.[28] What is gleaned from all of these objective measures? To complete a PhD requires a great amount of self-discipline; a doctorate demonstrates an ability to finish things that require intense concentration over a process filled with twists and turns. In the overheated dot-com environment, so many grad students, especially in technical areas, accepted job offers rather than completing their dissertations. Those with PhDs ostensibly care more about the quality of their work than the size of their bank accounts.

Having hired self-motivated experts, Google can encourage their employees to follow their bliss. Google got powerful by turning their engineers loose through "innovation time off." The ground rules: for every four hours Googlers spend on official company projects, they are encouraged to invest an hour on their own pet projects. Fooling around has been a successful business strategy. "Over 50 percent of Google's new products derive from Innovation Time Off hunches," from AdSense to Orkut and Gmail. Krishna Bharat, principal scientist at Google, built a system called StoryRank (modeled after the original PageRank algorithm) to organize and cluster news items. StoryRank eventually blossomed into Google News.[29] It launched in the wake of September 11, 2001, when our appetite for updates and information exploded.

While the Protestant work ethic made everyone's vocation equally valuable before God, it also could promote drivenness. Google, on the other hand, rewards a work hard/play hard ethos. They promote a sense of fun—in their work space, in their colorful logo, and through their daily Google doodles. Massive goals need not rule out the opportunity to discover, to innovate, to play. Google may be seeing the benefits of adopting Jesus's kingdom perspective. Jesus said, "Unless you change and become like children, you will never enter the kingdom of heaven."[30] While Eric Schmidt was brought in as CEO to provide "adult supervision" at Google, Page and Brin clearly retained a child-like sense of wonder, right down to their Google glasses. Google has built their kingdom by retaining the sense of discovery and play too many of us have lost.

Temptations

Google is guided by an ambitious mission statement—organizing the world's information. And to some degree, their work resembles the origins of the universe itself. In Genesis 1, God faced a mass of disorganized chaos. The earth was formless, a jumble of genetic code looking for structure. Through powerful words and actions, the world was transformed into something tangible and knowable. In a bit of inspired creativity, PageRank brought order to the chaos of the internet. It ascribed value and worth to a jumble of bits, bytes, and data. Google's algorithms enabled us to get our arms around the web. It put form to the information.

With such a firm grasp of the web, Google must resist the temptation to possess it. If the original temptation in the garden was too much knowledge (the serpent promised, "You shall become like God"), then Google is flirting with ancient lures. The hunger for knowledge can evidently overtake us, taking God out of the center of our world and thereby decentering us. An iGod can become unmoored. The Ten Commandments served as a corrective for a fallen people. The law provided a foundation to keep our worst instincts reined in. How appropriate that Page and Brin put forth ten commandments to guide Google's ethos. While never acknowledging God as the source of all knowledge, they did offer ethical standards that would guide their nascent behemoth. Their mantra was boiled down to the simple dictum, "Don't be evil." As a search engineer at Google acknowledged, "We're not evil. We try really hard not to be evil. But if we wanted to, man, could we ever."[31]

Now Google does the searching for us, combing through countless webpages to deliver the most pertinent links. While a quick search might produce twenty or thirty pages of links, how deep do we dive into the results? After a few clicks we may stop searching. We may settle for what Nicholas Carr refers to as "the shallows."[32] But what if the more profound and prescient answers are five or even ten pages into the search results? We may be grateful that Google sorted through a billion pages. But should we stop with the top ten or twenty links? How many pages do we visit before we find the answers we seek? In the internet era, seeking is fast, finding is easy. With Google, you get instant results.

There is almost no (visible) work involved. And our faith in Google's answers is nearly absolute. We rarely question their algorithmic authority. In fact, we imbue it with an almost mystical power. Type a few letters into its search engine, and Google will fill in the blanks, anticipating our intentions. It autocompletes us—in almost any language. With the rise of personalized search, Google seems to do more than half the thinking for us. So how should we think about Google? Have we defaulted to blind faith in the wisdom of their engine?

Jaron Lanier, one of the early artificial intelligence pioneers, suggests we've ascribed too much power to search engines, making them magical and all-knowing iGods. In his troubling manifesto, *You Are Not a Gadget*, Lanier suggests, "People degrade themselves in order to make machines seem smart all the time."[33] We bow before Google in an act of self-reduction. Lanier asks, "Did that search engine really know what you want, or are you playing along, lowering your standards to make it seem clever? While it's to be expected that the human perspective will be changed by encounters with profound new technologies, the exercise of treating machine intelligence as real requires people to reduce their mooring to reality."[34] I think of the powerlessness adopted by nondigital natives like my father who feels as if he is too old or dumb to learn how to even make a computer or cell phone work. He assumed that his capabilities and power were surpassed by the VCR and the answering machine!

If we've already convinced ourselves that machines are smarter than us, in Web 3.0, search engines will do even more of our work. Scientific research is expanding at such a maddening pace that learned doctors couldn't possibly keep pace with current breakthroughs. So with just a few instructions, tomorrow's search engines and semantic web will not only look for key words, but will also actually read through the articles, making thoughtful determinations about which findings deserve our time and attention. Do we want to surrender that kind of authority? Or will complex thinking by our computers allow us to concentrate even more on the problems we desperately need to solve? A large part of the future seems to reside in Google's formulas.

With so much authority extended to algorithms, what role does the Word of God play in the twenty-first century? To Israelites exiled in Babylon, God promised, "You will seek me and find me when you seek me with all your heart."[35] But this was not a quick search. This was a long period of waiting and wondering, of feeling lost and confused. An entire generation of exiles died without finding an answer to their prayers. Perhaps their heart wasn't truly in it. Or perhaps seeking is much harder than we think (even two thousand years later). Jesus promised his disciples, "Ask and it will be given to you; seek and you will find; knock and the door will be opened to you."[36] This formula sounds simple enough. It seems easier to implement than PageRank. And yet, the disciples consistently struggled. They asked for the wrong things, sought the wrong virtues and social standing, and found that following Jesus involved far more sacrifice than they ever imagined. Seeking has always been an essential (and costly) part of the Christian journey. But search engines make seeking seem like such a quick and immediate process because the complexities are completely hidden. So how might the surrender of our search function alter our hearts and minds? If Google seems to give us what we want, will we build in enough time and perspective to even consider what we need? I wonder what happens when we outsource searching. How do we decide what matters and what to pay attention to?

The triumph of Google raises key questions of authority: Who decides what matters? Will God still serve as a norm when our questions are answered by "Googling"? Arguments about facts can be sorted out at the touch of a button. Does "I saw it on Google" become a twenty-first century equivalent to "God said it, I believe it, and that settles it"? Both assumptions are shallow. And what about key life decisions like where to go to college or who to date? The ability to put preferences into a search engine might result in prospective college students traveling greater distances to go to school. Campus visits and financial aid packages will still factor into decision making. But when Christian college students are asked how they ended up enrolling, will "I prayed about it" be replaced by "I Googled it"? The algorithms that drive search engines are also being applied to the dating game. Are the engineers at eHarmony doing God's will by matchmaking? The founders of eHarmony are committed Christians who incorporate the best of psychology with the power of algorithms. Do their beliefs make their engines more inspired than competitors like Match.com or OkCupid?[37] Will the many happy couples forged by online dating services reduce the credit we used to give to God as divine matchmaker? Or will we come to see such technology as a means of finding the will of God? Churches have responded to this shift in authority by comparing faith over and against Google. How should Christians respond to this seeming shift in authority? Will the most gifted pastors of tomorrow be the ones able to sort through the most information? How do today's teachers develop the sage's ability to cut through the clutter with enduring wisdom? Perhaps in learning how the system works, we will feel less fearful, powerless, and intimidated by Google. Could we eventually thank God for algorithms that bless and enrich our lives?

Decision Making

"Information wants to be free!" The cry of techno-enthusiasts sounds appealing, democratic, and inherently American. Google famously wrestled with Chinese government authorities over freedom to search. But thousands of journalists and authors might argue with that dictum. They discovered that if information were free, they were likely out of a job (providing information). Free information came with a cost. Yet, Google never seemed to return the favor by revealing their trade secrets.

Google can be commended for aggregating news and organizing data, but some wonder if the company has already consolidated too much power. Siva Vaidhyanathan, in *The Googlization of Everything*, suggests that their algorithms contain inherent biases that alter our search results and perceptions. Vaidhyanathan warns that Google is "a system of almost universal surveillance, yet it operates so quietly that at times it's hard to discern."[38] While we were captivated by the Street Views obtained from Google's roving cars, we didn't realize how much personal information they were gathering during their drive-bys. An alarmed Vaidhyanathan advocated for regulation. Chastened by such criticism, Google opened up their data centers, not to the public, but to photographers who chronicled the computers processing our queries. The photos focused on the beauty of the hardware rather than the power residing in their databases. Google keeps their formulas secret even as they devour more of our habits. CEO Eric Schmidt believes that what customers want is for Google to "tell them what they should be doing next."[39] Such pronouncements awaken fears of Big Brother or *The Matrix*. We may need to reclaim our agency, our responsibility.

We must reflect more thoughtfully about the role of information. Does more information alter our behavior and change our actions? Can information transform lives? Or does it slow us down, turning our decision making into something unwieldy? Do we hesitate to act because there is always more to know before we buy? How can we dare to write or preach with any authority when there is so much more information to wade through? What is our proper relationship to TMI, too much information?

Information can humble us and make us realize how much we don't know. It can inspire us—to read more, to learn more, to dig deeper—but only if we're curious. It can paralyze us because we are overwhelmed by the avalanche before us. Too many choices can leave us stymied. It can also prepare us to make the best decisions possible. I fear that too much information has resulted in the abdicating of our responsibility. We see the creeping effects of too much information on the job or in public policy. Decisions are not made by a boss trusting his gut or a committee searching for the most compassionate route, but by an algorithm.

Writing in 1973, Daniel Bell saw the coming of postindustrial society, where "an *intellectual technology* is the substitution of algorithms (problem-solving rules) for intuitive judgments. These algorithms may be embodied in an automatic machine or a computer program or a set of instructions based on some statistical or mathematical formula; the statistical and logical techniques that are used in dealing with 'organized complexity' are efforts to formalize a set of decision rules."[40] That's how Google sorts through the information avalanche. They follow the numbers. But Bell warns of "a shift from the government of [the people] to the administration of things, a move to administration based not on intuitive judgments but on logical and statistical rules and algorithms."[41]

A decade later, James Beniger wrote in *The Control Revolution*, "How do inert programs manage to influence concrete technologies, not to mention living organisms, guiding both toward predetermined goals? Work in a wide range of disciplines converged by the 1930s on a single answer: programs control by determining decisions."[42] These are the origins of the form letters we receive in the mail. This is how people get their insurance coverage canceled. We punch buttons as we desperately try to get a person on the other end of the phone. We have stories we want to tell that might influence the decisions the corporation already made.

Beniger points out the origin of the word *decision*. It springs from the Latin verb *decidere*, to cut off from the source.[43] Computers have always been rooted in decision trees. When we encounter an automated voice message system, we are given the opportunity to indicate who or what we are seeking. We press one or two or three in an effort to reach our destination (often an elusive operator). Pioneering computer theorist Alan Turing noted the relationship between decidability and computability. The Church–Turing thesis has become one of the most influential concepts in mathematics and thinking: "What is human-computable is machine-computable." The de facto values of the Google search engine are rooted in Turing. In each search, some results are cut off, others elevated. In a world of too much information, the Google method is efficient, effective, and decisive. And yet, we rarely look at the links (or branches) in our search that are cut off. "Turing's man" may be "less aware of history than his predecessor and is not likely to see the historical currents in which he is caught. He tends to project the present indefinitely in both directions."[44] In other words, our decisions are driven by data rather than history, context, or collective wisdom. We are satisfied with skimming off the top of Google's search. We feel satisfied with what is given, but should we extend so much faith to Google engineers? Pariser suggests we need more programmers to go beyond Google's famous slogan, "Don't be evil." His plea: "We need engineers who will do good."[45]

It is remarkable how quickly we adapted our behavior to Google's standards. As bloggers and businesses, we conform to Google's methods for Search Engine Optimization. Once we learned how to play to their algorithms, we altered how we titled our posts or linked to articles throughout. (As Google changes their algorithms, different patterns and priorities emerge.) They can create safe searches, burying pornography (which is a good thing). Websites still aspire to game the system with key words. Yet, Google is always a step ahead, figuring out smarter ways to filter information. And without many users realizing it, Google has actually become the most efficient (and valuable) advertising delivery service.

Internet pioneer Jaron Lanier is horrified that the free range of the web has now reduced us to better advertising delivery systems. "At the end of the rainbow of open culture lies an eternal spring of advertisements. Advertising is elevated by open culture from its previous role as an accelerant and placed at the center of the human universe."[46]

How does too much information drive advertising and consumption (and lead toward passivity in our decision making)? The sheer avalanche of choices can inhibit us from taking action. It is great to have options at our fingertips, but there always seems to be another consumer report or Yelp review to read. For larger decisions like planning a vacation, hotels and itineraries may not be booked until we've consulted Trip Advisor *and* Fodor's *and* Lonely Planet. So many experts offer so much information that we can become weary and exhausted before we buy. Jacques Ellul suggested too much information creates a confused sense of impotence:

> The infinite multiplicity of facts that I am given about each situation makes it impossible for me to choose or decide. I thus adopt the general attitude of letting things take their course. But the course that things take is essentially that of the process of technical development. . . . The more the number and power of means of intervention increase, the more the aptitude and ability and will to intervene diminishes. . . . Information is the main carrier of contraception.[47]

Perhaps we struggle to commit to a single career path or religious denomination or even a spouse when we're presented by seemingly boundless possibilities via the iGods.

Personalized Search

The basic architecture for search engines has not changed in over forty years. It consists of three major components—a crawler, an index, and a query processor that connects the crawler and the index.[48] BackRub crawled across the web, devouring as much information as possible in its path. Webmasters were not sure how to respond to such an invasion. In this sense, search engines are invasive. They crawl through a website uninvited, taking note of any links embedded in the webpages. BackRub turned this data into an index. It made a list of words associated with the URL (what we now know as tagging). The speed of Google's search came from comparing the query against the index. It could not take the time to crawl through the web. It merely scanned the index with the search word in mind to return prioritized results—a ranked list of URLs. PageRank analyzes the index using a series of algorithms. John Battelle says, "At the end of the day, the holy grail of all search engines is to decipher your true intent—what are you looking for, and in what context."[49] The more that Google knows about you—interests, locations, history—the more effectively it can ascertain your intent. This is the promise (and lure) of personalized search.

Critics like Ellul suggested information without context can cripple or confuse. It can leave us literally dumbfounded. Having solved the initial problem of too much information, Google tackled a new challenge: how to make searches more relevant to the seeker. Kevin Kelly notes, "The solution to the problems that technology brings, such as an overwhelming diversity of choices, is better technologies. The solution to ultradiversity will be choice-assist technologies. These better tools will aid humans in making choices among bewildering options."[50] But we generally don't like to think of ourselves as needing assistance. We value our independence. Thus was born the new concept of "personalized search."

To what degree will personalized search limit our exposure to new ideas? Jesus began so many of his revolutionary teachings with the phrase, "You have heard it said, but I say. . . ." There are no "buts" in the Google search process, just "You have heard it said." Will Web 3.0 reinforce our assumptions and fossilize our beliefs?

Google offers different search results depending on where we are, what it knows about our interests. When we arrive in Portland or Miami, Google knows we're there—and our local news shifts to match our locale. It is nice to get news tailored to our favorite teams or our most pressing issues, but it is somewhat creepy to consider how our location is targeted so invisibly.

Pariser understands why we embrace personalized recommendations: "Our media is a perfect reflection of our interests and desires. By definition, it's an appealing prospect—a return to a Ptolemaic universe in which the sun and everything else revolves around us."[51] This is the iGods' alluring and dangerous promise—to place us in the center of our own self-reflexive universe. But what if we don't necessarily know what is best?

What if our limited experiences are further delimited by our choices so far? Instead of expanding our world and understanding, we could become consumed by what we already see and hear. At the 2009 Web 2.0 Expo, sociologist danah boyd warned, "If we're not careful, we're going to develop the psychological equivalent of obesity. We'll find ourselves consuming content that is least beneficial for ourselves or society as a whole."[52] Isn't education and growth about pressing into new arenas or unexplored areas? What is the danger in the personalization era? Psychologists call it confirmation bias—"a tendency to believe things that reinforce our existing views, to see what we want to see."[53] What happens when we encounter new information that contradicts our beliefs? Researchers at Stanford monitored subjects' brain activity to trace how they responded to cognitive dissonance. Democracy is endangered when we only listen to people we agree with.

Representative Lindsey Graham (R-South Carolina) laments that Congress is no longer the most deliberative body in the world; now it is just an extension of the political moment. Thomas Friedman and Michael Mandelbaum wonder how America fell behind in the world it invented: "This new-media environment reinforces hyper-partisanship in Washington, because the new media generally aim at smaller audiences than the old. Talk radio and cable television are not trying to attract people from different points on the political spectrum, as the three networks and the major newspapers did when they had a virtual monopoly on news dissemination."[54] Christians who have a tendency to flee the culture could wind up in a confirmation spiral. Plenty of our schools and media outlets proudly operate as a filter bubble, "safe for families." I respect the desire to preserve the innocence of children. But how do we create mature disciples? Could we stop growing with God because we only hear the things we are already convinced of? If we aren't really seeking, then we're not likely to find. Yet, Jesus consistently adopted cognitive dissonance as a teaching and preaching device. The Sermon on the Mount is a collection of sayings that challenged the conventional wisdom of the day. After his countercultural blessings for the poor, he expands on the implications of the Beatitudes. When Jesus opens with "You have heard it said . . . ," rest assured he will take his audience to uncomfortable places. Laws like "You shall not murder" are extended to apply to any kind of anger harbored against a fellow disciple.[55] Those who are confident they've never committed adultery are forced to reexamine their lustful glances and fantasies tucked deep inside their hearts and minds.[56] And Jesus subverts the saying, "Love your neighbor and hate your enemy" with a challenge to "love your enemies and pray for those who persecute you."[57]

How do filter bubbles work in churches? It comes with the Bible passages that are read and preached. Some pastors focus on the Gospels. Others drill into Paul's letters. But which letter should we listen to? Corinthians warns against wanton sex while Galatians stresses our need for more freedom. Far too often, we return to passages that reinforce our blind spots. So preachers who are already uptight seem to find their way back to Corinthians. And churches that may have already lowered their code of conduct preach the freedom of Galatians. A biblical faith will be informed by the whole of Scripture. It may depend on a lectionary more than a pastor's chosen subject. By allowing the church calendar or a lectionary to determine our Bible readings for the week, we submit to Scripture rather than lording over it. We pop our potential filter bubble by refusing to bend the Bible to conform to our will.

Seeking and Following

I started reading the newspaper as a young boy, seeking out the box scores for my favorite baseball team, the Pittsburgh Pirates. As I grew older, my interests spread from the sports section toward entertainment and eventually politics. I have read the newspaper from front page to last almost every day of my adult life. It is a ritual tied into my morning routine. I have rarely questioned why I read the paper. It seems inherently important to know what is happening in the world, to be aware of the heartaches and crises that deserve our attention and care. But now, as the news flows toward us by the hour, I have begun to wonder why I want to be informed. How often do I need updates? How quickly do I need to know who won the game or which celebrity was arrested now? As a follower of Jesus, I question whether more information helps me be a better disciple.

Yet, the metaphors of our time define us as information processors. In his book *Turing's Man*, J. David Bolter chronicles how the computer succeeded the clock and the steam engine as the defining technology of our era "chiefly because it can reflect the versatility of the human mind as no previous mechanism can do."[58] We see ourselves "as software more than hardware, as the program run by the computer more than the hard-wired machine itself."[59] Our minds program themselves to solve problems, achieve goals, and mold themselves to the environment. Media theorist Neil Postman points out how we use computer terms to describe our brains. We retrieve data, a busy day was a big download, and when necessary, we deprogram ourselves. And now we describe computers in human terms—like suffering from a virus. We all want healthy hard drives.[60] But does God call us to be more efficient or more human?

So much of our information gathering is now a reflex action. We check for messages and updates on our smartphones as soon as we leave the classroom or have an idle minute. Such busyness flies in the face of the psalmist's call to "be still, and know that I am God" or Paul's challenge to "be anxious for nothing."[61] If I am constantly checking my iPhone for sports scores or status updates, then I may be falling into what Quentin Schultze calls "informationism." In

Habits of the High-Tech Heart, he rightly critiques "a non-discerning, vacuous faith in the collection and dissemination of information as a route to social progress and happiness." We can place too much faith in our Google news feed, somehow believing that knowing what's happening is akin to knowing what matters. Schultze cautions us to be skeptical when informationism places "the is over the ought, observation over intimacy, and measurement over meaning."[62] The iGods would prefer that we are always online, always seeking updates, and rarely stopping to consider what it all means. Given the remarkable access we have to information via Google search, what is the proper relationship to information?

French philosopher Jacques Ellul was no fan of technology. He challenges us to recover earlier notions of information. Ellul writes, "Etymologically, information (*informare*) has the sense of giving form. It shapes conduct. If the same information is given to many people, by being led to adopt this conduct, they form a coherent group."[63] While we might cite the regimen placed on military personnel, Ellul points to the animal kingdom. Bees depend on other bees to identify sources of sustenance. Thus the information given by bees tells other bees "where there is nourishment, in what direction, and how far away, so that they all know where to fly. All the information that members of tribes receive is classified by them as useful or not."[64] We do the same thing with tasty restaurants and exceptional discounts. With the rise of social media, we are an active hive, telling others where to find the best deal. So perhaps our problem is not information itself but sorting out the essential from the mundane.

Kevin Kelly, the original editor of *Wired* magazine, sees information as the ground of our being. If who we are is driven by DNA, then the packets of information contained in our genetic code determine who we are, what we're like, and what we like. James Beniger sees DNA as the most foundational of all "control technologies," the basis of human society. Given the information exchange that happens on a cellular level within every living thing on earth, he marvels how critics could be skeptical or even hostile toward information processing. Beniger insists, "Information processing is also arguably the most human of life functions in that particular capabilities of our brains to process information best distinguish us from all other species."[65] We are made (and sustained) by sophisticated, cellular codes. Dr. Francis Collins was animated by his robust Christian faith to crack the genetic code, to discover the design and information driving us.[66] He saw his direction of the Human Genome

Project as groundbreaking science *and* an act of worship. It uncovered "God's instruction book." But it could never account for inherent knowledge of a moral law or our ongoing search for the divine. Collins sees greater understanding of where we come from as responsible stewardship. And the medical advances that enhance our health and extend our lives are viewed as a God-given capacity to think, create, and heal. Sure, there are temptations to "play God" with emerging technologies, but we cannot blame more information for our inability to keep it in perspective.

Clearly, more information has improved our lot in life. The advances in science, especially health and medicine, are staggering. The rise in literacy has lifted many out of poverty. A Maasai warrior with an Android smartphone has access to more information than the president of the United States did just fifteen years ago.[67] Farmers in Central and South America are helped by their newfound ability to know the fair market value of their goods via smartphones. Thanks to more accurate and accessible information, they negotiate from a position of greater knowledge, strength, and profitability. So where does information lead? Can it lead to wisdom? Kelly suggests, "Theologians should team up with nerds to study information as the entity closest to God."[68]

Big Data

In the comedic movie *Bruce Almighty*, Jim Carrey is given the opportunity to play God. When the prayers of the planet descend on him, the voices are overwhelming. Our collective hopes and dreams leave Bruce stupefied. Google too gathers information about what we're seeking, and this offers Google a Godlike perspective, what Battelle calls "a database of intentions." He writes, "Link by link, click by click, search is building possibly the most lasting, ponderous, and significant cultural artifact in the history of mankind: The Database of Intentions."[69] It is a snapshot of not only what exists but what we want more of. Google and their competitors can measure not just what we seek but the intensity of our search, how it ebbs and flows with the seasons. While promising us the illusion of knowledge, Google acquires a proprietary omniscience. Here in the early years of Google's efforts to organize the world's information comes the firstfruits of their vision: Big Data.

The rise of Big Data awakens metaphors previously reserved for the Almighty. Our smartphones make the internet (and us) omnipresent—available at all times in nearly any venue. Google is omniscient and gives us a taste of omniscience—having all knowledge at our fingertips. The sheer scope of the algorithmic engine capable of sorting and retrieving search results in seconds should make us marvel. From the beginning of time until 2003 we generated 5 billion gigabytes of data (5 exabytes)—all the books and news and movies and information in history. We now generate five exabytes of data *every ten minutes.*[70] We should wonder what kind of brain could possibly track all of the data swirling around the universe. And how does that Search Engine in the Sky know where I am and what I care about? It recognizes me amid a sea of swirling TMI. But by reserving the big picture for themselves, Google makes Big Data the real, elusive omniscience. For techno-enthusiasts like Kelly, Big Data is close to Big Daddy, the uber-lord of the clouds, who curates our daily dose of information every single day.

A robust definition of omniscience moves beyond a fixed body of knowledge. It transcends space and time. So when Jesus responds to his critics' claim that he is too young to truly understand Abrahamic law, he retorts, "Before Abraham was born, I am."[71] When questioned outside Jerusalem's temple in Matthew 21, Jesus sees into his future, promising to tear the temple down and rebuild it in three days. Such cryptic allusions undoubtedly left his contemporary audiences confused. After the fact, we recognize Jesus's prescient and prophetic understanding of the future as well as the present circumstances. While grasping the big picture of what has happened, what is happening, and what will be revealed, Jesus still manages to keep his attention to others deeply personal. God's knowledge is pinpointed, as when Jesus declares, "Even the very hairs of your head are all numbered."[72] Such far-reaching knowledge suggests that God knows everything we've done in private from our giving to our prayer life.[73] Doesn't Google keep similar records? Our political giving becomes retrievable, public knowledge if it exceeds $200 to a single candidate. And would we blush if we thought our children or spouses knew every search we'd ever made via Google? The immutable nature of our online footprint is a serious threat to our efforts to experience forgiveness.

Are we content to say, "Google knows me better than I know myself"? It remembers our digital footprint, tracing where we've been before. Do we really want to reduce ourselves to our interests? Aren't we much more than the key words in our searches? Pariser points out the differences between our Google selves and our Facebook selves: there's a big difference between "you are what you click" and "you are what you share."[74] Both systems box us into our web imprint. They feed us more of what they think we're searching for. But what if our interests change? What if we don't want to get mired in the past? How do we move from immature searches rooted in our younger selves to deeper, more thoughtful searches in the future? As people of faith, we are inherently committed to the possibility of fresh starts. Shouldn't we be freed from our search history? Why is Google built to revert to our old habits? Pariser says, "If we don't erase our Web histories, in other words, we may be doomed to repeat them."[75]

What does it mean to be born again in Google's world? How do we break free from our past if the internet already has clear ideas of who we were, what we liked? The cookies attaching themselves to our online persona may make being reborn even more attractive. Alas, we can't change our online persona as easily as we can change our beliefs. We have to change our name to be born again online. Who wants to start over with a new Gmail address and new Facebook friends? But the Christian story is filled with shifts from Saul to Paul, from persecuting Christians to persecuted Christian. We must actively subvert expectations if we hope to pop the filter bubble. Perhaps we need to approach our Google searches with more gamesmanship. What kinds of intriguing and unexpected searches could we conduct today? What untested word combinations could allow us to forge a new digital trail? I want to blaze some digital rabbit trails, to give the autocomplete functions something new. Google offers us a chance to start a new trend, to push their algorithms into uncharted waters.

If we feel like Google's grip has exceeded what is healthy in our lives, then the onus is on us to remove ourselves from that temptation. Brin said, "Some say Google is God. Others say Google is Satan. But if they think Google is too powerful, remember that with search engines, unlike other companies, all it takes is a single click to go to another search engine. People come to Google because they choose to. We don't trick them."[76] The heavy weight of Google's responsibility may reside behind Brin's statement. Evgeny Morozov makes a provocative observation: "Google's spiritual deferral to 'algorithmic neutrality' betrays the company's growing unease with being the world's most important information gatekeeper. Its founders prefer to treat technology as an autonomous and fully objective force rather than spending sleepless nights worrying about inherent biases in how their systems—systems that have grown so complex that no Google engineer fully understands them—operate."[77] Our challenge is their challenge: not to succumb to the temptation to know everything. Embracing our limits while expanding our hunger for knowledge and understanding is practical wisdom. While Google indexed the world wide web, they still have a ways to go before their engines unlock the subtleties of our searches, the emotions and motivations behind our key words. When asked how long he thought it would take for Google to organize the world's information, Eric Schmidt referred to a three-hundred-year timeline.[78] The innovations incorporated over the past short decade, from Google Earth to Sky Maps, demonstrate how voraciously Google is pursuing such mastery.

Many will undoubtedly continue to get their arms around the internet, the next wave of the semantic web. But none of us will live three hundred years. So we must also step back, marveling at the vastness, measuring our minutia. Instead of trying to see how many people we can reach, how many pingbacks our posts receive, how many "likes" we can generate, we could also focus on how much we can't grasp, letting go of that will to possess, to organize, to know it all. The temptation of Google is to build a tower to heaven, to become like God. The response must be to resist temptation, to acknowledge how little we know despite the resources available. Humility remains a prerequisite for genuine wisdom.

Will we come to understand our relationship with God as a relationship to Big Data? If Google knows us and anticipates our thoughts, how much more does God know our hearts and minds? Can we be comforted by how closely we are tracked? No matter where we are, God is already there, revealing what we need to know. We cannot make Google into an iGod; that is foolish idolatry. We can develop a deeper appreciation of how much we don't know, how overwhelming it is to be God, how marvelous it is to feel noticed by a risen Lord amid a world of too much information. We are loved by the initiator of information, animated by the source of our creation, and sustained by the original code writer. When we seek God, we may discover that we are already found.

Discuss

1. What are your primary sources of informationa? How deep a search do you conduct for answers?
2. When have you felt overwhelmed by too much information? How do you deal with it and order the flow?

A Brief History
of Social Networking

What should young people do with their lives today? Many things, obviously. But the most daring thing is to create stable communities in which the terrible disease of loneliness can be cured.

—Kurt Vonnegut, commencement address, 1974[1]

The primitive Church was a kind of Internet itself, which was one of the reasons it was so difficult for the Roman Empire to combat it. The early Christians understood that what was most important was not to claim physical power in a physical place but to establish a network of believers—to be on line.

—Bishop Jacques Gaillot of Partenia[2]

The internet has always been social. It was created to bring people together across distances and disciplines, to make it easier to connect. It has always been a place to share research and information, to find out who was doing what.[3] Yet who could have imagined the complex web of relationships that has resulted in all kinds of mutual benefits. Is God pleased with how the internet has drawn us closer together? As a pioneering online educational program, the PLATO computer system inadvertently spawned the online communication tools that drive social networking. By 1976, PLATO featured early versions of email, chat rooms, instant messaging, remote screen sharing, and even emoticons.[4] The first computerized Bulletin Board System followed in 1978. Initial conversations matched computer enthusiasts' interests, like hacking instructions or infamous passages from the Anarchists' Cookbook. (Pinterest may be seen as an extension of this electronic corkboard.) The arrival of Usenet in 1980 allowed articles to be posted to newsgroups without a central administrator. Popular topics and threads included news, recreation, science, and computers, and the catchall "alt." Usenet was a precursor to RSS Feeds. In 1985, the online community that followed the *Whole Earth Catalog* exchanged information at The WELL, the Whole Earth 'Lectronic Link. It sprang from the hippie ethos of the Bay Area, displaying an enthusiasm for the Grateful Dead and alternative lifestyles. In the nineties, CompuServe, Prodigy, and AOL all commercialized the chat room. People enjoyed meeting strangers online. Stories of finding an online romance began to appear in the press. AOL popularized the notion of member profiles.

Dating websites arose; people paid to create a profile and scan the profiles of others. Web addresses, like kiss.com and match.com, were purchased. Classmates.com was founded in 1995, making it easier to track down old friends. While you might be able to track down a former flame or teammate via friendfinder.com, these sites didn't offer the ability to keep lists; friends or contacts were not part of your profile.

GeoCities made it easy to publish personalized websites. Users could choose where to position themselves based on their interests. They could select the neighborhood or street where they wanted their webpages to reside. "Hollywood" was a natural gathering place for entertainment-themed sites. "WallStreet" became the hub for business-related webpages. GeoCities' web addresses followed a protocol that resembled the real world. A site on the "SunsetStrip" or "Rodeo Drive" would even be given a URL that ended with a street number.

To promote virtual communities, we still needed the ability to respond with more immediacy. How to get beyond checking in to see what others had posted? Real-time status updates arose with Internet Relay Chat (IRC). Created by Jarkko Oikarinen in 1988, IRC was used to share links, files, and breaking news (especially during the first Gulf War).[5] In 1996, four Israelis invented an instant messenger system for personal computers. America Online recognized the commercial potential of instant messaging and purchased the technology that spread avatars and emoticons far and wide.

Inspired by John Guare's popular play *Six Degrees of Separation* (also a 1993 film starring Will Smith), SixDegrees.com put the theory to the test. As part of setting up a profile, SixDegrees.com required users to list ten friends. SixDegrees extended invitations to these contact lists to join their burgeoning social network. Users could post messages to people in their first, second, or third degrees of contact (like a precursor to LinkedIn). But so much spam flowed to the friends we listed (outside the network) that potential members were turned off. Niche-driven sites like Asian Avenue, Black Planet, and Mi-Gente were founded in the wake of SixDegrees' initial success. They provided a place for people to gather around shared cultural backgrounds and interests. Even games like World of Warcraft offered a prototype for social networking, forming guilds from players around the world.

With the burst of the turn-of-the-millennium internet bubble, nascent sites like SixDegrees were snuffed out before they had an opportunity to prove profitable. While many websites were founded on finding like-minded strangers, the best social networking sites were extensions of our real-world relationships. Launched in 2002, Friendster was the first to turn "friend" into a verb. It demonstrated the multiplying power of friends' friends—connecting us with those just one or two degrees apart. Friendster was embraced by subcultures, such as gay men and "burners"—those who gathered for the annual Burning Man festival in the Nevada desert east of San Francisco.[6] Los Angeles-based MySpace copied Friendster's innovations (and code) but took off by embedding music. Bands and fans could personalize their pages to reflect their tastes and interests.[7] Sexual come-ons were rampant on MySpace. Voracious self-promoters like Tila Tequila built a quick following that turned them into early internet celebrities. LinkedIn was also founded in 2003 but as a much more business-related social network. The sharing of photos expanded with Photobucket and Flickr. Del.icio.us introduced social bookmarking. DIGG allowed users to vote articles up or down. By 2003, all of the elements we've come to expect in social networking (personal profiles, the sharing of favorite music and movies, posting our photos, voting for what we like) were in place.

We were all becoming curators, blasting and blogging about our tastes, our passions, our interests. Social networking began to spread around the world: Cyworld in Korea, mixi in Japan, QQ in China, Bebo in England, and

Orkut in Brazil and India.[8] So, how did Facebook manage to overtake social networking pioneers like Friendster and MySpace that had such a significant head start?

Facebook distinguished itself from MySpace by its presorting of clientele. Social networking sites open to anybody devolved quickly into a creepfest. You were always getting hit on. Facebook was initially offered only to upscale university students, catering to the elite. Researcher S. Craig Watkins found that "college students describe MySpace as crowded, trashy, creepy, busy, uneducated, open, immature, crazy, and predators. Facebook was seen as selective, clean, trustworthy, simple, college-educated, authentic, private, mature, and addictive."[9] While MySpace encouraged personal expression, Facebook insisted on standardization. Facebook's minimalistic design made creating a profile quick and easy; its interface was airy, open, and bright. In allowing their users to create with their own HTML code, MySpace may have allowed too much personalization. The designs and colors on MySpace came across as garish, communicating a desperate cry for attention. In contrast, Facebook's pages were always white, echoing their primarily Anglo-American users. It may have reminded us of Apple products, where crisp design created a sense of calm and confidence. We didn't really notice how much time we were spending on Facebook. Like Steve Jobs, Mark Zuckerberg created a walled garden of such serenity and delight we didn't want to leave. With each search result, Google drove their users away, all across the internet. Facebook sucked us in with the promise of reunions with friends far and wide. The mass migration from MySpace to Facebook felt like it happened overnight. I still remember one of my students' first posts on Facebook. He wrote on his wall, "I guess everybody is over here now."

Despite being depicted as the loneliest billionaire in *The Social Network*, Zuckerberg's revenge became *the* gathering place. The Facebook, as it was originally named, started as a bit of an exclusive club for Harvard students only. But the clamor for access spread across campuses into the awkward space of moms and dads (and even grandparents) with Facebook profiles. The lure of social media has proved irresistible. Over a *billion* people are now linked via this one social media service.[10] What other seemingly innocuous website has been credited with fueling social revolutions in the Middle East? After Egyptians organized via social media to depose Hosni Mubarak, one family even named their baby Facebook! So what is Facebook's power and appeal? It combines elements of a dating service, a class reunion, and a calling card.

We can project a version of ourselves that announces what we're about in remarkably diverse (yet strategically delimited) ways. Although it connects people across all types of borders, Facebook has reinforced some ongoing gaps between class and race. What made Facebook such a force to be reckoned with, a place that attracted audiences around the world? What special problems did Facebook solve?

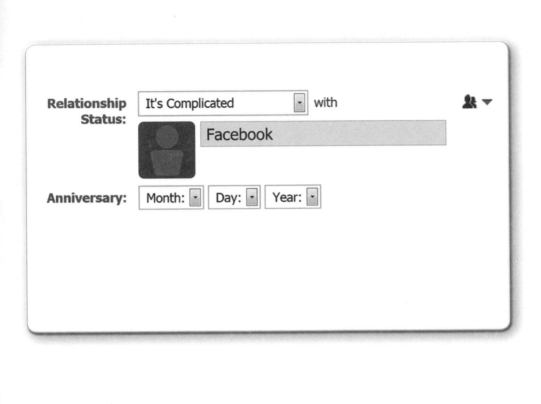

Facebook

Authentic Frenemies

We're a utility. We're trying to increase the efficiency through which people can understand their world.

—Mark Zuckerberg[1]

The early years were full of surprises. You never knew when a friend request would show up; posts would pop up on your wall from unexpected people. Some even dared to offer a provocative poke. There was not much netiquette to guide us. An academic eddress was an advantage because you were immediately dialed into a network of college students—early adopters—who dragged you onto Facebook. They seemed genuinely delighted to see a professor on the 'Book. (My students hadn't really thought through the fact I could see everything they'd been up to!) So they helped newbies like me scale up with friend recommendations. We extended access to each other. "Friend" became a verb in everyday conversations.

In this virtual game of six degrees of separation, we quickly realized how reachable our favorite artists might be. I friended musicians like Moby, filmmakers like Kevin Smith, and entrepreneurs like Mark Cuban. The world seemed so knowable. You were encouraged to fill in your backstory—how you knew each other. But as the network of relationships extended, this got trickier. And more annoying. So we let it go. And eventually, so did Facebook.

While many continue to question the validity of virtual friendships, it was clear that Facebook primarily served as a digital representation of real-world friendships. It made our web of interconnections visible. It became common to conclude a first-time meeting by saying, "Facebook me." And we were also glad to accept friends of friends into our network. We could stalk them beforehand to make sure we were compatible. We didn't consider such lurking inappropriate. We didn't reflect too much about what social networking meant. It was cool that people from the other side of the country or world wanted to connect. Facebook made our circles of influence seem larger. We loved this glorious new time suck.

The friendship requests increased with each month and year. Parents joined. Professionals signed on. We accepted friend invitations from almost anyone we vaguely recalled. Our network of friendships was expanding so rapidly, we didn't pause to consider that the thrill wore off rather quickly. There were always more people to find and to friend. But what happened when we reached the end of our circle? Facebook doesn't seem as dynamic when our friend lists stop growing. Even grandma got access to our Facebook profile. We were stuck within our friendly confines. By 2010, the purpose of Facebook shifted.

We started treating our friends more like an audience. Our posts had less enthusiasm and more calculation. Facebook was an extension of our brand, turning all of us into managers, carefully measuring our status updates. The "like" button allowed us to feel supportive of friends. It was easy to "like" a post, a song, or an upcoming event. It also required a bit of discernment. We wondered, "What kind of message am I sending?" "How will this play on my timeline?" Facebook was a place to connect with friends, but it was also the most visible online representation of ourselves. It was still fun; but photos posted by others could become a source of worry or embarrassment. We needed to monitor where we were tagged. Profile management could turn obsessive. Impression formation took work. The constant bragging by our friends grew wearisome. Their status updates might leave us feeling lonely or left out. We considered "unfriending" Facebook. Yet, it was such a ubiquitous platform, on the web, on our phones. Where else could we connect with as many friends as easily? While our feelings about Facebook were decidedly mixed, it still helped us check in with colleagues, coordinate events, and tell people what's happening. It was the annoying friend we needed and the abusive enemy we abhorred. Facebook was becoming our "Frenemy."

This chapter will consider our conflicted feelings about Facebook. How did Mark Zuckerberg and Facebook become the dominant online gathering place? What purposes does social networking serve? The initial stories passed into pop culture via the film *The Social Network* painted Zuckerberg in shadowy tones, as a revenge-driven iGod. Is there more to his story? We are actively debating the Facebook effect. Some researchers suggest, "Facebook users have higher levels of total narcissism, exhibitionism, and leadership than Facebook nonusers. . . . In fact, it could be argued that Facebook specifically gratifies the narcissistic individual's need to engage in self-promoting and superficial behavior."[2] Yet, Facebook's fans wonder, "Could it become a factor in helping bring together a world filled with political and religious strife and in the midst of environmental and economic breakdown? A communications system that includes people of all countries, all races, all religions, could not be a bad thing, could it?"[3] After a very messy initial public offering, investors are still trying to decide.

I want to dig deeper into Zuckerberg's motivations and mission. What were his goals and has he fulfilled them? In what ways have we altered our behavior to conform to Facebook's standards? What happens to our spirit when we think, "I can't wait to post this on Facebook"? Even more importantly, what are the implications of Facebook for communal institutions like synagogues and churches? What types of status updates could encourage our friends and bless those within our network? How might our online communities hinder or expand our efforts to support, encourage, and love each other?

Social Beings

We have always been social beings, designed to live in community. Amid all the initial glory of creation, one glaring weakness stood out. In Genesis 2:18, the Lord God said, "It is not good for the man to be alone." We were not created for isolation. We were born to be in relationship. God offered a practical solution to loneliness: "I will make a helper suitable for him." Animals and birds did not suffice as companions. While it is nice to have a pet, Adam needed a more suitable helper.

Yet, suitability is elusive. In school, we scanned the lunchroom for someone to sit beside. We entered classrooms and parties in search of the suitable. After graduation, we turned to churches, gyms, or bars in a hunt for a suitable helper. Social networking is an extension of an ancient dilemma. It takes time to develop relationships. Asking questions to ascertain interests can be a frustrating process. People who may share our passion for certain bands or teams may have divergent religious or political beliefs. Those we seemingly should like may turn out to be annoying or even hostile. How to solve the suitability problem?

Apple solved our computer problem—making technology more beautiful and human. Amazon covered our shopping needs—making infinite choice just one click away. Google addressed our information problem—making the internet more navigable. Facebook solved our human problem—connecting us in an era prone to depersonalization.

We often leave our hometowns in pursuit of work, yet fewer companies offer long-term employment and benefits to anchor us. Civic organizations like Kiwanis and Rotary have lost their appeal. Even bowling leagues that once offered a night of communal fun have shut down.[4] Churches that once served as the central gathering place for the community have long since splintered into competing denominations. Ecclesiology, the discussion of what it means to be God's gathered people, has faded. The independence we sought has left us increasingly alone.

The anonymity made possible by emails and avatars was alleviated by Facebook's insistence that we be ourselves. While the web was encouraging multiple virtual personas and second lives, Facebook got us back to our real selves—or at least, the best version of ourselves we could fashion from photos and a few identifying passions. The Facebook profile covered items that might emerge on a first date: favorite movies, bands, television shows, and quotations. Religious and political affiliations may also arise as an early test of compatibility. So rather than hide such convictions, Facebook encouraged us to put them out in the open for everyone in our network of friends to see. It promoted transparency rather than privacy.

Facebook was a new technology that enabled us to deal with the effects of other technologies. It put us back in touch with people we lost contact with along the way. Facebook restored community at a time when bonds seemed more fragile than ever. Zuckerberg's revolutionary code seemed like a dating site but was actually a simple way to connect to our past and unite our current contacts in one place. It combined business and pleasure, erasing the lines between public and private, work and play. Zuckerberg called his service a utility, like the phone company, so efficient and innocuous that you don't even think about how it works. The profiles also functioned like a free, global yellow pages—a place to be easily found.

This utility also gathered more of our personal data than previously imagined. We volunteered our age, our education, and our interests. The more time we spent on Facebook, the more data we revealed. We created social graphs that would allow advertisers to target us like never before. While Google aggregated information, Facebook aggregated us. We didn't realize that we were becoming the news. We didn't fully understand how we were becoming the product. While some worried about privacy, most of us happily surrendered our personal photos in exchange for access to others.

From Facemash to Facebook

Zuckerberg's programming prowess was established in high school. He was captain of the fencing team at Phillips Exeter Academy in New Hampshire, but his passion was computers. "Zuck" developed a music recommendation program called Synapse that anticipated later services like Pandora. It was nicknamed "The Brain." Microsoft offered Zuckerberg a million dollars for the technology. AOL also recruited him to work with them, but he declined their offers.[5] What teenager would turn down that kind of payday? This burgeoning iGod clearly had different dreams and ambitions. He wasn't motivated by money. Zuck enrolled in Harvard instead.

As a sophomore at Harvard, Zuckerberg created a program called CourseMatch. It allowed students to find classes based on other students' recommendations (like a smarter version of RateMyProfessor.com). But the goodwill generated by CourseMatch was undermined by his second project, Facemash. It allowed users to rank one another's hotness. The opening page asked, "Were we let into Harvard for our looks? No. Will we be judged by them? Yes." Zuckerberg started with photos from his fellow residents of Kirkland House. He also hacked into databases and files from Harvard's other residence halls to gather headshots. His program allowed users to compare students, and like DIGG, people were essentially voted up or down depending on their looks, "Hot" or "Not." Such brazen online judgment became quick and controversial news on campus. Facemash was chided by the *Harvard Crimson* for catering to the worst side of students.[6] Zuckerberg risked expulsion for violating security, copyright, and privacy according to Harvard's code of conduct. He apologized to the campus in the student newspaper.

Despite the affront of Facemash, Harvard students were still interested in an electronic version of the freshman register. The university had promised to provide one but got cold feet when it came to notions of privacy. During Zuckerberg's sophomore year, the *Harvard Crimson* published an editorial, "Put Online a Happy Face: Electronic Facebook for the entire college should be both helpful and entertaining for all." While universities around the country dallied, enterprising students forged ahead. *The Social Network* put the Winklevoss twins at the forefront of the idea. It chronicled how Zuckerberg started as their employee before grasping the power of his programming and launching an alternative with his roommates. Plenty of lawsuits followed. *Fortune* magazine's David Kirkpatrick offers an alternative history in his book, *The Facebook Effect*. Kirkpatrick reports Zuckerberg's side of the origin story, "Dustin [Moskovitz] and Chris [Hughes] [his Harvard roommates] and I would sit around and talk with other people I was taking computer science classes with. And we'd talk about how we thought that the added transparency in the world, all the added access to information and sharing [enabled by the Internet] would inevitably change big-world things. But we had no idea we would play a part in it. . . . We were just a group of college kids."[7]

Facebook could have been described as "Friendster for College." It began as a practical solution to an annual university problem. First-year college students wanted to know who was in their class, who was on their hall, what their roommate looked like. For upperclassmen, a freshman class directory offered an easy way to spot potential fraternity brothers or sorority sisters. Snap judgment could be rendered for potential friendships or romance. Universities like Harvard had hesitated to create an electronic database to facilitate such social interactions due to privacy concerns. Yet, every college student was potentially interested in such a dynamic database.

The question remained, "How could Zuckerberg (or anybody) avoid the legal problems that got him into so much trouble with Facemash?" The breakthrough came with a simple innovation: "What if students voluntarily uploaded their photos?" Facebook began in 2004 as an (unofficial) electronic form of the freshman register at Harvard. Half of Harvard's 19,500 students signed up in the first month. The only requirement to join was a Harvard .edu eddress. For a campus that was already competitive and status conscious,

the ability to create your own profile proved irresistible. The Harvard im-
primatur also added to the allure. If the elite were already signed in, then
the other Ivys would surely want to register. Zuckerberg describes what
happened once Facebook launched: "Little by little—'Oh, more schools
want this'; and 'Okay, more types of people want this.' . . . And it just kept
getting wider and wider, and we just went, 'Wow.'"[8] Moskovitz took the
lead in expanding the service to Columbia, Stanford, and Yale. Adoption
at tech-savvy Stanford was especially rapid and enthusiastic. Dartmouth,
Cornell, MIT, Penn, Princeton, Brown, and Boston University were added
next.[9] Facebook spread among highly educated status seekers. It expanded
due to snob appeal.

Initially, students could only friend each other within their campus network.
How could you cross-connect beyond your school? Facebook expanded by
creating an "opt in" system. People became friends beyond their university
network via mutual agreement. A friend request could be ignored, or it could
be accepted, initiating a low-key social contract. As users expanded, your
college affiliation defined you, posted right beneath your photo. The gradual
rollout from campus to campus allowed Zuckerberg and his friends to scale
up gradually. Waiting lists formed with students begging Facebook to come to
their campus. Zuck and his team didn't add servers until demand was already
established. And they didn't expand to new universities until the servers were
in place. Problems of scalability that plagued Friendster were modulated by
Facebook's campus-driven model.

Zuckerberg and his roommates moved to Palo Alto for the summer of 2004.
Advisors like Sean Parker moved in, and early financial partners like Harvard
classmate Eduardo Saverin got eased out. After a summer being wooed by
Silicon Valley investors, Zuckerberg thought Harvard looked a lot less appealing. Despite the parade of lawsuits that dominate *The Social Network*,
Zuckerberg's actions suggest that it was never really about the money. Facebook
was opened up to high school students in 2005 and to everyone (over thirteen)
in 2006. The mission was clarified: to give people the power to share and make
the world more open and connected. Zuckerberg turned down takeover offers
from Viacom and Yahoo! that valued the young company at a billion dollars.
A fresh, young iGod was resisting the temptation to cash in. In *The Facebook
Effect*, Zuckerberg comes across as idealistic: "We can make the world a more
open place. . . . Let's build something that has lasting cultural value and try
to take over the world."[10] It didn't take long.

Authenticity and Anxiety—Why We Love (and Hate) Facebook

The proliferation of email accounts means that many of us juggle correspondence from work in one account while checking in with friends and family in another. We also may hold on to email addresses from our college days. (I even keep an old AOL account open for nostalgia.) A change in jobs might result in a new email address, and despite our best efforts to migrate relationships to a new professional space, we might lose valuable friendships and business contacts along the way. It is tough to manage so many relationships, to keep so many different people apprised of our activities. It became more attractive to have one place as the central hub for our internet activities.

Facebook stepped up as the place to gather and update friends. In *The Facebook Effect*, Zuckerberg revealed his vision: "You have one identity. . . . The days of you having a different image for your work friends or co-workers and for the other people you know are probably coming to an end pretty quickly." So perhaps sites like LinkedIn that focus on our professional networks will become outmoded. It seems easier to have one place to check in, one place to be found, one site to maintain. But Zuckerberg goes further, adding, "Having two identities for yourself is an example of a lack of integrity."[11]

What a big statement. It borders on presumption, especially in the internet era when we routinely create avatars to play games. My children generated multiple "Miis" when they started playing with the Wii. Guitar Hero offered choices between male and female characters with an array of outrageous costumes for each. Personalizing an avatar with gear was part of the fun, the reward for "winning." Psychologist Sherry Turkle of MIT was an early advocate of the role-playing offered by the internet. She was enthusiastic about the opportunities for young people to try on various identities, to experiment with "the second self" available online. Turkle notes, "In the course of life, we never 'graduate' from working on identity; we simply rework it with the materials at hand. From the start, online social worlds provided new materials."[12] Her early enthusiasm for "life on the screen" has waned. In interviews with adolescents, she noticed how much energy was expended juggling their various profiles. In *Alone Together*, she writes, "The life mix is the mash-up of what you have on- and offline. Now, we ask not of our satisfactions in life but in our life mix. We have moved from multitasking to multi-lifing."[13] In a world of rapidly escalating virtual personae, Zuckerberg promoted Facebook as the source of veracity, the place where only authenticity would be accepted. This could be an important corrective to the splintered selves we build. So what kind of profile does Facebook promote?

Note Facebook's original features, like relationship status and religious and political views. It offered a quick way to define ourselves and put our faces out there. In a college context, Facebook was the ultimate form of speed dating. With relationship status, we could send a clear message regarding our availability—no awkward questions at a crowded bar necessary. Users could quickly scan through pages, noting one another's passions, convictions, and appearance. If you only wanted to go out with people who shared your beliefs, then Facebook sorted your friends as Christians, Jews, agnostics, and atheists. And if those broad groupings didn't suffice, you might personalize your faith with phrases like "Love God, Serve Others," or "Follower of Jesus," or the playful "gee oh dee." Same with political convictions; if you didn't want to wade into potential painful discussion of public policy on a first date, Facebook allowed us to separate Republicans from Democrats. Plenty opted for "other." Perhaps the most open-ended response to religious or political views was a simple "yes." Thanks to social media, we could judge countless books by their covers.

By delimiting our profiles to a few key signifiers, Facebook may inadvertently have added to our anxiety. It crammed the formality of a résumé (education, job titles) and personal interests (relationship status, "likes") into one minimalist profile. For Ivy League students used to performing on paper, such profile building came naturally. But what about those already worried about their public persona? The pressure to be funny or witty increases when we're reduced to a single quotation. The ability to change our profile picture may bring us back to those multiple selves that Zuckerberg seemingly wanted to avoid. Sometimes we feel serious and picture ourselves professionally. Other times, maybe on vacation or amid friends, we can come across as carefree. Which photo should we choose to define "me"?

Turkle describes the presentation anxiety that can arise from managing our profiles. She writes, "Creating the illusion of authenticity demands virtuosity. Presenting a self in these circumstances, with multiple media and multiple goals, is not easy work. Learning to make a me via profiles, profiles, profiles."[14] On Facebook everything becomes a token or marker for who we are. The pressure can be crippling. In her research, Turkle interviewed Brad, a high school senior, who described his anxiety: "When you have to represent yourself on Facebook to convey to anyone who doesn't know you what and who you are, it leads to a kind of obsession about minute details about yourself. . . . You have to know everything you put up will be perused very carefully. And that makes it necessary for you to obsess over what you do put up and how you portray yourself . . . and when you have to think that much about what you come across as, that's just another way that . . . you're thinking of yourself in a bad way." The pressure continues to pick the right bands, the hip quotes.

So why did so many of us sign up? Was it social pressure, not wanting to be left out of the crowd? Facebook became the social network not by being new but by becoming big. It provided one place to connect with the most people. This new technology became a way to deal with effects of other technologies. Facebook is a place for keeping up to date with people we already know without having to make the effort. It is the perfect follow-up to a fraternity or sorority party or a class or a conference. A chance to scope out people after the fact—"Do I want to know them better?" Not having a Facebook account could be even more socially damaging than a mismanaged profile. That old bugaboo, peer pressure, reared its ugly head.

Facebook also offered casual ways to gauge interest. It encouraged flirting. We could poke each other, seeing if a gentle electronic nudge prompted a reaction. A friend request could be accepted or ignored with a similar level of commitment. Some may complain that Facebook devalued the notion of friendship, making it too quick and too easy. Friendships in the real world can occur quickly. First impressions can be enough to cement lifelong commitment. Most friendships begin with a trial period where we are discovering shared interests. On Facebook, those interests are shared up front, potentially allowing us to simply proceed. The surprise and delight that arises from bouncing opinions off each other is an art in and of itself. So perhaps, Facebook facilitates friend-seeking but reduces our ability to make real-world friends. It may have inadvertently undercut dating. All of those questions that you might discover over coffee or dinner were now out in the open. Things that may not have arisen on a first or even second date were answered before the questions were asked. Our social circles are spread wider but thinner.

Facebook also quickly became a preferred time waster, a convenient way to avoid homework or any other obligation, aka "social notworking."[15] Hours could be spent checking friends' pages, tagging photos, engaging in live chat. By opening up their API (application programming interface), Facebook encouraged third-party programmers to develop addictive games like Mafia Wars and FarmVille. Zynga made millions off of social gaming. Some Facebook enthusiasts mysteriously disengaged. But after six months off the network, their friend requests might reappear. Zuckerberg responded to criticism that Facebook is addictive by comparing it to an ancient tool that we now find innocuous (and helpful). He asked a Stanford University class, "You wouldn't say you're addicted to your glasses because you wear them every day right?"[16] Is Facebook already so ingrained in our daily life that we check our notifications the way we wear a pair of glasses? What makes Facebook so attractive, so irresistible, and so annoying at the same time?

Social Capital

Some have questioned whether social networking undercuts friendship, but researchers are increasingly finding it can increase our social ties. Anthropologist Daniel Miller studied the impact of Facebook on residents of Trinidad. The island has long-established social traditions regarding kinship. It could be assumed that Facebook might undermine friendship, keeping people indoors, cut off from their neighbors. Yet, Miller found that while Facebook could substitute for face-to-face relationships, "it enables people to gain more experience and confidence, which in turn facilitate offline relationships."[17] Israeli sociologists studied the effects of information and communication technologies like social networking on adolescents in Israel. They acknowledged the increase in networked individualism that accompanies technologies like Facebook. Teens can now belong to many groups that extend beyond their families, their classmates, or their physical borders, but that doesn't mean they leave those real-world friends. "The internet is typically used by adolescents as an additional space of activity and social interaction, which often complements rather than replaces offline spaces of social communication, activity, and gathering."[18] It is a safe place to practice sociability.

Facebook is an interesting experiment in "social capital." An obscure West Virginian educational reformer, L. J. Hanifan, coined the term *social capital* in 1916. Robert Putnam retrieved Hanifan's progressive notions from the dustbin of history in his influential book, *Bowling Alone* (2000). He cites Hanifan's quotation:

> The individual is helpless socially, if left to himself. If he comes into contact with his neighbor, and they with other neighbors, there will be an accumulation of

social capital, which may immediately satisfy his social needs and which may bear a social potentiality sufficient to the substantial improvement of living conditions in the whole community. The community as a whole will benefit by the cooperation of all its parts, while the individual will find in his associations the advantages of the help, the sympathy, and the fellowship of his neighbors.[19]

Hanifan merged the wisdom of English poet John Donne with economic principles: "No man can succeed as an island." When we cross paths, when we work together, there is a multiplying effect that generates something far beyond our original capacity. Theorists seeking to understand the phenomenon of social network also turned to sociologist Mark Granovetter's 1973 paper, "The Strength of Weak Ties." Granovetter noted how our social networks are structured into strong ties and weak ties. Strong ties are those family members and close friends; weak ties are more like acquaintances. Granovetter argues that social networks are essentially well-defined, small groups. While weak ties are tough to measure, they still connect groups to additional social circles, eventually involving much larger groups of people than do strong ties.

An example of the strength of weak ties is a college alumni association. While we may not have attended school at the same time (or even on the same campus), the weak tie formed by alumni can sometimes suffice to score an internship or even a job. In joining my college alumni association, I not only benefit myself but also expand the power and reach of the entire network. We see the same pay-it-forward principles taking place through Kiva.org. When my wife and I make a microloan to a cobbler in Mongolia, our capital is creating a ripple effect among his community. Social networking makes such empowering websites possible. The weak ties of near strangers on Kiva bless the strong ties to his family, friends, and neighbors. As the cobbler repays the loan, we can then extend that capital to others. Through social networking, we discover, "If strong ties are the connections that help you get through the day, weak ties . . . are the connections that help you get ahead in life."[20] In his survey of American adolescents, S. Craig Watkins concludes, "Whatever the trade-offs—more casual, shorter, and distant conversations—the use of social and mobile media should not be interpreted as inherently adversarial to how humans bond, build community, and cultivate social networks. The long-term net effect may be that computer-mediated and mobile-based communication complements, and in some cases, even invigorates both the strong and weak ties that humans build."[21]

As a free service, Facebook allows us to keep our weak ties active with minimal investment of time and energy. Sometimes it feels like Facebook is training us to exploit our friends. We know that our recommendation has value. Users famously bristled when Facebook launched Beacon in 2007. We didn't want our friends to know what we purchased. It felt too personal and invasive. Class action lawsuits were filed, and Facebook shut Beacon down. Zuckerberg eventually admitted it was "a high profile mistake."[22] Facebook has persisted in monetizing our taste in other ways. Now, Facebook is even trying to charge for introductions—making users pay $100 to get an email to Zuckerberg.[23] It raises the questions, "How much would you pay for an introduction?" and "What is friendship worth?"

What Are Friends Worth?

The new category of "Facebook friends" raises the question of what constitutes "true friends." Aristotle identified three kinds of friendships in his *Ethics*. We all have people with whom we enjoy hanging out, going to the mall, playing games. He called those friendships of pleasure. We also have friends we work with, business associates, who enable us to get things done. Aristotle recognized these as friendships of utility. Most worthwhile relationships are friendships of virtue. They may include entertainment; they may prove useful. But virtuous friends bear goodwill to each other and wish good things for each other. They are delighted when a friend prospers. In Facebook terms, they "like" it when others get promoted, are in a relationship, have a baby, and post pictures from their exotic vacation. Aristotle considered such friendships rare.

All the Facebook friends in the world may not equal the importance of one true friend. As Proverbs indicates, "One who has unreliable friends soon comes to ruin, but there is a friend who sticks closer than a brother."[24] Christianity begins with the incarnation—Emmanuel, "God with us." Jesus came near and discovered that his friends abandoned him in the garden of Gethsemane. They denied him three times when confronted by the threat of the cross. Peter rebounded from his failures. In the Gospel of John, Jesus reestablished his faith in Peter during a postresurrection appearance on the beach.[25] Peter passed a three-part quiz centered on his care for the most vulnerable. True friendship is tested (and often forged) in times of crisis.

I vividly recall in high school when a friend lost his father in a river rafting accident. The shock that rippled across our social circle was palpable. None of us knew what to say in a time of such rapid and tragic reversal. I didn't have that much in common with my friend. I played football; he played soccer. We ran in different but overlapping groups. Yet, as we asked our friend what he wanted or needed, he valued our presence. He asked us to spend the night, to sleep in the basement with him while a phalanx of adults scurried around upstairs. Many of our companions bailed, but I stuck around. We passed the painful hours, and then days, together. Playing ping-pong. Shooting pool. Passing the time. We didn't need to say anything in particular. I wasn't especially useful. My presence in a time of crisis spoke volumes. Years later, I discovered a biblical passage with parallels. In 2 Kings, Elijah faces a crisis. He says to Elisha, "Stay here; the LORD has sent me to Bethel." Elisha responds, "As surely as the LORD lives and as you live, I will not leave you."[26] Three times Elijah invites Elisha to stay behind. Three times, Elisha vows to journey with him. So they went down to Bethel, to Jordan, to Jericho—together. Elisha accompanied Elijah until he was transported to heaven. Friendship involves presence.

Eight years after my friend lost his father, I was blindsided by similar circumstances. My sister was killed in a car accident. She was a college senior on her way to work at a hospital. She swerved to miss a dog in the road that turned out to be dead already. Her car flipped over, and my sister's neck snapped. The impact from such a sudden loss knocked me to my knees. Those whom I had stood beside rallied in my hour of greatest need. After hours of receiving fellow mourners at the funeral home, I was faint and weary. Condolences and sympathy from the crowd did not suffice as sustenance. Their words sounded as hollow as the cold comfort of Job's "friends," Eliphaz, Bildad, and Zophar. The trio meant well, as Job 2:11 indicates: "They set out from their homes and met together by agreement to go and sympathize with him and comfort him." But simple answers quickly sound like trite aphorisms. At my sister's wake, one friend recognized the depth of my need. He did not direct words to me but to God. He leaned over and whispered a prayer to God in my ear. He both invoked and embodied presence. I was literally lifted up, buoyed for the remainder of a draining night. I experienced the promise of Ecclesiastes 4:9–10, "Two are better than one, because they have a good return for their labor: If either of them falls down, one can help the other up. But pity anyone who falls and has no one to help them up." The temptation on Facebook is to offer quick answers or clichés. But how much depth can we pack into a comment? Presence is not possible. True friendship is more than a post. It extends beyond a "like." Friends get in the car, board the plane, and deliver dinner.

Jesus outlined the active nature of friendship in the Gospel of John: "This is My commandment, that you love one another as I have loved you. Greater love has no one than this, than to lay down one's life for his friends. You are My friends if you do whatever I command you. No longer do I call you servants, for a servant does not know what his master is doing; but I have called you friends, for all things that I heard from my Father I have made known to you."[27] Such sacrifices may seem easier to make on a battlefield or amid a natural disaster. It is tough to lay down your life via a status update. Clicking on a "like" button signals some support, but not nearly as much support as wielding a hammer or carrying a cup of cold water.

Facebook's unfriending option means we can welcome people into our network without long-term complications. One click and we are shielded from those who turn out to be creepers. If only the real world were equally efficient. Yet, the Bible provides ancient criteria for unfriending someone. Proverbs encourages us to "stay away from a fool, for you will not find knowledge on their lips" (or in their posts).[28] Paul challenged the Corinthians, "Do not be misled: 'Bad company corrupts good character.'"[29] Political elections have probably been responsible for the most unfriending activity. The anger and vitriol spilled across our timelines in the 2012 Obama–Romney election reached disturbing heights. The wisdom of Proverbs seems particularly resonant: "Do not make friends with a hot-tempered person, do not associate with one easily angered, or you may learn their ways and get yourself ensnared."[30] How many hours were wasted arguing with people equally entrenched in their political convictions?

We can also lose friends via social networking. We can get dragged into drama, forwarding updates that are none of our business. Proverbs 16:28 warns, "A perverse person stirs up conflict, and a gossip separates close friends." Facebook makes it so easy to share news or photos about others. We can escalate misunderstandings by posting inappropriate photos or gossip. I get annoyed when somebody tags me in a picture that I didn't necessarily want to be public. It is not that I was embarrassed to be pictured, but maybe the depiction is so unflattering that I'd rather it not be blasted across Facebook. Proverbs 17:9 offers sound advice when considering whether to post an unflattering photo: "Whoever would foster love covers over an offense, but whoever repeats the matter separates close friends." Yes, social networking can enhance our weak ties and strengthen our close bonds, but it can also strain relationships and pull people apart. We are wise to remember, "A friend loves at all times."[31]

Seeking Status

Social media can appeal to our worst instincts. We can fall into a voyeuristic pattern of electronic stalking. It can slip into judging others. But my biggest temptation is labeled clearly: "update status." What is happening when we think, "I can't wait to post this on my timeline"? What mania drives us to declare what we ate for dinner? Or compels us to share our location? Virtual exhibitionism can devolve into genuine narcissism if we don't monitor our motivations.

I live in Malibu and teach at Pepperdine University. My neighbors are among the wealthiest and most famous people on the planet. On any given day, we may see Angelina Jolie riding a bike or Adam Sandler at the grocery store. It is so easy to mention that we saw Natalie Portman at our local sushi bar, but what lies behind these casual updates? Why are we so eager to share our news? Status updates provide a quick way to feel validated. It is such an easy attention-seeking device. Note the promise in the word itself: *status* can be a report on our current situation, but it is also a word that implies aspiration. Facebook seems to confer status, a standing within our community. We sense that we have a captive audience at least passively paying attention to our thoughts, whims, and recommendations. Our updates can range from playful to desperate, but we hope they'll generate a response from somebody. They can range from a cry for help, a plea for prayer, or a way to bolster our self-esteem. If we can't get people to notice our updates, then we can always leave a note on their timelines. This privilege can easily be abused when we promote our event by posting it far and wide on friends' timelines. Status updates tap into our search for status in many places, circles, and settings. What a rare and valuable opportunity in a fluid, aspirational society—especially when the service is free. Consider them status upgrades.

Facebook allows us to elevate our social standing. One key person can open access to an entirely new social circle, but this can also result in rejection. We judge friend requests based on our friends in common. Strangers may pass muster if they're Facebook friends with even one of our friends. Social media turns six degrees of separation into a lived reality. It is one thing to "follow" a celebrity on Twitter, but who wouldn't welcome the chance to consider a favorite actor or musician a Facebook friend? We can also increase our social standing by padding our friend lists. My perceptive wife skewers me for adding friends on Facebook that I've never met. Facebook can feel dangerously close to a popularity contest.

In his landmark book *The Lonely Crowd* (1950), sociologist David Reisman suggested that Americans had turned from tradition-directed to inner-directed to other-directed selves. As we stretched toward the suburbs in postwar America, we increasingly turned our gaze to our neighbors. We measured our success and self-worth via comparison. We can blame the mad men who were tapping into our search for status via advertising. In the eighties, designers like Ralph Lauren and Calvin Klein and their labels grew into literal status symbols. Psychologist Sherry Turkle sees Reisman's assessment as a mere warm-up for the social networking era. She writes, "Today, cell phone in hand, other-directedness is raised to a higher power. At the moment of beginning to have a thought or feeling, we can have it validated, almost prevalidated. Exchanges may be brief, but more is not necessarily desired. The necessity is to have someone be there."[32]

Social media heightens the temptation to self-promote. In the status update, we are invited to talk about what we're doing, where we're going, who we're meeting with. It is our wall, our timeline after all. Yet, Jesus never said, "Blessed are the self-promoters."[33] The Christian calling is to get beyond ourselves, to take the focus off our needs, our wants, our desires. We are to follow God and reach out to our neighbors—to bless others as we have been blessed. Jesus challenged us to follow him, not to create our own fan pages. Facebook offers countless ways to build an audience and expand my reach, to declare my status as an iGod.

Do we post and tweet to say, "Validate me," "Show me I'm not alone"? That is a form of prayer, but it is misdirected. It points outward, but not upward. An outward-defined self will ultimately be dissatisfied. How many followers or "likes" will suffice? The temptation toward more will push us to ever more extravagant or desperate posts. "If my last post received fifteen 'likes,' then what do I need to say to get twenty 'likes'?" And how often do I have to update my picture to stay current/relevant/in the spotlight?

Facebook can be a great way to reach out to others. You can quickly connect to friends far and wide. It is touching to have someone seek you out—however minimally. But let's engage in a bit of introspection. What percentage of our

Facebook posts and messages are outreach oriented versus self-promoting and attention grabbing? Perhaps the ideal attitude for social media is gratitude. What if we brought things worthy of praise, thanks, and celebration into the public square? What if we figured out subtle ways to praise God in our posts? Not necessarily by preaching at our Facebook friends but by highlighting the beauty and wonder that surrounds us each and every day. Could we create a conspiracy of kindness, a litany of appreciation, and a cascade of poetry forwarded and shared across cyberspace? Could I offer a spark of hope, a ray of light, a bit of laughter each day?

Oversharing and Underbragging

It has been said that Facebook is where you lie to your friends and Twitter is where you tell the truth to strangers.[34] Why is Facebook characterized by so much braggadocio? Is it too tempting to one-up old friends? Are we always looking for a little edge over rivals? The status update invites us to post where we are and what we're up to. We can brag by announcing the concert we're attending or our vacation site. A photo communicates plenty. Proximity to the stage or court demonstrates your ability to score the best seats. We can also raise our standing by talking about the friends we're with (and which friends, presumably, we're not with). A quick tag or two can say plenty about our social standing.

Oversharing on Facebook also makes us look a bit desperate. Are we going to certain restaurants or clubs because of the cache they offer? Those island photos make the beach vacation even more worthwhile. Friends can express their envy in real time—no need to wait until returning home to rub it in. Is my joy really enhanced by showing people what they're missing? Sometimes the sheer volume of photos communicates our desperate longing for attention. One well-timed photo may say enough. Twenty photos of beaches or bikinis in the middle of winter definitely constitutes oversharing.

Sophisticated Facebook users perfect the art of the underbrag.[35] Rather than tooting accomplishments, the underbragger manages to seem humble while still getting out the overall message, "Look at what I'm doing." It is a question of tone. Instead of saying, "Woo hoo, graduating cum laude today" or "Fastest three and a half years of my life," the underbrag might post, "Pleased to have saved my parents some tuition money" or even, "Time to start paying back those college loans." When it comes to romance, while it is nice to praise a spouse or significant other as "the best in the world," maybe a more modest moniker would do: "She makes each day brighter," or "He even knows how to cook." Underbragging allows others to fill in the blanks, to keep their feelings of inferiority to a manageable level.

Neither oversharing nor underbragging falls within the big book of biblical virtues. Humility used to be something to aspire to. Proverbs 22:4 suggests, "Humility is the fear of the LORD; its wages are riches and honor and life." And Saint Peter added, "All of you, clothe yourselves with humility toward one another, because, 'God opposes the proud but shows favor to the humble.'"[36] So Facebook bragging about your cool new shirt, hat, or outfit is not recommended. Self-promotion doesn't even make the list in the Pauline Epistles. Check out this radical anti-Facebook rant: "Do not think of yourself more highly than you ought, but rather think of yourself with sober judgment, in accordance with the faith God has distributed to each of you."[37] According to Jesus, even prayer is not slated to be a public announcement.[38] Sure, it can encourage a friend to know we're praying for them, but perhaps that could be a private message rather than a public pronouncement. By taking the conversation out of the public arena, perhaps you invite more honest sharing. Maybe there is more to the story than they've even let on. When we initiate a private conversation, we send a signal—we can be trusted with secrets, we understand the need to keep things quiet. Surely, those kinds of friendships remain in short supply.

Oversharing and underbragging are a plea to be noticed. We want a witness to our accomplishments or our pain. It is interesting to think about Facebook as an opportunity to witness. Not by preaching to our friends but by acknowledging their struggle, celebrating their promotion, sharing in their rites of passage. There could be a positive side to oversharing on Facebook—if it results in forwarding others' news, supporting their projects, broadcasting their needs. Oversharing could be another constructive response to abundance. Jesus taught oversharing in the feeding of the five thousand, turning loaves and fishes into leftovers. He multiplied the meager holdings of his community into ample food for all.

Facebook Envy

While we can control our posts on Facebook, we can't always restrain the oversharing or underbragging of others. What happens if spending time on

Facebook makes us feel lonely and inadequate? Can we learn to celebrate others' accomplishments, to "like" their successes? There are many ways to become jealous on Facebook. We can envy someone's status updates, their friends, even their "likes." Perhaps the most jealousy springs from photographs posted of parties, of friends, or of exotic vacations that invariably shout, "I'm here and you're not." Gossip and envy are two of the most insidious vices. They take root in our hearts slowly, but once planted, they can be tough to remove. They can yield bitterness, depression, and doubt. Jealousy even gave birth to murder.

The green monster of envy turned brother against brother in Genesis. Cain was the older brother, working as a farmer. Abel was the younger brother, serving as a shepherd. Each made an offering to the Lord from their work. The Hebrew Bible says, "The LORD looked with favor on Abel and his offering, but on Cain and his offering he did not look with favor. So Cain was very angry, and his face was downcast."[39] We can speculate on what separated the two offerings. Perhaps Cain withheld the best of his crops. Maybe he offered a portion of his yield begrudgingly. Maybe Abel's livestock produced more than Cain's land. But "the Lord's regard" for Abel made Cain furious. The Lord questioned Cain about his anger and warned him in Genesis 4:7, "Sin is crouching at your door; it desires to have you, but you must rule over it." There will always be people with more than us, who are seemingly more blessed, more appreciated. And the temptation to be jealous crouches around every status update. Cain did not master his feelings. They grew into murder, fratricide, the killing of his baby brother.

I have read about a couple who was murdered after defriending a woman.[40] And there will undoubtedly be some spouse who seeks revenge following an adulterous Facebook affair. But most of us will keep our most murderous thoughts in check. Nevertheless, studies are emerging that illustrate how status updates and friends' photos can make us feel much, much worse. German researchers found that among six hundred Facebook users, one-third felt worse after visiting the site—especially if they viewed vacation photos. Hanna Krasnova of the Institute of Information Systems at Berlin's Humboldt University said, "We were surprised by how many people have a negative experience from Facebook with envy leaving them feeling lonely, frustrated or angry."[41] Besides vacation photos, Facebook users were also depressed by the greetings and comments others received on their birthdays. We may not even realize how our happiness can depress others. In the report "Envy on

Facebook: A Hidden Threat to User Satisfaction," German scientists wrote, "Overall, however, shared content does not have to be 'explicitly boastful' for envy feelings to emerge. In fact, a lonely user might envy numerous birthday wishes his more sociable peer receives on his FB Wall. Equally, a friend's change in the relationship status from 'single' to 'in a relationship' might cause emotional havoc for someone undergoing a painful breakup."[42] Are we responsible for how our posts make others feel? After Cain killed Abel, the Lord asked a simple question, "Where is your brother?" Cain responded with an evasive question, "Am I my brother's keeper?" God's implicit answer is, "Yes, yes, a thousand times yes."

In the German study, envy was highest among those who didn't post much to Facebook themselves. "Passive following triggers invidious emotions, with users mainly envying happiness of others, the way others spend their vacations and socialize."[43] This coincides with research done by Moira Burke as a grad student at the Human-Computer Institute at Carnegie Mellon. In her longitudinal study of 1,200 Facebook users, she is finding that "the effect of Facebook depends on what you bring to it. Just as your mother said: you get out only what you put in."[44] Those who come to Facebook out of loneliness and lurk on others' timelines without posting are likely to come away more depressed. Burke doesn't consider that the end of the story: "If people are reading about lives that are much better than theirs, two things can happen: they can feel worse about themselves, or they can feel motivated."[45] Burke parlayed her research into a job at Facebook. This may be an important challenge to us when we are intimidated by others' posts and progress, but it doesn't absolve me of responsibility for my own status updates. The German scientists found, "The spread and ubiquitous presence of envy on Social Networking Sites is shown to undermine users' life satisfaction." They concluded with a warning to Facebook's bottom line: "From a provider's perspective, our findings signal that users frequently perceive Facebook as a stressful environment, which may, in the long-run, endanger platform sustainability."[46] I am not worried about Facebook, but I am troubled by the implications for people of faith.

Can our happiness, our photos of family celebrations, birthdays, and vacations be depressing others? Of course, we would never blame Cain's murderous actions on Abel's bragging, but this study may veer into what Jesus warned about, not causing others to stumble. The Christian community invests a lot of time worrying about women's modesty in clothing and dress. We strive to uphold Paul's directive regarding apparel.[47] We even extrapolate how Paul's concerns about meat sacrificed to idols could apply to our language or our movie going.[48] So why wouldn't I apply a similar ethic to my posts on Facebook, Twitter, and Instagram? Just because I have the freedom and ability to document my vacation doesn't mean that others want to share it. While they struggle to pass a course or pay the bills, we may make them feel worse with our accomplishments. Facebook was born among elites and may be set up to broadcast success. That doesn't mean we must succumb to these iGods' values. Jesus took our effect on others quite seriously. He told his disciples, "Things that cause people to stumble are bound to come, but woe to anyone through whom they come. It would be better for them to be thrown into the sea with a millstone tied around their neck than to cause one of these little ones to stumble. So watch yourselves."[49]

By now, you might be depressed, worrying about how the simple joys of Facebook have been ruined by all these ethical dilemmas. Yet, as one of our major daily public activities, posting on Facebook deserves plenty of thoughtful reflection. It is one of the most visible places we live out our convictions. If they shall know we are Christians by our love, then we must also consider whether they will know us by our "like."

The Problem with "Like"

Note how Facebook satisfies different social needs. College students welcomed a tool for navigating their campus clubs and circles. Adults relished the opportunity to reconnect with far-flung friends. Fans embraced the chance to rally around their favorite bands, films, or shows. Having attracted so many people for so many different reasons, Facebook suddenly faced the challenge of keeping users engaged. The initial thrill of who might join on any given day was gone. The blasts from the past slowed down. The novelty of social gaming wore thin. So the next wave of Facebook fell on the "like" button.

To some degree, the "like" button turns Facebook into a simple democracy. Building on the notion of sites like Digg.com that allowed us to vote our favorite articles to the top of the charts, Facebook encouraged us to share our passions and support far and wide. On February 9, 2009, Facebook's Leah Pearlman described the new "like" button as a simple way to congratulate people on accomplishments, from running a marathon to having a baby. We could join the celebration of getting accepted into college or being hired on a new job.

"This is similar to how you might rate a restaurant on a reviews site. If you go to the restaurant and have a great time, you may want to rate it 5 stars. But if you had a particularly delicious dish there and want to rave about it, you can write a review detailing what you liked about the restaurant. We think of the new 'like' feature to be the stars, and the comments to be the review."[50] About a year later, the two features were combined into the ability to "like" a comment.[51] We "like" things on Facebook almost three billion times per day.[52]

Clicking on a "like" button is a form of voting, especially when it is aggregated around a pop cultural phenomenon like a band, a movie, or a team. The Dallas Cowboys, long revered as "America's Team," had over 5 million "likes" on Facebook while the lowly Jacksonville Jaguars mustered less than 300,000 "likes." In the run-up to the 2012 election, Barack Obama had over 28 million people who "liked" him on Facebook[53] while Mitt Romney had just over 6 million "likes."[54] Yet, both presidential candidates paled in their Facebook reach compared to Lady Gaga's 53 million "likes." What essentially became a point of self-identification—"liking" a show like *Glee* or a singer like Bob Dylan—eventually morphed into a literal fan base, a simple way to blast an update to millions of dedicated followers. "Like" moved from a show of support to signing up for electronic newsletters. We hardly noticed when the "like" button was released across the internet, driving all of our thumbs-up straight back to Facebook.

All of this seems innocent enough, so what's not to like about the "like" button? It works splendidly when passing along pleasant news. But what happens when we're sharing our pain or sorrow? We've all been confronted by status updates that might suggest dire circumstances such as "Mom is in the hospital for an MRI, still waiting for a diagnosis" or "My Dad passed away today, getting in the car for long drive back to my hometown." While such updates may trigger a wave of condolences, they are certainly something we would not "like." Facebook doesn't offer a "dislike" button. Eli Pariser of Upworthy .com notes how this simple software option may force us to rethink our status updates, shading them in hopeful terms. Slight shifts toward "Mom is in the hospital for an MRI, doctors working on a diagnosis" or "Dad passed away today, know he's in a better place" make our updates much more "likeable." While I am all for projecting hope, we must acknowledge that not all our prayers will be answered and not all of our experiences are positive. The introduction of emoticons to Facebook allows for a broader range of responses but it still tends towards the shallow. Facebook offers a way to reach out to friends and family, but it isn't predisposed toward depression, doubt, or loneliness. I've seen updates that beg for a response ("Is anybody out there?" or "I'm so lonely") linger because they ask for a bit more than we may be used to offering via Facebook. A casual comment does not seem sufficient to address the conflicted feelings on the other end of the post. The same thing happens with friends who use, and maybe even abuse, the instant messaging function. We can count on certain people to pop up for a quick "hello" every time we log into the system. We may be tempted to block them from seeing our status. A software feature designed to bring people together in real time becomes a source of annoyance requiring an ability to hide. While Facebook was built to connect us, it also keeps us a safe distance from one another. An occasional "like" may suffice rather than an extended conversation via phone or live chat.

The "like" button may also limit the kinds of links we share. It is much easier to pass along a funny video than a poignant news update. One generates plenty of "likes," while the other forces a level of reflection and introspection that, frankly, we may not "like." I could never "like" an article about genocides or floods or institutional injustice. I might find it timely, important, relevant, enlightening, but "like" seems too small an emotion to apply to complex issues that defy easy answers. Pariser suggests that by only offering an ability to "like" things, Facebook may inhibit our knowledge of wars, conflicts, and social problems. There isn't much to like about the conflict in Darfur or homelessness in America.[55] Importance must be inscribed in the update itself: "An article worth thinking about." While it is certainly helpful to have a news feed that can sort through the world wide web and allow my friends to forward the best stories, we are also somewhat limited by the format itself. Pariser calls for new buttons that offer a wider range of emotions. Facebook would still offer programmatic shortcuts (perhaps offering three or four different emotional buttons to click), but users would also be invited to consider a wider range of responses.

I often find the "like" button insufficient. I need a "love" button to suggest the depth of my passion, the strength of my support. It doesn't take much to "like" a band. One hit song may compel us to "like" their music, but it may not translate into buying seats for a concert. I may have twenty bands I like, but only two or three that I truly love. There is no way to measure intensity.

A friend recently told me he was "discipling" thousands of people online. I was intrigued. He pointed me toward a Facebook page that included a daily Bible verse and photo. Those who "liked" the page received a daily update, comparable to a thought for the day, tied to a particular passage of Scripture. We were both impressed by the global reach of Facebook; people from seemingly closed countries like Pakistan and China had "liked" his Facebook page. While I affirm the power of spreading God's Word, I could hardly consider the distribution of a gauzy photo and a single verse "discipleship"; it feels far removed from the personal discipleship that Jesus called his disciples to practice. He called twelve and invested heavily in three of his followers. They weren't challenged to "like" everything Jesus said and did. Some of his words were confounding; others undercut the prevailing wisdom of the day, challenging Jews to care for Samaritans. And, certainly, there was almost nothing to like about the Passion, the most important part of Jesus's ministry. "Liking" the teaching of Jesus will never suffice. Adopting the way of the cross may not be something we enjoy either.

Being Used

When we express our opinions and share articles, links, and photos, we engage in democratic actions. Facebook celebrates transparency and free speech. We didn't realize that each "like" also became a quicker way to join groups. The "like" button opted us in for updates on our favorite baseball teams, even real-time highlights. Facebook was suddenly more like Twitter, a way to blast out updates, promoting books or articles or opinions. Twitter never hid the public side of their service. Unfortunately, Facebook turned our connection tool into an advertising agency and public relations firm. Turkle notes this subtle but significant shift: "When we Tweet or write to hundreds or thousands of Facebook friends as a group, we treat individuals as a unit. Friends become fans."[56] In setting an upper limit of five thousand friends, Facebook set a tangible number or goal—what it takes to turn people from friends to fans. Unfortunately, that also turns people into numbers or a goal. Turkle suggests, "Online, we invent ways of being with people that turn them into something close to objects. The self that treats a person as a thing is vulnerable to seeing itself as one."[57]

Now Facebook is turning our "likes" into profits—linking them to random sponsored ads.[58] Things we've "liked" in the past are being connected to sponsored ads that may only be loosely affiliated with our passions. If I "liked" a photo tagged as the Malibu Pier, I may find my name associated with a realtor's paid ad. If you "like" the Miami Dolphins, you may find your fandom turned into a recommendation for a hotel on South Beach. This associative advertising can create false impressions about what we like and recommend. The key thing that Facebook offered—an aggregation of my friends' honest assessments—is now being used deceptively. We are slowly discovering the ways in which Facebook is using us.[59]

Such shifts in Facebook's policy have given us pause. It made Facebook look a little less cool. Call me old-fashioned, but I don't post my birth date on Facebook. I've never filled in my timeline with the year I graduated from high school or my wedding anniversary. I don't always announce when I'm on vacation. I don't want to make it easy for scammers, spammers, or Facebook to exploit me. An older generation of critics and scholars seems far more concerned about the loss of privacy via social networking than today's students. Most Facebook users seem content to exchange their personal information for access. Facebook offered each of us free advertising, a personal internet billboard. Yet, how much private information are we sharing in exchange for this "free" service? What are the implications of revealing our passions and interests and webs of relationships on the web?

In *Cognitive Surplus*, Clay Shirky notes the blame game that adults play with young people, particularly when it comes to the collapse of privacy on Facebook.

> People in my generation and older often tut-tut about young people's disclos-
> ing so much of their lives on social networks like Facebook, contrasting their
> behavior with our own relative virtue in that regard. "You exhibitionists! We
> didn't behave like that when we were your age!" This comparison conveniently
> ignores the fact that we didn't behave that way because no one offered us the
> opportunity (and from what I remember of my twenties, I think we would have
> happily behaved that way if we'd had the chance).[60]

What resides behind the exhibitionist impulse? It may be more than a plea for attention.

The rise of Facebook reveals some of our deepest, ongoing needs. It demonstrates our strong communal longing. We hunger for connection, for interaction, for feeling like a part of something larger. In *The Church of Facebook*, Jesse Rice states, "At the root of human existence is our great need for connection: connection with one another, with our own hearts and minds, and with a loving God who intended intimate connection with us from the beginning. Connection is the very core of what makes us human and the very means by which we express our humanity."[61] Perhaps connection is the very foundation of the universe, with Father, Son, and Holy Spirit present together at the dawn of creation. We were not only born to be *in* relationship, we were born *out of* relationship. So the act of revealing ourselves via Facebook is the first step in being known.

Does revealing ourselves online result in the kind of relationships and community we hunger for? Turkle writes of the transition from adolescence to adulthood: "Traditionally, the development of intimacy required privacy. Intimacy without privacy reinvents what intimacy means. Separation, too, is being reinvented. Tethered children know they have a parent on tap—a text or call away."[62] Electronic connection can offer a sense of security. Being reachable is a form of mutual reassurance for parents and kids. It may also hinder development. Turkle points out how valuable time away from family and friends can be: "Adolescent autonomy is not just about separation from parents. Adolescents also need to separate from each other. They experience their friendships as both sustaining and constraining. Connectivity brings complications."[63]

What type of mystery and secrets are worth preserving? God practiced progressive revelation, withholding the full portrait of his will and his ways until a deeper relationship of trust was established with his people. How do we take back our privacy or at least obscure our digital footprints? There is evidence that people are starting to resist the tracks that Facebook leaves on every website we visit. What do we only share in strict confidence either with God, with our ministers, or with our Christian community? Surely, such sacred moments shouldn't be sold out for a quick "like." And yet, postmodern ministry must contend with the strong sense of ownership people feel with Facebook. We want to be known. We want our thoughts, opinions, and passions to be heard. What kinds of forums can the church create for people to express their hopes and hunger, to share their glee, and mark signposts along their journeys? The walls of the church once housed our communal records from weddings to baptisms. Facebook provides the ability to publish, to promote, and to create a public record without the attending ritual. No priests are needed to document our timeline. At one time, people longed to be buried on sacred ground, in a place where people visited regularly—the church. I've had several friends who've passed away, yet their Facebook page still offers a place to gather, to post, and to mourn as a community. Facebook offers electronic immortality without the funeral or the cross. To millions around the globe, the exchange of privacy for Facebook's form of eternity makes sense.

Unfriending Facebook

Have you been tempted to unfriend Facebook? We have such strong feelings about changes made to our profile, shifts in the rules we thought were established. Also, we may find Facebook too tempting, too addictive, feeding narcissism we're trying to resist. Many of us bristle at the loss of control over our most public face. I noticed many of my friends giving up Facebook for Lent as a spiritual discipline and cleansing. Rebecca Cusey posted news of her breakup with Facebook on Patheos.com. She explained her reasons: "You're a creeper, Facebook. Now you watch my every keystroke, even when I'm not logged in. You tell people what I've been reading, even my insomnia-driven reading on mating whales. You even tried, without my knowledge, to take over my email. And you seem hell-bent on revealing my location to the world, even when I'd rather not. . . . Facebook, you manipulate, you control, you pimp me out, and potentially tell me what I can or can't say. That's not love. That's abuse."[64]

I didn't opt out of Facebook while I taught for a semester in China, but the Chinese government's filters severed my online connections with friends and family. What did I miss when I was away from Facebook on a daily basis? Evidently, I missed lots of baby photos, wedding pictures, and status updates. The bulk of those status updates were rather mundane. But occasionally, I missed friends' news of health scares or cancer diagnoses that I would have wanted to know. Facebook gave my friends a false sense that everyone was following their status, and my friends assumed (like everybody on Facebook) I had already heard. Facebook can give us a false sense of how closely we are being watched and followed. It so effectively removes the need for phone calls that it can make us a little lazy. Since we don't have to actively seek out information, we may not reach out to those in need. We may assume that everyone saw an important update.

We end up defining ourselves outwardly in ways that may not always be honored. In other words, we expect more from our friends via Facebook than they can possibly deliver. The affirmations we seek via a status update may not engender as broad a response as we hoped. The temptation to up the ante, to make our updates even more dramatic or clever, may rise to unsustainable heights. While being creative and generating a well-turned phrase is an art, it probably shouldn't become our sole preoccupation. Turkle notes our misplaced faith: "We build a following on Facebook or MySpace and wonder to what degree our followers are friends. We recreate ourselves as online personae and give ourselves new bodies, homes, job, and romances. Yet, suddenly, in the half-light of virtual community, we may feel utterly alone."[65] We end up perplexed by the results: "These days, whether you are online or not, it is easy for people to end up unsure if they are closer together or further apart."[66]

We have questioned whether social media undercuts or facilitates embodied relationships. Researchers are finding we are more connected to friends and family as a result of social networks. But the presence of virtual relationships may still distract us from spouses and children and roommates who are often right beside us.

Technology can provide an easy way to hide. Turkle recalls,

> The answering machine, originally designed as a way to leave a message if someone was not at home, became a screening device . . . over time, voicemail became an end in itself, not the result of a frustrated phone call. People began to call purposely when they knew that no one would be home. People learned to let the phone ring and "let the voicemail pick it up." In a next step, the voice was taken out of voicemail because communicating with text is faster. E-mail gives you more control over your time and emotional exposure. But then, it, too, was not fast enough. With mobile connectivity (think text and Twitter), we can communicate our lives pretty much at the rate we live them.[67]

This is an amazing advance. I am stunned by how I can connect with people instantaneously over Facebook. Nevertheless, I must not confuse possibilities with presence. Texting can be the next best thing to being there, but only if I recognize the enduring power of presence. Turkle warns, "In text, messaging, and e-mail, you hide as much as you show. You can present yourself as you wish to be 'seen.' And you can process people as quickly as you want to. Listening can only slow you down."[68] We are still called to be present to those in need. Not just via Facebook, but via hugs and kisses and meals and meetings.

Jaron Lanier wants to reclaim the human side of social media. He suggests, "The central mistake of recent digital culture is to chop up a network of individuals so finely that you end up with a mush. You then start to care about the abstraction of the network more than the real people who are networked, even though the network by itself is meaningless. Only the people were ever meaningful."[69] He wonders if Facebook has dumbed us down, reducing who we are to a few key identifiers. Lanier worries that "the new designs on the verge of being locked in, the web 2.0 designs, actively demand that people define themselves downward. . . . Emphasizing the crowd means deemphasizing individual humans in the design of society, and when you ask people to not be people, they revert to moblike behaviors. This leads not only to empowered trolls, but to a generally unfriendly and unconstructive online world."[70] Facebook has the potential to become the civil gathering place, but we are often unkind and far from civil. It can bring out our inner troll or unleash the green monster of envy. While Reddit or 4Chan spiral out into all manner of misbehavior, could the social standards established on Facebook restrain our worst impulses? Proper netiquette is still forming. Will we turn Facebook into a competitive contest or a glorious celebration of the blessings that surround us?

The Gift of Community

Religion binds people together via a shared set of rituals or values. Is a social networking site—gathering people around shared networks, passions, and interests—inherently religious? Facebook binds us together. It connects us, however loosely and voluntarily. The church of Facebook can be quite affirming. We may share the joys of graduation, of college acceptance letters, of promotions, of weddings, of births. We also share the pain of sickness and the sorrow of death. It is a place to ask for prayer, to express unwavering support. But the unity is based on Facebook's rules, which can change at any time.

Like a religion, Facebook places demands (or at least expectations) on us. You have to reveal yourself in some way. And while we can control our privacy settings, we can't hide our information from Facebook itself. If we just lurk, we don't gain much from the community. We must share if we long to feel connected. Status updates can be a form of prayer, alternating between praise and pleas. They can also devolve into bragging, which helps none of us. We can learn to celebrate the things that surprise and delight us, and lift up the things that bewitch or frustrate us.

How many friends or followers do we need? How big a circle of influence is enough? How many relationships can we truly be committed to? Jesus hurt for the crowd. He saw how lonely and aimless we can be, even when we're surrounded. Jesus saw the crowd as harassed and helpless, like sheep without a shepherd.[71] He spoke to the masses, offering bread and wisdom. But he also fled from the crowd, seeking isolation. We can't be all-public-all-the-time. We must maintain downtime, quiet time, time to connect with our core values, to commune with our God. This may include taking a break from Facebook, stepping away for a season or even a day. Turkle worries about how the always-on culture beckons us: "Increasingly, people feel as though they must have a reason for taking time alone, a reason not to be available for calls. It is poignant that people's thoughts turn to technology when they imagine ways to deal with stresses that they see as having been brought on by technology. They talk of filters and intelligent agents who will handle the messages they don't want to see."[72] Technology may answer our calls or filter our friends, but it cannot provide peace of mind.

In bringing us closer together and encouraging more openness, Zuckerberg and the Facebook investors and employees have acquired massive riches. Yet, his motivations still point beyond money. He asked David Kirkpatrick of *Fortune*, "Are you familiar with the concept of a gift economy?" Zuck explained, "It's an interesting alternative to the market economy in a lot of less developed cultures. I'll contribute something and give it to someone, and then out of obligation or generosity that person will give something back to me. The whole culture works on this framework of mutual giving." Zuckerberg may be proudest of the fact that Facebook (and other forces on the internet) now creates sufficient transparency for gift economies to operate at a large scale. He suggests, "When there's more openness, with everyone being able to express their opinion very quickly, more of the economy starts to operate like a gift economy. It puts the onus on companies and organizations to be more good, and more trustworthy."[73] Zuckerberg has also seen how "it's really changing the way that governments work. . . . A more transparent world creates a better-governed world." He has backed up this core belief with actions. Even before Facebook's initial public offering poured billions into his pocket, Zuckerberg vowed to give his fortune away. Zuckerberg and Dustin Moskovitz joined Bill and Melinda Gates's "Giving Pledge." As the youngest billionaire on the list, Zuckerberg said, "People wait until late in their career to give back. But why wait when there is so much to be done? . . . With a generation of younger folks who have thrived on the success of their companies, there is a big opportunity for many of us to give back earlier in our lifetime and see the impact of our philanthropic efforts."[74] On the same day that Facebook had its IPO, Zuckerberg gave away $500 million dollars in stock to the Silicon Valley Community Foundation.[75] Facebook may hide all the ways it makes money off our posts, but Zuckerberg seems quite committed to public acts of charity, giving, and social transformation. Given the notoriously tight pockets of the original iGod, Steve Jobs, this is a trend that I like.

A gift economy can be realized through crowdsourcing—from something as fun and simple as a mall flash mob singing the "Hallelujah Chorus"[76] to people supporting each other through sites like Kickstarter and Indiegogo. Even more satisfying are the microloans we can extend across the world through organizations like Kiva, which has distributed over $300 million in loans around the world, with a 98 percent repayment rate. That is a powerful source of change, particularly for women and children previously cut off from capital. David Fischer, vice president of business and marketing partnerships at Facebook, notes, "The tools we have today to reach a new audience work for nonprofits and important causes, too. . . . They find Facebook to be a really engaging place to build up awareness."[77] We are created for communion, co-uniting with God and his people around a shared table. We have rightly elevated technology because it facilitates communication. It makes sociability easier. It extends our reach. It is a complement to, but not a substitute for, God's gathered community, the church.

Christianity is one of the original social movements. Membership grew via word of mouth and exploded via vigorous actions. Amid the opulence of ancient Rome, plenty of people suffered. Christians distinguished themselves by caring for the sick, supporting widows, rallying around orphans. Universities arose because monks preserved ancient texts and priests passed on knowledge to succeeding generations. Social reformers like William Wilberforce fought long and hard to abolish slavery, inspired by a vibrant biblical faith. In the Industrial era, Christians took to the streets of England with the Salvation Army. In America, committed Christians like Jane Addams and Donaldina Cameron fought for the working class, creating a network to stop the exploitation of child laborers, the abuse of alcohol, and the subjugation of women. At its best, the church is a social network that organizes to make a difference. It shares status updates of people who need food, shelter, and clothing. We may not always like each other, but we're learning how to love instead.

We've all been disappointed by Christians on almost a daily basis. I've had to modify my expectations, to understand the wisdom contained in Dietrich Bonhoeffer's description of life together. A genuine community is bound to disappoint us because it is composed of fallen people who gossip and fight, overshare and overbrag. But it is equally hazardous to try to follow Christ on our own. Bonhoeffer understands the push and pull inside us. He warns, "Let him who cannot be alone beware of community. Let him who is not in community beware of being alone." Bonhoeffer had previously explained, "Each by itself has profound perils and pitfalls. One who wants fellowship without solitude plunges into the void of words and feelings, and one who seeks solitude without fellowship perishes in the abyss of vanity, self-infatuation, and despair."[78] He challenges us to rise above our experiences to mystical truth. For Bonhoeffer, Christian community is not an ideal but a divine reality.

We have all experienced the gift of community. I have seen the people of God in action responding to a tragedy by filling a friend's house with food or even mowing our lawn to prepare for mourners. I've been a recipient of the gift economy. When my wife was battling cancer, relative strangers would show up at our door with dinner. We didn't know how far the caring bridge extended, but we saw the results in countless casseroles filling our fridge. Christians can be infuriating (especially on Facebook!). Communities of faith regularly fall short of their ideals (Lord knows, I do as well). But when God's social network gets it right, there is nothing more powerful, humbling, and inspiring. With or without Facebook, such true and transformative friends remain a rare blessing.

Discuss

1. Do social networks broaden and deepen your friendships? Does Facebook make you feel more connected to others?
2. How do you feel after spending time on Facebook? Envious? Covetous? Loved? How can you be an encouragement to your friends online?

YouTube, Twitter, Instagram

Audience Participation

> God dazzles us by excess of truth.
> —French composer Olivier Messiaen[1]

It arrives as a link, posted on our Facebook timelines or tweeted to the world. A simple click will often snap us into strange and wonderful sights. We laugh when we watch "Charlie Bit My Finger—Again," and we laugh at the woozy "David after Dentist" and at "Debbie," who loves every kind of cat in her "EHarmony Video Bio." The shortest and silliest links, like six seconds of "Dramatic Chipmunk," travel the fastest and the farthest. With "Sneezing Panda," "Keyboard Cat," and "Goats Yelling Like Humans," we get a peek into the wonder of God's creation. These snippets of animals reveal things we've never seen or believed or realized. We laugh at the absurdity, marvel at how much we don't know. At its best, YouTube celebrates the weird, wild diversity of God's kingdom. The mobiquity (mobility/ubiquity) of cameras allows moments like the "Battle of Kruger" between buffaloes and lions on the African savanna to be shared by millions. YouTube is a place where almost anything seems possible.

It is easy to see why some videos go viral. They are such pure, disposable pleasures, a quick laugh, sometimes at others' expense like "Miss Teen USA 2007–South Carolina" or "Yosemitebear Mountain Giant Double Rainbow." In the midst of busy days, a blast of laughter goes a long way. Now, thanks to autotune, we can enjoy the Double Rainbow song remixed! We don't need to understand Psy's lyrics to relish the infectious energy he conveys in "Gangnam Style." The gaudy color and silly dance drew us in again and again. As the first billion-view video on YouTube, "Gangnam Style" blanketed the planet with K-pop. It demonstrated how viral videos transcend language and borders. From Seoul, South Korea, to *Saturday Night Live*, Psy was a global phenomenon.

Not all viral videos are silly. Some, like "Kony 2012," are remarkably serious. Almost 100 million people watched a thirty-minute video about an African warlord who deserves to be brought to justice. It became the most viral political cause of the YouTube era. In the stylish video, filmmaker Jason Russell spells out why he wants to make Joseph Kony famous. He documents the atrocities committed by Kony and his ill-named "Lord's Resistance Army," kidnapping thirty thousand children in Uganda and turning them into child soldiers. Russell uses his own son, Gavin, as a case study, both why African children deserve better and how little attention it takes for Gavin (or the audience) to identify Kony. Having made the plight of Invisible Children visible, Russell's goal was to shine a spotlight on Kony, to give him no rest or hiding places. "Kony 2012" implores celebrities like George Clooney, Rihanna, and Jay-Z to use their clout to bring Kony's crimes to the attention of policy makers. And it invites viewers to put on a Kony 2012 bracelet to raise awareness. It is a video about how to create a viral phenomenon that became a viral phenomenon.[2]

Unfortunately, the rapid rise in popularity shifted the focus from Kony to the filmmakers. Many questioned the effectiveness of the campaign, denigrating it as easy "slacktivism."[3] Russell was put on the defensive, having to answer questions about his organization and its finances.[4] The video spread so rapidly that Russell nearly snapped, eventually explaining to Oprah why he ran through the streets of San Diego naked.[5] The strange saga demonstrated how fast and wide an idea can spread across new media. Internet success, whether for Psy or Invisible Children, can be overwhelming in its scale and suddenness.

An amateurish, fourteen-minute video, created to provoke, also stirred up audiences in 2012. "The Innocence of Muslims" was filmed in Southern California under false pretense, dubbed into Arabic afterward, and distributed by anti-Muslim groups in America to clerics in the Middle East. It lampoons the origins of Islam, suggesting that Muhammad was a pork-eating adulterer who encouraged child rape. The cheap sets, costumes, and lighting demonstrate the unprofessional nature of the production. Alas, the suspect production values did not dull the effects of such premeditated blasphemy against Islam. When violent protests erupted in Cairo, the filmmakers pointed to the results as proof of Islam's volatility. This irresponsible video posted on YouTube created undue policy problems for peacemakers throughout the world. United States Secretary of State Hillary Clinton and President Obama both made statements condemning the film as reprehensible. YouTube blocked the video in most Muslim countries. Our freedom of speech was abused. The United States government arrested the producer on prior parole violations, but the damage was seemingly done. "The Innocence of Muslims" demonstrated the power of technology to spread slander and disinformation with lightning speed. The Bishop Ijaz Inayat of Pakistan reframed our perspective on blasphemy in the internet era:

> On YouTube, you can find videos insulting every religion on the planet: Jews, Christians, Hindus, Catholics, Mormons, Buddhists, and more. Some clips are ironic. Others are simply disgusting. Many were posted to bait one group into fighting another. Mockery of your prophet on a computer with an Internet address somewhere in the world can no longer be your master. Nor can the puppet clerics who tell you to respond with violence. Lay down your stones and your anger. Go home and pray. God is too great to be troubled by the insults of fools.[6]

Each of these viral videos was created outside the standard Hollywood system. The creators bypassed mainstream media to take their message directly to the people. Infamy enabled them to elevate their profile—whether deserved or not. They demonstrated how the communication pyramid has been inverted. People tend to refer to YouTube, Twitter, and Instagram as new media. They are all new means of communicating, but they mostly take preexisting notions of communication and put them in the hands of the people. Rather than being run by a single guiding entrepreneur (like the iGods), they are collective efforts to enhance our abilities to reach an audience. They can potentially turn anybody into an internet idol. YouTube and Twitter turned the old, top-down, one-to-many forms of communications (such as television broadcasting) into a democratized, many-to-many forms of narrowcasting.

Now, anybody can have his own show or network; anybody can aggregate her own following to create a news feed; and anybody can instantly tweet or publish a photo. As the old barrier of network executives or publishers have fallen, the power has shifted to what Jay Rosen of NYU calls, "The People Formerly Known as the Audience."[7] Communication no longer flows from central clearinghouses. It is a rowdy, aggregated mélange. The implications for churches and synagogues are profound. Lecture-based education is on notice. We are not satisfied with listening. We expect to participate.

Viral videos and services like Twitter and Reddit are quite democratic in nature. They are rooted in what's hot, what's trending, what is being voted up. They are new forms of popularity contests, reflecting the best and worst of human nature. We've seen the benefits of going viral for democracy in the Middle East, but the ubiquity of devices can also be turned against a community. The aggregation of what's trending can also be controlled and monitored by totalitarian regimes. Smartbots can spread rumors and disinformation across these new platforms. This chapter will consider the upside and the downside of viral videos and instant communication. Short messages and viral videos can pack powerful messages, but they may also undercut thoughtful analysis and reflection. Snarky is not a substitute for substance. We may now be settling for the circus without even the bread.

Why do we share things via YouTube, Twitter, or Instagram? Word-of-mouth communication can be a form of warning others, "Go back," "Be careful," "Turn on your lights." It can also be a way of helping people find water, shelter, or bargains. Christianity was originally a viral network, a community blessed to be a blessing. The church is uniquely positioned to aggregate audiences and encourage participation. Still, how much faith should be placed in the wisdom of crowds? Jesus often fled from the masses right after addressing them. He sought solitude when he needed solace. While we may celebrate the fun of flash mobs, let us remember that the crowd that loved Jesus on Palm Sunday turned on him by Good Friday. Social networking can be a blessing and a curse. We will consider how people of faith can tap into the possibilities of YouTube, Twitter, and Instagram while avoiding the self-importance that accompanies a motto like "Broadcast Yourself."

YouTube

In retrospect, the idea behind YouTube seems so simple: sharing videos via the internet. It is one of the most ubiquitous activities on the planet—taking videos—a feature of basic smartphones. Yet, Chad Hurley, Steve Chen, and Jawed Karim birthed their idea at a historic confluence of feasibility. They were all former employees of PayPal. They had all witnessed how wealth could be generated around early web innovations. Napster created a firestorm of protests when it made music so shareable. Flickr provided a pioneering format for sharing photos. Broadcast.com made a mint with an early example of internet radio and podcasting. In 2005, Hurley, Chen, and Karim cobbled together enough programming know-how and capital investment ($10 million) to launch a video-sharing service. The rise of YouTube was meteoric. It grew at the nearly inconceivable rate of 75 percent *per week*.[8] Within sixteen months of the company's founding, YouTube was streaming more than 30 million videos a day.[9] A year and a half after it began, Google bought YouTube for $1.65 *billion* in stock. The *Time* 2006 Person of the Year featured a reflective computer screen that honored "You." *Time* celebrated the shift to user-generated media and participatory culture: "It's about the many wresting power from the few and helping one another for nothing and how that will not only change the world, but also change the way the world changes."[10]

By inviting users to "Broadcast Yourself," YouTube disrupted old media in lasting ways. Traditionally, new forms of electronic mass media took a decade to develop and another decade to find an audience. The pattern was followed in the adoption of AM radio, VCRs, DVD players, personal computers, and cell phones.[11] YouTube is the product of an accelerated era. It went much wider much faster. In its first five years, YouTube had amassed more hours of video than the entire history of American television programming. The hours of videos being uploaded *every minute* boggles the mind (and challenges YouTube's servers and bottom line).[12] The company struggles to keep up with our ability to create, no matter how inane the subject. It has also become the de facto archive of all the video that preceded it, from vintage music performances to seminal political speeches. For those poets and artists never recorded for posterity, one may wonder if their legend will survive the YouTube era where seeing is believing. Yet, fortunately, poets like Emily Dickinson and Gerard Manley Hopkins are already well represented in readings and documentaries on YouTube.

There is also plenty of inanity and banality on YouTube. Amid the avalanche of cat videos and pratfalls is genuinely useful information. Many YouTube videos are how-tos—practical demonstrations of things such as doing a dance move, playing the ukulele, shucking an oyster, baking a soufflé, or repairing an auto. While a video demonstrating the art of unboxing a new iPhone may seem superfluous, the information to be gained from others' experiences can undoubtedly save hours of frustration. Could YouTube become a valuable educational resource? Radio and television were initially considered potentially revolutionary technology for educators. And we know how far those movements got in comparison to the lure of sitcoms and variety shows. Will a participatory audience eventually return to passivity?

I am encouraged by the growing influence of TED talks distributed via the web. By packing potent ideas into a fast-paced format (under eighteen minutes), TED talks have become high-brow viral videos. Wouldn't we prefer to watch "How to solve world hunger" or learn how to raise social capital rather than watch why we should "Leave Britney Alone!" The rapid rise of MOOCs (Massive Open Online Courses) is causing ripples within higher education. Khan Academy (offering free lectures online) has brought instructions in math and science to the masses in unprecedented numbers. While the efforts of Khan Academy and Udemy (a website that hosts classes) were easy for established institutions to dismiss, the partnerships between Stanford University professors via Coursera and MIT's edX initiative have given smaller schools serious pause. Can a community of learners arise from aggregated videos? Can online instruction spark active participation?

My nine-year-old son learned the art of origami via YouTube. He found new videos and designs every day and has littered our home with paper cranes, ninja stars, and even a miniature Millennium Falcon. YouTube channels like Ehow, Howcast, and Make have loyal subscribers who browse through countless crafts and projects. As a gamer, my son turns to YouTube for cheat codes to guide him through particularly vexing levels of a game. YouTube illustrates the power of showing versus telling. We appreciate the opportunity to *pull* media toward us, rather than deflecting the *push* of traditional broadcast networks.

Religious institutions are used to pushing. For centuries, synagogues, churches, and mosques have dispensed wisdom and advice to nearly captive audiences. They had minimal competition for time, attention, and resources. Churches served and the people received. Religious leaders now compete with so many more distractions; they wonder how to make our faith and practices visual and appealing, something that people seek. Churches now need to change from *pushing* their practices to *creating a pull* from seekers. Worship experiences can be enhanced by stirring background videos, but I am not sure a countdown video (which projects a clock image counting down to the start of the service) fulfills the original purpose of a prelude. These videos start five minutes before a worship service and are an ingenious way to get a congregation's attention; they get us ready to watch the show, but they do not necessarily prepare us to participate. Are they designed to calm our hearts and minds, focus our attention, and invoke the Spirit of God?

How do we model discipleship in the YouTube era? The temptation is to create five-minute how-to videos for following God. But the way of the cross cannot be compacted into small, digestible links. Nevertheless, the seeds of faith, particularly how people are living out their convictions, can be captured in a short video. For example, the visual liturgies from *The Work of the People* show how potent and powerful video meditations on faith can be. In them, Travis Reed, using lush images, has interviewed some of the most challenging theologians. How great to tap into the spontaneous thoughts of Tom Wright, Marva Dawn, Barbara Brown Taylor, or Richard Twiss in short bursts of insight. These can be catalysts for fruitful discussions. *The Work of the People* still needs to be translated into our local liturgies. What actions are we taking that are stories worth sharing?

There has been an explosion of creative expressions from religious communities such as worship songs and church videos. The remarkable range of material available on sites like SermonSpice.com demonstrates how a new generation of leaders embraces word and image. Rob Bell's groundbreaking work with Flannel Media resulted in the influential Nooma series. These short video sermons became a surprisingly popular and portable format. The Skit Guys and Igniter Media have created a vibrant business selling short, seasonal videos to congregations. It is encouraging to see the potential of short films previewed on YouTube for positive purposes.

I would like to see more people of faith setting the pace on YouTube. All too often, what passes for creativity is parroting or satirizing a trend started by somebody else. Biologist Richard Dawkins coined the term *meme* to describe the spread of ideas in genetic terms. It combines the Greek word for "imitation" with the viral nature of mutated genes.

The "McKayla Is Not Impressed" meme was first captured at the 2012 London Olympics medal ceremony when the American gymnast McKayla Maroney made an "unimpressed" face after receiving her silver medal. The image mutated its way across the internet, pasting McKayla's face onto pictures of "Double Rainbow" or the Mona Lisa. Viral videos mutate like memes. When we create a "Harlem Shake" video, we spread the virus, disseminate the idea, often without understanding its origins or intent.[13] For example, many churches tapped into the popularity of the Mac-vs.-PC commercial campaign to create their own "Christian vs. Christ Follower" or "Christian vs. Atheist" parodies. It is a tribute to the simple power of the original Apple campaign, but it also shows how often we revert to simple us-vs.-them tendencies. Sadly, the church is still playing catch-up, resorting to pale imitations more suitable for GodTube than the broad and sometimes cruel marketplace of ideas on YouTube. Social media is our Areopagus, the marketplace where ideas and worldviews bump into each other. Weak videos and genes are squashed, the stronger memes voted to the top. It is often survival of the wittiest.

A few inventive church productions crossed over to become original YouTube sensations, like the skit set to Lifehouse's "Everything" or Anita Renfroe's paean to motherhood set to the William Tell Overture.[14] Jefferson Bethke sparked plenty of debate thanks to his provocative spoken-word video, "Why I Hate Religion, But Love Jesus."[15] This video opens with a blast of political incorrectness: "What if I told you Jesus came to abolish religion? / What if I told you voting Republican really wasn't his mission? / What if I told you Republican doesn't automatically mean Christian—and just because you call some people blind doesn't automatically give you vision?" Bethke packed a load of theology, sometimes witty, sometimes wise, into four potent minutes. The video generated almost 200,000 comments and perhaps even more significantly, almost 200 answer videos,[16] including "Jesus = Religion" from Orthodox Christians in Florida.[17] The conversation about God has stepped outside the walls of the church and the province of preachers. David Kinnaman of the Barna Group notes the rise of general revelation: "Anyone could be a theologian as long as you're persuasive, able to create a great Internet video, and the luck of the draw that your video gets selected out of the thousands that are uploaded." Kinnaman adds a caution, though: "But is there a possibility that this is going to create a new breed of people that are great at performance but light on theology? . . . I think so."[18] The rise of YouTube should prompt a deeper commitment to disciple making as well as media creating. We need thoughtful and grounded participants.

As a film professor for the past fifteen years, I've been honored to work alongside Christ's followers who are moving from imitation to innovation. At the Los Angeles Film Studies Center, I had the privilege of teaching talented storytellers, like Destin Daniel Cretton, Michelle Steffes, and Joshua Church. Biola University grad Scott Derrickson has directed haunting films like *The*

Exorcism of Emily Rose and *Sinister*. My work with Reel Spirituality at Fuller Theological Seminary focused on creating media-savvy ministers. I started the Center for Entertainment, Media, and Culture at Pepperdine University to launch a new wave of media entrepreneurs. I've proudly watched our students launch viral videos, like "Wes Anderson's Spider-Man" and "The YouTube Movie," a hilarious parody of *The Social Network*.[19] Yes, our students have engaged in the most meta of new media—viral videos on YouTube about viral videos on YouTube.

WeTube

While the original invitation on YouTube was to "Broadcast Yourself," the user experience is much closer to what Henry Jenkins calls "WeTube."[20] He notes that the word *you* can be plural as well as singular. Yes, a do-it-yourself ethos pervades many of the homemade videos, particularly those that involve a direct address to the camera. But the ability to talk back via YouTube, to respond to videos with our own, makes it a genuinely participatory culture. Clay Shirky sees the rise of YouTube as an encouraging throwback to the days before radio and television, when we entertained each other with stories and songs that we shared without an ear toward profit. YouTube is a threat to broadcast networks because "the simple act of creating something with others in mind and then sharing it with them represents, at the very least, an echo of that older model of culture, now in technological raiment."[21] YouTube pushes past passive reception into participation, the recovery of agency, the possibility of an active response.

So many corners of God's world are captured on YouTube that it cannot be contained. It is an endless chronicle of creativity and fecundity and stupidity—a perfect mirror of humanity circa Adam and Eve (and their offspring Cain and Abel). When we capture something rapturously beautiful and post it on YouTube, we are engaging in a form of praise. We are placing God's beauty before others—and inviting a response. It is a type of doxology, an opportunity to join the chorus. The flash mob that surprised unsuspecting Christmas shoppers with Handel's majestic "Hallelujah Chorus" spread joy to over 40 million YouTube viewers.[22] Two of my students got up every morning to film the sun rising over Malibu. They collapsed a month of sacrifice into a beautiful, two-minute time lapse, "The Sunrise Project."[23] Transcendent television moments like Susan Boyle's rendition of "I Dreamed a Dream" can be forwarded and shared across borders. Roger Ebert described Kseniya Simonova's "Sand Animation" (which won Ukraine's Got Talent competition in 2009) as "the most beautiful thing I've ever seen."[24] The Piano Guys' inventive take on One Direction's "What Makes You Beautiful" is a three-minute marvel. These are not mere financial plays but genuine gifts shared with the world.

Unfortunately, YouTube can also descend into a desperate cry for attention. To put ourselves out there on YouTube or Vimeo is an act of courage and foolishness. If we haven't found our worth beforehand, in the love of family, friends, and a faith community, we may be devastated by the affirmation that fails to arrive. We must not measure ourselves in relation to our YouTube views. Your talent or worth is much more than a number. We are acting in a much larger drama, authored by God, starring Jesus, and directed by the Holy Spirit.[25] We can take comfort that we are acting alongside Jesus, performing for an audience of One. If we do not understand the importance of that lifelong role, our videos may grow more frequent or cloying in an effort to attract an audience. Jealousy and backbiting in the comments and responses on YouTube can descend into the murderous ways of Cain's attack on Abel. What Abel offered up as an appreciative gift evoked envy and rage in his brother, Cain. Far too much of the attitude on YouTube is cutting and cruel.

Justin Bieber was discovered on YouTube. Music executive Scooter Braun stumbled across the videos of a talented twelve-year-old in Canada by accident. Bieber became YouTube's first superstar, entertainer as iGod. It also launched the notion that internet fame could potentially be bought. Companies have stepped in to serve teenagers eager to attract an audience.

Ark Music Factory offered to write songs and shoot videos for hopeful teen idols for $2,000 to $4,000. Producer Patrice Wilson said, "It was based on the idea of Noah's ark . . . in other words, a place to gather people together, where they could be safe."[26] Rebecca Black's parents hired Ark as a birthday present. The awkward video for "Friday" became a global pile on, stacking one snarky comment on another.[27] It was reviled as "the worst video ever." Frankly, the songwriting and production value were laughingly bad, instant YouTube kitsch. Although Rebecca didn't write the song or produce the video, the thirteen-year-old was singled out for abusive comments like "I hope you cut yourself, and I hope you get an eating disorder so you'll look pretty. And I hope you go cut and die."[28] Anonymity in the comments allows a certain amount of jealousy to run wild. The cruelty can be devastating.

Why are we so harsh toward each other on YouTube? The short videos arrive in isolation, devoid of context, without any prior knowledge of the people who made them or the intent of the performers. They are largely viewed as isolated moments in time. YouTube is increasingly coalescing around channels and subscribers, the opportunity to follow performers over time. There will undoubtedly still be countless home movies and awkward moments to ridicule. What may have been personal and profound is available for all to see. The privacy settings on YouTube are rarely invoked. Videos intended for family may be subject to abuse. It is a communal broadcasting service, like cable access gone wild. While it can be great to have an audience, the anonymity of the creators and the viewers affords a little too much distance. In participatory culture, we can all become broadcasters, but we can also all become critics. We can objectify the actors or performers because they are far removed from our everyday experience. Things we would never say face-to-face can be unleashed in a litany of online abuse.

The decontextualized nature of delivery, often arriving via a link or random search, keeps us from reflecting on why the video was created and who it was intended for. The fusillade of unfiltered comments on YouTube demonstrates how desperately we need new media literacy. A phenomenon like "Gangnam Style" breaks down borders and brings us closer together. The possibilities when everybody becomes a broadcaster are remarkable (as evidenced in the viral embrace of "Kony 2012"), but the opportunity requires responsibility (eschewed by the makers of "The Innocence of Muslims"). Not everyone will exercise the option to be a producer, but as viewers, we can approach the plethora of possibilities with humility and wonder. We may be surprised, delighted, or infuriated by what we encounter. But in the marketplace of ideas, we must pause long enough to consider the heartfelt cry residing in the song, poem, or rant being shared. Shirky reminds us that "the essence of amateurism is intrinsic motivation: to be an amateur is to do something for the love of it."[29] YouTube is a form of freewill offering, a sacramental act. And while rarely directed toward God, it should be received with appreciation as from Abel, rather than rejected with the murderous rancor of Cain.

Twitter

Your grandmother may have kept a daily diary. Nothing elaborate, just an ongoing record of what she was thinking, feeling, doing. Holidays, birthdays, special events would have been cited. Entries might have been as mundane as changes in the weather or as personal as heartaches and pains. Health updates, frustrations in a marriage, or the challenges of raising a child were all fair game. She may have developed her own style or abbreviations, a personal shorthand. Grandma might have listed her prayer requests and noted when or if they were answered. It was often a daily ritual, a way of collecting her thoughts, reflecting on her experiences. She may have kept the diary in a dresser drawer, somewhere it wasn't likely to be discovered. Many diaries featured a lock and key, a way to keep others from discovering private thoughts. Hopes, joys, jealousies, and insecurities were guarded. Privacy was valued back then.

The most famous extant diary was started by Samuel Pepys on January 1, 1660, in England. He started writing at age twenty-seven, long before he became a Member of Parliament. He recorded his daily activities—where he went, whom he visited, what he thought about the people he encountered. *The Diary of Samuel Pepys* offers scholars a rare window into the practices and concerns of England in the 1660s. Amid a decade of notes regarding food, wine, and errands, Pepys also recorded details about the Second Anglo-Dutch War, the Great Plague of London, and the Great Fire of London. The extraordinary emerged amid the mundane.

Twitter feels like that. Most days are ordinary, filled with notes about things we saw, people we met, thoughts that occurred in passing. Except the private is now public. Extraordinary individuals are revealing their personal thoughts to legions of adoring followers. And ordinary people are talking to their friends and followers in 140-character bursts. The diaries are unlocked in real time before enough space elapses to judge their relative merits or importance. Things that seem crucial at the time may fade. Mistakes made on Twitter can undo a public career in 140 characters or less (#CongressmanAnthonyWeiner). Our hunger for an audience can prove costly.

Twitter merges the daily diary (now more commonly called blogging) with instant messaging. The 140-character limit makes the thoughts on Twitter more compact, the speed of the posts often faster than they should be. Notes to self can become broadcasts to the world instantaneously. Never have so many shared so much with so many. For sociologists and trend seekers, it has become a cultural snapshot, an instantaneous poll of what's hot and what's not. Twitter is our town hall, with all the perks and perils of democracy included.

The idea for Twitter percolated inside Jack Dorsey back in 2000. He was launching a company in Oakland to dispatch taxis, couriers, and emergency vehicles via the web. He signed up for a new blogging service called LiveJournal. He recalls,

> One night in July of that year I had an idea to make a more "live" LiveJournal. Real-time, up-to-date, from the road. Akin to updating your AIM status from wherever you are, and sharing it. For the next 5 years, I thought about this concept and tried to silently introduce it into my various projects. It slipped into my dispatch work. It slipped into my networks of medical devices. It slipped into an idea for a frictionless service market. It was everywhere I looked: a wonderful abstraction which was easy to implement and understand. . . . The 6th year; the idea has finally solidified (thanks to the massively creative environment my employer Odeo provides) and taken a novel form. We're calling it twttr.[30]

As with YouTube, Twitter arrived when technology aligned with a bright idea. Our longing for personal expression met the ability to aggregate a private audience.

So what was the creative environment at Odeo? It depends on who you ask. Odeo was planned as an audio blogging service combining Noah Glass's programming with Evan Williams's and Biz Stone's business acumen. Williams was already renowned as the cofounder of Blogger, which he had sold to Google. Odeo was aiming to do for podcasting what Blogger had done for online diaries until Apple scooped up the podcasting market on iTunes. With Odeo's plan derailed, Glass seized on Dorsey's idea to combine instant messaging and status updates. While Glass invested his creativity into the project, ultimately he got squeezed out by Williams, Stone, and Dorsey in machinations that may make *The Social Network* look like *Sesame Street*.[31]

Dorsey says the Odeo team settled on the name "Twttr" because it was both a short burst of inconsequential information and the chirps from birds. What seemingly modest ambitions. Many who sign on to Twitter complain about the inconsequential aspects of it. They wonder why they would want to know what people are eating for breakfast or watching on television. The abbreviated nature of tweets is necessarily limiting. The 140-character limit came from taking the 160-character range of SMSs (Simultaneous Messaging Systems) on cell phones and leaving 20 characters to designate a name (like my Twitter handle, "@craigdetweiler").

Some have worried that short messages are inherently shallow. But in an era of too much information, the need to reduce things to the essentials may actually enhance communication, like an electronic haiku. To the uninitiated, the emoticons and abbreviations that drive Twitter and instant messaging may be frustrating. It doesn't take long to figure out that "RT" means "Retweet." But those emotional icons (emoticons) are a way to suggest plenty in a compact way. They need not mask emotion but rather pile lots of complexity into a short, smart message. Japanese, Chinese, and Korean languages have their own particular emoticons. The sophistication required to decode these symbols could be commended rather than critiqued. At its best, Twitter cuts through the clutter, forcing us to pare our thoughts down to their core notions.

Perhaps we can think of the biblical Proverbs as the original Twitterverse. It is a collection of pithy, random observations from a variety of sources, both inside and outside the Hebrew people, culled together into a coherent whole. When we read Proverbs, we are perusing the best of the best, the most inspired and enduring wisdom from the Ancient Near East. I would never equate the updates of Kanye West with the inspired Proverbs of the Hebrew Bible, but the Proverbs arose amid sayings that passed via word of mouth, retweeted so often that they were recognized as enduring, inspired, divine wisdom worth preserving across eons. How many tweets would we have to sort through to find a similar level of insight? The challenge in ancient Israel remains the same today—learning to find sustaining gold amid much dismissible dross.

The origin of the word *tweet* is captured in their blue mascot, a smiling bird. Dorsey told the *Los Angeles Times*, "Bird chirps sound meaningless to us, but meaning is applied by other birds. The same is true of Twitter: a lot of messages can be seen as completely useless and meaningless, but it's entirely dependent on the recipient."[32] Users choose whom to follow, whom to listen to. It is a user-generated news filter and as such, far more personalized than the algorithmic authority exerted by Google or the ads targeted by Facebook (at least until we're limited by tweets or trends "tailored for you"). The early decision of "whom to follow" is a big question for a first-time user. Our sources will expand or contract our view of the world.

Birds' songs are fanciful throwaways, inconsequential information to humans, except in a culture whose ears are tuned to the nuances. In Indonesia, the bird markets are remarkably popular. In Asia, birds are treasured pets, sources of endless amusements and delight. In the jungles of Belize, locals can distinguish birds by their chirps. Humans can learn to appreciate the aviary world's sophisticated communication. It is a language that we can train our ears to discern. Interestingly, Jesus spoke so often about the need to develop ears to hear.[33] His parables were impenetrable to a large portion of his audience.

They couldn't dial into what Jesus was saying. Evidently, listening has always been a virtue in short supply, even before social networking. Yes, Twitter could become a distraction, but it is also an opportunity to hear clearly, to test the tweets, to figure out whom we should be listening to.

It is easy to imagine why many Christian leaders have been early adopters of Twitter. The notion of building a following comes naturally to preachers. We are comfortable speaking to large audiences on a regular basis. I am still wrestling with the power disparities on Twitter between the follower and the followed. It is a remarkable broadcasting service for celebrities or authors to reach their fan base. For some unknown reason, Twitter is constantly recommending I follow Mariah Carey. I am not sure that the popular or the famous deserve my attention. I am also disturbed that I can acquire more followers on Twitter in a week than Jesus had in three years of ministry. Our notions of influence are often equated with numbers. Yet, Jesus proved that enduring influence is much more than an initial popularity contest.

Jesus's ministry began with a call to Peter and Andrew to follow him.[34] He promised that if they followed, they would become fishers of men, ostensibly catching many. The multiplication of the Christian movement is vibrant, living proof how networks of influence can build. We've seen how quickly the crowd can turn against someone who challenges the prevailing wisdom. Jesus demonstrated that ten or eleven committed disciples can unseat an empire like Rome. He went from a handful of followers in the first century to two billion today. Deep, real-world ties can exceed a broad but shallow commitment from Twitter followers.

Despite their popularity today, Ashton Kutcher and Lady Gaga aren't likely to produce the same kind of results from their followers. Evidently, our sources of information, the authorities we turn to, matter. Psalm 37:30 declares, "The godly offer good counsel; they teach right from wrong" (NLT). Psalm 40:4 says, "Blessed is the one who trusts in the LORD, who does not look to the proud, to those who turn aside to false gods." By aligning ourselves with wise sources to follow, we may end up with a more mature take on the world around us; otherwise we could wind up following the trials of the Kardashians. Discipleship remains a test for those who have ears to hear.

Twitter took off when it was adopted by attendees at the 2007 South by Southwest interactive conference in Austin. It was an easy way to navigate the conference, to share relevant information, to figure out who was playing where. Six months later, actor Chris Messina proposed the use of hashtags to form groups on Twitter.[35] It made aggregation of information much more possible. Two months later, San Diego resident Nate Ritter added #sandiegofire to his updates on brush fires racing across California.[36] Friends and family cut off by the fires could get real-time updates from Ritter's tweets. Twitter was becoming a potential source for following breaking news, a place to figure out what's trending.

Twitter use peaks around shared events when we want to follow a thread as it unfolds. Tweeting the World Cup or the Grammy Awards is an opportunity to express our opinions in real time. There is a certain joy that comes from joining a crowd, adding our voice to something much larger than ourselves. Twitter measures what we're watching in an active way, which people or events are seemingly worth talking about. Hashtags are used to signal our interests and aggregate our activity. The "#" sign on the hashtag is also a cultural marker that immediately defines us as someone in the know, part of the club. The commentary on these large public occasions (usually centered around traditional media events like the Super Bowl, the Olympics, a presidential election) is rarely elevated. It often descends into a snark-fest, a one-liner contest that rivals the most contentious sitcom writers' room. The temptation to play "Can you top this?" is so great that the humor can devolve into putdowns and sexual innuendo. When everybody is a comedian on Twitter, who is left to laugh? Occasionally, genuine wit cuts through the clutter. Imagine what Oscar Wilde would have done with 140 well-chosen characters. I'm honored to know the Pepperdine grads who created the clever "Historical Tweets."[37] Their most popular tweet comes from Honest Abe (Lincoln) in 1863, who asks, "Anyone got a more creative way of saying '87 years'?"

In times of crisis, Twitter can also become a place for collective grieving. The shocking news of an earthquake in Haiti, a tsunami in Japan, or a school shooting in Newtown can pull out the best in us. We send prayers and support and donations via our cell phones. While retweeting a condolence or a place to give hardly constitutes a sacrifice, it is a simple way to take a step toward others rather than away from community. Twitter will never replace face-to-face communication, but as a disembodied collective, it can move us from ignorance or indifference toward engagement.

It is easy to tweet our favorite Bible verse or report an answered prayer with the hashtag, "#blessed." How do we go deeper? Perhaps church leaders can challenge their Twitter followers to make a pledge. Read one biblical proverb for every tweet we send or receive. There must be a way to even program such a process into your phone. What a simple rule: one proverb for every tweet. Weigh that rumor or innuendo that just popped into your mobile against a time-tested tradition. Perhaps the inanity will abate. Add a biblical filter to Twitter and we may end up a little less foolish. Feed your soul before, during, and after you turn to the Twitterverse. I've been captivated by the clever "Twibles" crafted by @JanaRiess.[38] She has been summarizing each chapter of the Bible in 140-word bursts for over three years. Riess has merged a spiritual discipline with a new medium. Our ancient faith remains remarkably adaptive, portable, and incisive—an ongoing viral movement.

Instagram

Instagram merged the photo-friendly format of Flickr with the social networking of Twitter. Photos can be distributed to followers and labeled with hashtags to categorize and aggregate them. Instagram added the ability to stylize our photos with filters. How interesting that during an era of too many images, Instagram broke out by forcing users to look back. The square format and retro filters (like "Lo-fi" and "1977") place our current experiences into an idealized past. Instagram made it cool to look old, giving our present surroundings a classic feel. The filters evoke postcards that once told loved ones, "We remember you, even while we're having a fabulous time (without you)." Instagram has made it easier than ever to create classic moments and forward them to our friends. The company discovered how much we value our images when it tried to claim the right to sell our images. Personalized art rooted in precious memories proved a strange bedfellow for sponsored advertising. Our Instagrams felt sacred, not for sale, until Facebook bought the company for $1 billion.

The avalanche of images on Instagram (and Facebook's efforts to monetize them) prompts us to think more carefully about photography's power and purpose. Why do we take so many pictures? What purpose do they serve? One hundred years ago they were an expensive way to document special occasions. Photographers were hired for wedding days or to take pictures of our baby. Travel became an occasion or excuse for taking photographs, but in the digital era, they are just another form of mass communication. Whether on Instagram, Twitter, or Facebook, photographs are a fast way to convey where we are, what we're doing, who we're with. We are immediately (and sometimes permanently) associated with the people beside us in the frame. We are tagged with our "friends" regardless of what we might someday feel; that is, we may not always want to be measured by those people or surroundings. Our behavior might prove embarrassing to us in the future. Photographs fix us in time, becoming a permanent, frozen record of what we were like. Photos are among the most contentious areas on Facebook. The social standards and offenses we take vary from country to country.[39] What is objectionable in India may be normal in Japan, but we all have opinions about whether we want others to take and distribute our images.

Susan Sontag was among the first cultural critics to think seriously about the meaning of photography. She noted how tourists use the camera to distance themselves from the experience at hand. For people on vacation, taking photographs becomes an excuse or comfort for not working; instead of wasting time, we can prove via photographs how effectively we used our time.[40] She noted the possessive quality inherit in picture taking. Sontag saw the camera as a weapon, comparable to a gun that clicks. A photograph "turns people into objects that can be symbolically processed."[41] She even suggested that photographing someone is a soft, sublimated murder, a *memento mori* that freezes their mortality, vulnerability, and mutability. A photograph makes time stand still.

Perhaps we take more pictures than ever because we feel that life is passing us by. We post pictures of events as they happen because we have no time to pause or reflect. Instagram is a way to externalize what used to be an interior activity. With no time to think about what we're doing or what it means, we photograph it instead. Instagram acts like a giant note to self: "Think about why I'm here."

What about all the "selfies," the self-portraits we take on our mobile phones? French professor Roland Barthes associates photography with death. In *Camera Lucida*, he suggested when we pose for the camera, we lock ourselves in place, playing along with the whole photographic ritual. Barthes describes our mental process: "I lend myself to the social game, I pose, I know I am posing, I want you to know I am posing, but (to square the circle) this additional message must in no way alter the precious essence of my individuality: what I am, apart from any effigy."[42] But our hopes are almost always dashed because the photograph is so limited. Our efforts to construct an idealized self rarely satisfy. Barthes admits, "What I want, in short, is that my (mobile) image, buffeted among a thousand shifting photographs, altering with situation and age, should always coincide with my (profound) 'self'; but it is the contrary that must be said: 'myself' never coincides with my image."[43] Perhaps we post so many photographs on our profiles because we know how limited they are. We never settle on a single image to represent us because we always harbor grander visions of ourselves. Or perhaps it is a way of cheating death, trying to fix our digital eternity.

We don't want to be limited by a photograph or a quotation or a single profile page. Barthes notes, "Photography transformed subject into object, and even, one might say, into a museum object."[44] The process itself can be dehumanizing, turning us from a vital force into a still life. Barthes admits, "Each time I am (or let myself be) photographed, I invariably suffer from a sensation of inauthenticity, sometimes of imposture (comparable to certain nightmares)."[45] Think about the poses we adopt because we know the image might show up on Facebook or Twitter. We project a version of ourselves that we'd like to see forwarded to envious friends. Isn't such self-editing a trap? Barthes bristles under the feeling that in the photograph, "I am neither subject nor object but a subject who feels he is becoming an object: I then experience a micro-version of death (of parenthesis): I am truly becoming a specter."[46] Photography, even when shared via Instagram, becomes a bit of an embalming. Instagram encourages us to age the photograph immediately—to place it in both the immediate and eternal past.

How odd that something seemingly instant could be connected to the eternal. The nostalgic appeal of Instagram suggests how desperately we want our experiences to matter. We are memorializing them even while we're experiencing them. It is tough to be in the moment and document it at the same time. Jesus suggested that when we are concerned about saving (or preserving) our life, it is easy to lose it. Only when we're willing to lose our life can we save it. Perhaps only when we put down the cell phone and eschew the possibility of documenting an afternoon, can we completely enjoy it. We are freed from feelings of melancholy, the need to capture a lovely but fading moment. Like the manna that God supplied to the Hebrews during their exodus from Egypt, beauty cannot be hoarded or preserved. It can only truly be enjoyed in the moment itself as a fleeting gift of sustenance.

Photography is a longing for eternity, a desire for a lasting impact. When we blast our memories far and wide, we are hoping they will linger when we're not present and maybe even when we're gone. How odd that something seemingly instant can be rooted in a hunger for eternity. The compulsion to document our lives, even while living it, can put an odd filter on the present.

As someone who has taken thousands of digital photographs (my hard drives are full of pixels that I cherish), I know that I cannot make my life last any longer or my family grow any more ebullient by stopping to take a photograph or to create a fifteen second video. Instagram leads to instant nostalgia, but the Spirit can only meet me today, in this present moment.

What's Trending: Democracy or Faith in Technology?

The cameras on our cell phones are a challenge to our spirit, forever taking us out of the moment we're in. They are also an opportunity to document events of tremendous significance. YouTube, Twitter, and Instagram can turn the camera in our pocket into a news-gathering device. Clay Shirky notes, "The chance that someone with a camera will come across an event of global significance is rapidly becoming the chance that such an event has any witnesses at all. . . . Where we previously relied on professional photojournalists to document such events, we are increasingly becoming one another's infrastructure."[47] So what kind of punch does social media offer?

During a semester of teaching in Shanghai, I experienced the restrictions China placed on new media services, like Google, Facebook, YouTube, and Twitter. The communist government seemed to fear social networking's potential for organizing protests or promoting democracy. When protestors gathered in the center of Minsk to protest the 2006 election results in Belarus, President Aleksandr Lukashenko shut down cell phone service. United States Secretary of State Condoleezza Rice called Belarus "the last true dictatorship in Europe."[48] A similar example of electronic resistance occurred in Moldova during 2009, where tech-savvy young people took to the streets to contest election results that put communists back in power. A twenty-six-year-old native of Belarus, Evgeny Morozov, watched the protests in Moldova with great interest. He was impressed by the power of social media to organize resistance. Morozov declared, "While it's probably too early to tell whether Moldova's Twitter revolution will be successful, it would certainly be wrong to disregard the role that Twitter and other social media have played in mobilizing (and more so, reporting on) the protests" against the last remaining communist government in Europe.[49] Morozov hoped that social networking would prove more powerful than repressive regimes. While Moldova organized for democracy, Belarus continues to be ruled by the same dictator.[50]

Similar resistance accusations of voting fraud followed the 2009 Iranian presidential election. Supporters of Mir-Hossein Mousavi contested the results, claiming that widespread abuse resulted in the reelection of Mahmoud Ahmadinejad. Protestors took to the streets, brandishing green signs, banners, and ribbons signaling their solidarity with Mousavi. Ahmandinejad's government slowed down the internet and censored the media in an effort to squelch the Green Revolution. How did the protestors organize a week of marches despite police crackdowns? Echoing Morozov's youthful hopes for Belarus, uber-blogger Andrew Sullivan was quick to announce, "The Revolution Will Be Twittered." He suggested, "You cannot stop people any longer. You cannot control them any longer. They can bypass your established media; they can broadcast to one another; they can organize as never before."[51] Sullivan praised the power of microblogging to organize protests and undermine an oppressive government.

Forty brutal seconds of video captured in Tehran escalated the Green Revolution in Iran. An unarmed protestor was shot down in the street. The description on YouTube was painfully clear: "Iran, Tehran: wounded girl dying in front of camera, Her name was Neda."[52] As the camera rushes over, Neda's eyes glaze over, blood flows from her mouth and nose. Despite valient efforts to tend to her wound, Neda dies, becoming the first martyr for freedom in Iran captured on video. This is the immediacy of citizen journalism, when a medium like YouTube can make atrocities available for the world to see. Coverage and protests in memory of Neda Soltan followed. YouTube's head of policy and communication, Victoria Grand, says that during the protests "people were holding up their cameras as if it were a sword in a way. They really understood that if you can get the global community to see what's happening that will be your greatest defense."[53] And yet, that same regime still remained in place, and Mousavi and his family endured over two years under house arrest. YouTube and Twitter proved to be an effective way to report on a resistance, but they were not powerful enough to overturn a brutal government. Reflecting its newfound power amid activists and journalists, in 2009, Twitter changed its status question from, "What are you doing?" to "What's happening?"[54] It became *the* place to break news.

Additional examples of social networking's power spread throughout 2011 in what has been celebrated as the Arab Spring. Tunisia had aggressively censored the internet since 2005, blocking not just political sites but also social media sites and videos on Dailymotion.[55] The downfall of dictator Ben Ali in

Tunisia spread hope in Egypt. The traditional media outlets reported on the peaceful movement in Cairo that undermined long-time Egyptian President Hosni Mubarak. The real revolutionary actions were occurring via new media. Tech-savvy activists announced, "We use Facebook to schedule the protests and Twitter to coordinate, and YouTube to tell the world."[56] Wael Ghonim became the public face of the resistance. He had launched the Facebook group called Kullena Khaled Said (We Are All Khaled Said) that honored a twenty-eight-year-old resistor killed by the Egyptian police.[57] Ghonim called for a gathering in Cairo's Tahrir Square on January 25, 2011. He was captured and held shortly thereafter. After Mubarak's resignation, social media was credited as a more powerful force than tanks or guns. Pictures of a proud father who named his newborn son "Facebook" got massive press coverage.

The wave of democracy unleashed by social media spread to Libya. Images of a disgraced and disfigured Muammar al-Gaddafi dominated worldwide news. *Time* magazine named "The Protestor" as their 2011 Person of the Year. In 2012, the *New York Times* noted how Twitter had taken hold in Saudi Arabia. Faisal Abdullah, a thirty-one-year-old lawyer, declared, "Twitter for us is like a parliament, but not the kind of parliament that exists in this region. It's a true parliament, where people from all political sides meet and speak freely."[58] Social media was celebrated as a liberating, democratizing force.

Only after the fact did questions emerge about the impact of social networking. Deen Freelon of the University of Washington assembled a database of six million tweets on the protests in seven Arab countries: Algeria, Bahrain, Egypt, Libya, Morocco, Tunisia, and Yemen. When he sorted the data by location, Freelon discovered that most of the tweeting was happening outside those countries. Twitter was abuzz with new reports, primarily from outsiders discussing breaking news in places far removed from their location.[59] Amid a population of 80 million Egyptians, less than 15,000 were tweeting.[60] Persian blogger Hamid Tehrani estimates that under a thousand people were using Twitter during Iran's Green Revolution. Tehrani observes, "The West was focused not on the Iranian people but on the role of western technology. Twitter was important in publicizing what was happening, but its role was overemphasized."[61] Early advocates of the Twitter revolution, like Morozov, chastened their enthusiasm, suggesting that tech companies were taking credit for revolutions that were years in the making. In *The Net Delusion*, Morozov wrote, "Instead of talking about religious, demographic, and cultural forces that were creating protest sentiment in the country, all we cared about was

Twitter's prominent role in organizing the protests and its resilience in the face of censorship."[62] If social media was an irresistible democratizing force, then why has the revolution in Syria drawn out so long? Why did Twitter use wane when the fight took much longer than expected? Was democracy trending or was crediting Western technology like Google, Facebook, and Twitter as the force for democracy a movement that proved short-lived? Trends come and go, but real, lasting change, like forging democracy in Syria, takes time.

The fact that Belarus has not escaped the grip of a ruthless dictator undoubtedly informs Morozov's skepticism. He has shifted from a cyber-utopian idealist to an astute critic of our blind faith in technology. He questions, "The fervent conviction that given enough gadgets, connectivity, and foreign funding, dictatorships are doomed, which so powerfully manifested itself during the Iranian protests, reveals the pervasive influence of the Google Doctrine."[63] Americans are so convinced of technology's power that we would rather send Google into foreign countries than military advisors or financial aid. Morozov reversed his initial faith in technology, announcing, "I fundamentally disagree with the argument that technology favors only pro-Western and pro-democracy activists; it could easily favor the extremists too."[64] For all the benefits of social media, it also became a way to locate and arrest activists like Ghonim. Tunisian authorities engaged in "phishing" attacks to obtain information from activists' Gmail and Facebook accounts. The government-backed internet service provider obtained passwords that locked activists out of their own accounts and revealed email lists of presumed activists.[65] When protests erupted in Russia following contested elections in 2011, researchers discovered of 46,846 Twitter accounts that discussed the disputed elections, 25,860—more than half!—were bots, posting 440,793 tweets of disinformation.[66] Totalitarian regimes are getting smarter. Flash mobs can gather to launch a protest or squelch a resistance. A hashtag like "#Riot" cuts both ways.[67] Cyber-attacks launched by North Korea and China have demonstrated that the organizing power of technology can have a dark side as well. Americans have come to expect that the National Security Agency may well be monitoring our texts and calls.

Social media is a great tool for connecting people and tracking our passions. It has turned us from passive observers into active participants. It can also give us a false sense of power, turning genuine activism into the convenient click of "slacktivism."[68] Joining a Facebook group dedicated to raising awareness of the situation in Darfur may not result in any genuine change. The average giving generated from such Facebook activism was a paltry nine cents per "like." Malcolm Gladwell compares such "weak-tie" activism to the sacrifices made by those engaged in the lunch counter sit-ins during the civil rights movement.[69] At one time, people were willing to be arrested in order to protest inequalities. Now, we figure "favoriting" a cause on Twitter should suffice. Social media may be good for funding a movie via friends but fall short of generating sustained social change. For all the efforts of Invisible Children (and 100 million views on YouTube), Joseph Kony still remains at large. Morozov has seen young people in his native Belarus slip into "a very nice digital entertainment lifestyle that does not necessarily turn them into the next Che Guevara."[70] Our pleasures, from YouTube to Twitter to Instagram, can lure us into an active response or a comfortable complacency. We may be slipping into a self-assured digital activism that requires little of us beyond a click and a smile. How do we avoid becoming absorbed into a self-satisfied crowd?

The Wisdom of Crowds

Crowds equipped with a smartphone have usurped television networks and movie studios that used to serve as the arbiters of taste. Not only can audiences undercut months of marketing with immediate word of mouth via texts and posts, we can also create our own media stars without studio interference. Shirky marvels, "As mobile phones and the internet both spread and merge, we now have a platform that creates both expressive power and audience size. Every new user is a potential creator and consumer, and an audience whose members can cooperate directly with one another, many to many, is a former audience."[71] The upside of new media is affordable cameras and mass distribution via the internet. The downside is the sheer avalanche of images competing for our attention. Shirky notes,

> Mass amateurization has created a filtering problem vastly larger than we had with traditional media, so much larger, in fact, that many of the old solutions are simply broken. . . . Mass amateurization of publishing makes mass amateurization of filtering a forced move. Filter-then-publish, whatever its advantages, rested on a scarcity of media that is a thing of the past. The expansion of social media means that the only working system is publish-then-filter.[72]

In a democratic society, the idea that everyone has a voice is quite attractive. We are still left with the problem of which voices to follow.

In 2004, James Surowiecki celebrated "the wisdom of crowds."[73] He cites examples where the aggregated response of a crowd gathered at a country fair or in a game show audience will often outsmart a single expert trying to guess the weight of an ox or answer a trivia question. Surowiecki points to scientific studies and naval expeditions that were successfully navigated via aggregated wisdom. The implications for businesses, economies, and governments are substantial. We've seen the Facebook effect alter political history in the Middle East throughout the Arab Spring. But what if we overestimated the effects of the Twitter revolution?

Another way of describing the wisdom of crowds is the Hive Mind. As bees communicate wisdom across their hive, we are just learning how to spread knowledge across the internet. Content-driven websites routinely create lists of "the most viewed" and "the most emailed" articles. We assume that what's popular is also what is valuable. Of course, anyone who has been on the receiving end of chain letters or email blasts knows how much disinformation has been spread via social networking. Sites like Snopes.com have arisen to deal with false rumors and alarmist pronouncements that the crowds fail to sort out. The hosannas that greeted Jesus on Palm Sunday turned to shouts of "Crucify him!" in a single week. We've also seen the wisdom of crowds on display during the French Revolution and the Reign of Terror.[74] At their worst, crowds can descend into mob rule.

We need more accurate filters or more trustworthy crowds to navigate the information era. Sheryl Sandberg, COO of Facebook, told the World Economic Forum in Davos, Switzerland, "Now, due to social technologies and the way people are connected, we are moving away from this wisdom of crowds to the wisdom of friends."[75] The next wave of social networking is the Social Graph.[76] Those people we know best (and who ostensibly know us best) act as our news feed, a reliable source of information, from dinner recommendations to job searches. How often have we seen friends post a pithy review of a new movie? We know how much weight to give their response because we know how often they post and with what intensity. Someone who rarely opines about anything may have inordinate pull when they do speak up. Or the rarity of their endorsement may offer us too few points of comparison; we can't judge their taste because it is distributed haphazardly.

In a Graph Search, all our activities and posts can and will be advertised. As a hub tied into services like Yelp and Pandora, Facebook maps our passions and clicks across platforms and distributes them back to our network of friends. We are performing for our friends (and Facebook) whether we know it or not. Every time we link to an app via Facebook, we are allowing our relationships to be monetized. We give away portions of our privacy in exchange for services. "LinkedIn knows your resume, Google knows your web searches, Twitter knows who you follow, Apple and Amazon have your credit card number, and your phone's OS maker knows what apps you've downloaded."[77] Our real-life friends remain largely Facebook's domain. While encouraging us to be open, they are cutting off competitors like Twitter (and their Vine video service) from access to information about our friendships. Graph Search turns each click made with Facebook's knowledge into an opportunity for them to cash in. The Social Graph is participatory culture on steroids, the audience as advertiser. I don't want to treat my Facebook friends as an audience or turn my Twitter into a megaphone for the mundane. Can we make social networking a source of inspiration and insight?

There is wisdom to be found among friends who know us. They may see our blind spots with more clarity. They may call us back to our better selves. In Matthew 18, Jesus instructs his disciples in how to handle a dispute. "If your brother or sister sins, go and point out their fault, just between the two of you. If they listen to you, you have won them over. But if they will not listen, take one or two others along, so that 'every matter may be established by the testimony of two or three witnesses.' If they still refuse to listen, tell it to the church; and if they refuse to listen even to the church, treat them as you would a pagan or a tax collector."[78] The words and wisdom of close friends can supersede the wisdom of crowds. And sometimes, even public embarrassment isn't enough to humble us.

How much faith should we extend to the crowd gathered on Twitter or YouTube? The crowd can be great for finding the funniest videos, but what if we need something more substantive? When Jesus needed wisdom, he walked away from the crowd. He sought God's will in isolation, by withdrawing to a quiet place. After feeding five thousand people, Jesus broke away from the crowd. He put his disciples in a boat while he went up a mountainside to pray.[79] His ministry of healing continued to generate a following. Luke writes, "The news about him spread all the more, so that crowds of people came to hear him and to be healed of their sicknesses. But Jesus often withdrew to lonely places and prayed."[80] Turning his back on the crowd was a deliberate strategy for figuring out how to deal with the demands of his everyday life and ministry.

Even in the garden of Gethsemane, Jesus retreated to prayer. He dialed into an audience of One before returning to the challenge ahead.

Crowds can tell us what is trendy, what's popular, the most searched. Twitter can tell us what is happening. Rarely does the crowd provide the space to *think* about what it happening. What matters amid the chatter? There is still a gaping need for a well-timed word. Jesus did plenty of teaching in private, personalizing his message for his disciples. The time away from the crowd offered an opportunity to reflect. Luke recounts, "Once when Jesus was praying in private and his disciples were with him, he asked them, 'Who do the crowds say I am?'"[81] This discussion of public sentiment became an occasion to find out what his disciples thought of their relationship to Jesus. Jesus shifted the focus from public opinion to the individuals gathered around him: "But what about you?" he asked. "Who do you say I am?" We need contextualized direction from God. While it can be fun to participate in the latest meme, we must learn how to turn away from our followers toward God instead. Beyond the trending and the popular arises wisdom that endures.

Discuss

1. Who do you follow online and why?
2. Do you think of yourself as a broadcaster? What kinds of videos, photos, and posts are you creating or promoting?

Conclusion
The **Telos** of Technology

The world of technology is the sum total of what people do. Its redemption can only come from changes in what people, individually and collectively, do or refrain from doing.

—Ursula M. Franklin [1]

We live in a transitional era of profound pain and tragic identity quest, but the agony of our age is the labor pain of rebirth. I expect to see the coming decades transform the planet into an art form; the new man, linked in a cosmic harmony that transcends time and space, will sensuously caress and mold and pattern every facet of the terrestrial artifact as if it were a work of art, and man himself will become an organic art form.

—Marshall McLuhan [2]

What have we gleaned from our study of the iGods? Steve Jobs distinguished Apple by unleashing creativity. He harnessed the ingenuity of designers and an advertising firm to sell creativity in creative ways. Amazon employed algorithms to offer us recommendations, offering a more personal "touch" than our neighborhood merchants. Larry Page and Sergey Brin of Google undercut librarians with a revolutionary search engine, and Google tapped into our thirst for knowledge. We gladly exchanged a little privacy to get access to information. Facebook insisted on transparency and refined the recommendation by connecting us to friends who knew us best, whose opinions we could trust (or at least enjoy disputing). With YouTube, Twitter, and Instagram, we have been transformed from a passive audience into active participants (one of the transforming aspects of Christian worship). All these technologies fulfilled their lofty promises, granting us access, improving our aesthetics, operating with authority. Their rapid public embrace and unparalleled success made us hopeful about the future.

Apple, Amazon, Google, and Facebook have made billions by helping us manage the information overload. They solved practical problems that were encroaching on our efforts to keep the chaos of abundance at bay. When Napster unleashed the power of file sharing, we ended up with too much music. Apple solved our problem with the iPod. When our books threatened to overtake our apartments, Amazon responded with the Kindle, a handy way to lighten our load. When the world wide web expanded at a dizzying rate, Google gave us a way to find what we were looking for. And when our friends were spread across too many email addresses, Facebook stepped in as a way to organize too many relationships. When we developed too many friends (since Facebook limited us to *only* five thousand), Twitter emerged as a new form of broadcasting. The iPhone collapsed all of these space-saving tools into one potent handheld device. Once again, we could literally wrap our heads and hands around our harried lives.

But where are the iGods taking us? Over a decade ago, Bill Gates suggested that computers will gradually "disappear" into the fabric of our lives.[3] It is already occurring in our cars, our television sets, our heart monitors. Computers will become so small and so ubiquitous that we will no longer notice them. Many of the questions raised in this book may vanish, at least from our everyday thoughts. The focus on a technology crisis now will shift to other more pressing problems. We will still need to consider the implications of our blind faith in technology because the iGods' promises did not point to or include the divine. Instead, they suggested that *we* are becoming divine as we develop such amazing intelligence within smaller and smaller devices, so small that a point of Singularity will blur humanity with machine, our minds with eternity. Should we find this inspiring or distressing? What is the *telos* of technology—the end goal?

Thirty years ago, Gates was portrayed as a satanic monopolizer in contrast to the uber-cool iGod Steve Jobs. Now, the Bill and Melinda Gates Foundation is a world leader in philanthropy, health care, and education, and we fear the rebel outsiders like Apple who seemingly control too much. The iGods started pure—Google wasn't sure they wanted advertising. Going public with their stock resulted in the need for quarterly returns. It forced Google and

Facebook to bow down to the even greater gods of commerce. The question of access remains. Who will control the flow of information? Will a few get rich at the expense of others? Techno-enthusiasts at the annual TED conference envision a gift economy where the sharing of ideas leads to profound breakthroughs in science and education. Others fear the controlling power of information technology. What happens when the information we share freely is aggregated aggressively, when too much information lands in the hands of the wrong company or country?

This project began with a semester in Shanghai, where I was surrounded by the technology and people that will drive the twenty-first century. And yet, living behind the great firewall of China limited my access to the web services we hold to be self-evident: Google, Facebook, Amazon, YouTube, Twitter. I discovered the dangers of a central authority filtering our information. I saw how fragile democracy can be when somebody else decides what we can see, read, and hear. Chinese restrictions gave me a deep appreciation for the wonderful mess we call the internet, where anyone can express their craziest thoughts and notions.

Yet, I also discovered I could live without our most pressing technologies. For four months, I focused only on the people in front of me. I spent more time with my wife and kids. Nearly all day, every day, we were in face-to-face communication. At times, our nerves were frayed. We retreated to the comforts of laptops or television for private time, to collect our thoughts. Yes, I missed interacting online. While it is nice to have a broader audience to update on Facebook, I found that I could also be satisfied with living anonymously. I didn't need to feed the Twitter stream; it rolled along nicely without me. I missed so many faux controversies that my friends struggled to recall what they were after the fact. "What were we tweeting about?" They couldn't remember beyond the broad strokes. The Oscars, the Final Four, the primary elections occurred while I was gone. These are all notable events, worthy of our attention, but the view from behind the great firewall only hit the highlights. I only needed to know a few moments, select victories, exceptional events.

Before the internet (and even before the printing press), education and religion were predicated on privileged information. Only a few people could read and get access to the archive or sanctuary. Each book was treasured. Even one hundred years ago, families may have owned just a Bible and a few other classics. But even so, children were steeped in the wisdom contained therein. Knowledge may not have been broad, but hopefully wisdom ran deep. What about now, in our highly democratized information era? With an Amazon Kindle, our personal libraries can be nearly boundless. We have adapted, demonstrating a remarkable ability to process massive amounts of input. The internet is comparable to one massive book, still being written. Our personal hard drives and memory may not be full, but the notion of one more input may cause us to crash. A crying need for wisdom and discernment emerges in an era of too much information. What do we discover as we attempt to see through technology, to assess the promises it offers?

Technology has become an alternative religion. It has distinct values, celebrated saints, and rites of passage. We sacrifice our privacy in exchange for services. Our passions become quantifiable, often reducing us to a target market or a call to monitor. This conclusion will focus on the eschatology of technology. What does all the efficiency point to? Where does a world of smaller, faster, and smarter gadgets lead?

The church of the twenty-first century must contend with the significant cultural changes wrought by the iGods. Technology's rise as an alternative faith system (the power of progress, the need for speed, the efficacy of efficiency) may reveal plenty about our own blind spots and shortcomings. What can Christians learn from the iGods? Are we a backward-looking people in a time of remarkable leaps forward? An ancient religion may be attractive in periods of profound upheaval, yet the church still needs to be a force for unleashing fresh creativity. We must recover our appreciation of aesthetics. Our calling in the garden was to be like God, forging something good out of chaos. Apple has reawakened our calling to beauty and design. Amazon has excelled in its customer service. They have also made us into even more self-centered shoppers. We've grown accustomed to having the things we want find us. Are we still eager to seek, or will we be content with being fed by our feeds?

Google reflects our restless search for answers. Will churches make equal room for seekers? Instead of selling answers, perhaps we can learn from Google's faith in their algorithms. They are so confident in the accuracy of their search results that they do not need to embellish their ads. They have done their homework. They have dialed so clearly into our longings that their recommendations speak for themselves. Amazon has made shopping so convenient that we have become a less patient people. In a world of abundance, Facebook has tapped our friends for what to buy, who to listen to, what to see. We make informed decisions based on a like-minded community with shared values. And our friends can express their needs as they arise. Will involvement in a faith community make me smarter, more tuned into beauty? Can we respond to needs as quickly as they arise? And where is our faith headed? What future do God's people anticipate and participate in?

The biblical book of Revelation was addressed to people on the ropes, overwhelmed by a wave of change sweeping through the Middle East. God's people found the temple in Jerusalem destroyed. A sacred space had been desecrated. A former seat of influence had been leveled. As a Christian in exile, John received a message of hope, a vision for the future aimed at people who felt belittled, beleaguered, and banished. Christians were challenged to resist the dominant cultural paradigms of the day. The beast was so big, so overwhelming that resistance seemed futile. Yet, when it became a question of loyalty, John urged the people of God to stand firm, to resist the temptation to concede or to collapse in defeat. As we consider how to be the church in the twenty-first century, let us identify the prevailing assumptions that undergird a technocracy and that compete for our loyalty. What kind of faith are the iGods selling?

The Tenets of Technology—Newer, Faster, Smaller

Consider the core assumptions that accompany our information age. New is always advertised as improved. Every update of a computer, phone, or tablet packs more memory and more processing speed into a smaller device. In our devices, we prefer newer, faster, smaller.

Is new always better? Fruit rots. Bread grows stale. Rust can corrode a car. The creation groans from all the pain and sorrow that surrounds us. We have a strong sense that life is not the way it's supposed to be.[4] We cry out at injustices, rail against inequalities, long for things to get fixed. The long march for racial, gender, and economic equality is an ongoing struggle. Progress is rare. When it comes to electronics, the advances seem to arrive on a regular basis. Every holiday season, we're greeted by upgrades, by a new network from 3G to 4G to 5G. Products make progress seem easy and inevitable. The hard work of design and engineering is hidden. Yet, even the latest, greatest technology breaks down. Unfortunately, we don't know how to fix our gadgets. The mechanics that drive our devices often defy our comprehension. We toss out our old computers and cell phones, and we embrace the new and improved. Replacing isn't the same as redeeming.

The Bible insists that God is committed to making all things new. God doesn't cast us out as useless. Instead, he reclaims us, remakes us, restores us. God's steadfast love is described as new every morning.⁵ Perhaps this is a recalibration that we need to engage in each day. We are challenged to forget the old things and told not to dwell on the past because God says, "See, I am doing a new thing."⁶ God never lets go of us in the process of renewal. He holds on to his people, leads us out of exile, back into a promised land. Jesus puzzles Nicodemus with his admonition that "no one can see the kingdom of God unless they are born again."⁷ Baptism involves water and the Spirit—a cleansing, a fresh start. But we live out that baptism in the same body. We may be rewired, but the same physical elements make up our circuitry. The apostle Paul challenges us to put off our old selves.⁸ If we are in Christ, we are declared a new creation.⁹ We walk through this world with a fresh perspective and see things in new ways. It is with a deeper appreciation for all God has given us. We have a more sacramental approach to our physical surroundings. New gives us a deeper appreciation for the old. Revelation anticipates a new heaven, here on earth. The former things will pass away. Our tears, our mourning, our pain will cease.¹⁰ While the original creation was good, the new will ostensibly be better. In the meantime, we nurture and tend to what we've been given. New is a foretaste of glory divine, but it is rooted in the redemption of what already is.

The iGods have given us access to more—more knowledge, more content, more information. Is more better? We understand that more memory allows us to store more songs or photos on our hard drive. Last time I backed up a new computer, I discovered that my laptop contained more than one million unique files, folders, and items. I am a millionaire. Most of us are. What does more get us? Greater variety. We have music to match every mood. And what about all those photos? Our children will have a filmed record of almost every major milestone from first steps to first game to first concert. But have we increased our memory? No, we have merely outsourced our memory banks, storing them somewhere so we can retrieve them if and when we'd like.

We prefer more choices, but we can't always handle the freedom. As we discovered, the sheer volume of options can be crippling. We need wisdom to cut through the clutter. Driven by a robust Christian faith, Bill McKibben asks us to proclaim, "Enough." Just because we can have more doesn't mean we have to. Technological determinism suggests that we don't have a choice. We have to take the bigger piece, the better deal, the supersize. McKibben challenges us "to do an unlikely thing: we need to survey the world we now inhabit and proclaim it good. Good enough."[11] Getting back to the garden may not involve perfecting all, but accepting and embracing and celebrating what God has already provided, to rest and rejoice and relish all we've been given. A theology of abundance may turn us from a nation of hoarders to a generous people, echoing the words of Jesus, "Freely you have received; freely give."[12]

Is "more" satisfying? I am always up for another piece of cake. But it isn't always healthy or wise. More can also become a problem. Sorting through our stuff can be crazy making.

I remember a particularly frustrating summer day. It was hot in the Carolinas, and a friend invited me to his lake house. A dip in a freshwater lake sounded quite inviting to me. For my friend, going to his lake house also meant going water-skiing, which meant bringing along his boat. We spent the entire morning stocking supplies for the boat, packing the life preservers, getting out the skis, checking on the tow ropes, and getting the boat trailer hitched to the car. The hour-long trip to Lake Norman got sidetracked by the need to get gas for the boat.

And getting lined up to put the boat in.

And getting it in the water.

And getting the car parked.

And getting the boat started.

And getting out to open water.

And getting a preserver fitted.

And getting the tow ropes untangled.

And getting the water skis on.

And getting lined up with the boat.

So I could offer a thumbs up, ready to go.

Four hours into the journey, I was finally water-skiing. The ten-minute ride was exhilarating. But the half day involved in making those ten minutes possible seemed absurd to me. How could so much time have gone into getting machinery working for such a short ride? To my untrained eye, my friend was a slave to his equipment. The boat delivered a certain thrill, but at a high price. In this case, more did not feel better.

Researchers at UCLA studied life at home in the twenty-first century. In observing thirty-two middle-class Los Angeles families, they found that "all of the mothers' stress hormones spiked during the time they spent dealing with their belongings." Despite the high cost of living in Los Angeles, "seventy-five percent of the families involved in the study couldn't park their cars in their garages because they were too jammed with things."[13] Writing of his experiences in urban Atlanta, Jeff Shinabarger encourages us to ask, "What is enough?"[14] He suggests we create an excess bin (beside the recycling bin) for all the stuff we do not use on a regular basis. We must learn to recognize when we have more than enough, when we have excess, when our homes contain so much that we must start sharing.

Is faster better? Another core value of the digital age is our insatiable need for speed. Abraham Lincoln's inaugural address took seven days to reach the West via Pony Express. The telegraph was a miraculous breakthrough. Transatlantic cables continue to form the backbone of the internet and nearly instantaneous communication. The notion that faster is better is rooted in some deeper philosophical assumptions. We have wholeheartedly embraced efficiency. It is viewed as inherently good to do things quickly and efficiently. We are told from an early age that "time is money." So the faster we can deliver—a report, a response, a product—the better. The internet has only amplified the efficacy of efficiency. Book, music, and film purchases are instantaneous. There is almost no lag time between our desires and their fulfillment. We can get what we want when we want it.

How does "faster is better" square with biblical values? Patience is repeatedly celebrated as a virtue. Waiting seems to be an inherent part of Christian discipleship. Speed is never held up as something valuable or desirable. In fact, the notion of eternity challenges (and maybe even undermines) the entire notion of faster. The magisterial pace of an Orthodox Christian worship service could be viewed as slow. Or it could be seen as operating on an alternative clock, not measured by minutes or hours. Step into an Orthodox Church and the thick smoke from candles, the pungent smell of incense, the ringing of bells all point to a higher plane. Time doesn't stop; it ceases to be measured. The concerns of today or tomorrow fade in the glare of a timeless kingdom. How does doing things faster get us any closer to eternity? What does rushing achieve? We may answer, "More free time." But what is that free time used for? Our leisure time has largely become an opportunity for more consumption. We rush home to have more time to watch television or be on our computer. Or watch television while on our computer. So what did an efficient day yield? More time to waste? Is that our purpose or end? As Jacques Ellul said, "Time saved is empty time. . . . The faster we go, the more harassed we are."[15] Jesus aches at the sight of our overscheduled lives. So much to pack in, so little time to reflect.

We need not succumb to Moore's Law (which says that thanks to more transistors packed into integrated circuits, computers will get smaller and smarter and faster). We may feel the relentless pull of an accelerated culture, but that doesn't mean our pulse must necessarily quicken. All of our devices have the same option: an off switch. If we are feeling overloaded and overwhelmed, try turning off the Twitter feed. Take a break from Facebook. I have discovered the power of an electronic Sabbath—experiencing the slowest, most meaningful days ever. With the click of a button—shutting off our devices—we can get on God's time. My students are shocked by how much free time they recover if they get unleashed from the electronic beast. They may spend the day catching up on sleep, getting outside, making up for a semester's worth of reading in a single afternoon. By unplugging, we can rediscover our heartbeat. Remember what it feels like to breathe. See what is in front of us. Connect with the person beside us. Commune with the God in and around and above us. Christians can be a countercultural force by looking up rather than down.

Slower is better for philosopher Albert Borgmann. He has come to appreciate the focal points and practices that can shape our lives. He traces the Latin roots of "focus" to "hearth," the warm center of a home. Borgmann challenges us to recover the practice of family dinners, where we pause to celebrate the bounty of God's creation and share the stories of the day. The simple act of slowing down, gathering together in a daily ritual, creates room for reflection. A meal is not a momentary break between the consumption of information but the chance to hold the tyranny of email and social networking at bay. We turn off the electronic inputs so we can engage our senses in the tastes, the smells, and the light in our eyes. Borgmann insists, "If we are to challenge *the rule of technology*, we can do so only through *the practice of engagement*."[16]

We practice an ancient faith committed to renewal. To the loud, we can counter with quiet. To the fast, we can offer slow. And to the superficial, we can go deeper. So what about small?

Is smaller better? It is certainly easier on the environment (and on our homes and apartments). So much space used to be taken up by records and tapes and compact discs. Each update of an Apple product celebrates how much has been packed into a smaller, sleeker package. At the unveiling of Apple's new G5 Power Mac (back in 2003), lead designer Jonathan Ive opened up the computer, revealing the design inside the machine: "We wanted to get rid of anything other than what was absolutely essential, but you don't see that effort," he said. "We kept going back to the beginning again and again. Do we need that part? Can we get it to perform the function of the other four parts?" His basic philosophy: "It became an exercise to reduce and reduce, but it makes it easier to build and easier for people to work with."[17] Amid our pursuit of speed comes the accompanying search for small.

E. F. Schumacher famously declared, "Small is beautiful." He drew upon Buddhist principles of freeing us from attachments and wants, greed and envy. Schumacher wrote, "Ever bigger machines, entailing ever bigger concentrations of economic power and exerting ever greater violence against the environment, do not represent progress: they are a denial of wisdom. Wisdom demands a new orientation of science and technology towards the organic, the gentle, the non-violent, the elegant and beautiful."[18]

Wendell Berry suggested a simple shift in our thinking: "For most of the history of this country our motto, implied or spoken, has been Think Big. I have come to believe that a better motto, and an essential one now, is Think Little."[19] And what does the Bible say about smaller? Jesus thought that our stewardship of small things was a good test of our larger capacity. "Whoever can be trusted with very little can also be trusted with much, and whoever is dishonest with very little will also be dishonest with much."[20] He lifted up the mustard seed as a model of faith. Little children were cited as an example of how you humbly enter the kingdom.[21] "Let the children come to me" sounds like a small, smart, slow, and measured long-term plan.[22]

Social Networking as the Noosphere

Philosopher Martin Heidegger saw technology as a revealer, an art that uncovers what was residing within something all along. The windmill reveals the true essence behind it—unseen, previously immeasurable wind. The Hoover Dam reveals the massive power residing in a river. Michelangelo saw an angel in the marble and carved until he set the captive free. What does today's technology reveal? The computer revealed that our minds are like a computer—full of files, sorting information, able to retrieve and synthesize data in remarkable ways. In revealing the human mind, doesn't the computer also reveal the mind of God? Just as an earlier era came to see God as master craftsman, do we see God as the ultimate programmer, the great Google in the sky, hyperlinking all of creation (including communities) together?

French theologian Pierre Teilhard de Chardin was definitely a man out of time or ahead of his time. As a priest and paleontologist, Teilhard reconciled faith and science before they had officially split up. His interest in fossils and his work on archeological digs (like the Peking Man in China) made Teilhard an early advocate for evolution. Before the Scopes Monkey Trial drove a wedge between faith and reason, the Jesuits had already silenced Teilhard and forbidden him to publish. Yet, in embracing evolution as a dynamic, ongoing process, Teilhard insisted that evolution was also a divine process, that God was amid the movement. He saw all things being pulled together to a higher state of consciousness, humanity included. Writing in the 1920s, his work would not be cleared for publication until thirty or forty years later.

What did Teilhard suggest that was viewed with such suspicion? He said,

> We must enlarge our approach to encompass the formation taking place before our eyes . . . of a particular biological entity such as has never existed on earth—the growth, outside and above the biosphere, of an added planetary layer, an envelope of thinking substance, to which, for the sake of convenience and symmetry, I have given the name of the Noosphere.[23]

Such lofty terms and ideas must have sounded like science fiction to his contemporaries. "Noos" was taken from the Greek word for mind. Teilhard was suggesting that a collective mind was rising above our biological realities and limitations. When studying nature and humanity, he wrote in *The Phenomenon of Man*, "We are faced with a harmonized collectivity of consciousnesses to a sort of superconciousness. The earth not only becoming covered by myriads of grains of thought, but becoming enclosed in a single thinking envelope . . . a single unanimous reflection."[24] Perhaps people thought he was talking about a world government, about one body that would rule over human affairs. Teilhard's vision came into sharper focus with the rise of smart machines—computers. In 1947, he wrote, "To an increasing extent every machine comes into being as a function of every other machine; and, again to an increasing extent, all the machines on earth, taken together, tend to form a single, vast, organized mechanism. . . . And the basis, the inventive core of this vast apparatus, what is it if not the thinking-centre of the noosphere?"[25] He saw us becoming wired, connected together by a vast network of linked machines. With the noosphere, Teilhard was describing the world wide web almost fifty years before it arrived. Careful observation of biological processes enabled

Teilhard to envision a future where our collective thoughts were united via computers.

Where is the noosphere headed? Teilhard looked forward to what he envisioned as a mystical moment, "the Omega point." He anticipated evolution heading into a roaring fire that will consume the universe itself. Cosmic matter will collapse into absolute spirit. This sounds like bad news; why would we embrace collapse? For Teilhard, transcendence and consciousness arrive in absolute spirit, a love that pervades all of our brains and beings. He was attempting to bridge old divides, to awaken people to the possibility of people retaining their individuality amid a robust unity: God as the Hive Mind in the sky (or perhaps what is now referred to as the cloud). Teilhard was pulling strict materialists (who only believed in science) toward the spiritual, and believers (who tried to ignore biology) toward the physical world. He saw a convergence where machine and humanity all rise above our physical limitations, but we don't lose our individuality in the process.

In her fascinating book *CyberGrace*, Jennifer Cobb explains the implications of Teilhard's Omega Point: "The sharing and merging of our thoughts in this experiential realm does not result in a melting of identity. Quite the opposite. Although identity in cyberspace takes on a new fluidity, its presence remains central to experience of the environment."[26] This sounds like the strength of social networking. Facebook is only as vital as our profiles and posts. Twitter depends on our dissemination of important information. Social networking is not about spreading our personal brand but spreading the brand of love. Facebook and Twitter are more than information—"Did you know?"—and more than treating people as an object—turning our friends into an audience. Social networking at its best is an essence, capable of receiving and transmitting glorious, broken humanity.

These are heady thoughts and fascinating ways to think about social networking. Teilhard suggested that a neural network, covering the earth, could draw us together and toward God. He saw the physical world, the reality of biology and evolution, as building to a transcendent truth, a higher stage of Spirit. Our brains grew so advanced that we figured out how to rise above the limits of our bodies. We can now teleport via the internet, Skype to our heart's content. The noosphere is comparable to the Hive Mind, the way that bees communicate. In our case, Twitter's trending topics provide a window into what the Hive is buzzing about. Somehow I don't think Teilhard had in mind guilty pleasures like the television show *Scandal* or Kids' Choice

Awards on Nickelodeon. Our network of friends and friends-of-friends on Facebook and LinkedIn can be a lofty extension of ourselves. They give us a peek into the potential reach of the noosphere. Social networking extends our social capital and increases our options. It allows us to support a farmer in Pakistan through microfinancing services like Kiva. Every time a microloan is repaid, we get a sense of how interconnected and supportive we can be in the wired era.

While such notions of advanced consciousness are attractive, I find they don't wrestle enough with human evil or bodily limitations. Having served as a stretcher carrier during World War I, Teilhard witnessed plenty of suffering, but he saw our pain as redeemable in Christ. The soldier/priest wrote, "Only the image of the crucified can sum up, express and relieve all the horror, and beauty, all the hope and deep mystery in such an avalanche of conflict and sorrows. As I looked at this scene of bitter toil, I felt completely overcome by the thought that I had the honour of standing at one of the two or three spots on which, at this very moment, the whole life of the universe surges and ebbs places of pain but it is there that a great future (this I believe more and more) is taking shape."[27] Despite witnessing the horrors of war, Teilhard remained remarkably optimistic. He foresaw us learning and progressing, evolving even amid our capacity for evil. I like the notion of noosphere that takes us all to a higher, interconnected plane. The end result feels a bit too disembodied. We have great thoughts and intentions, but we are limited by our physical capacities. While I might be able to talk with others around the globe via Skype, it is still not the same as being there in person. A note of encouragement to a sick friend on Facebook is lovely, but a cup of soup in their hand might be better. We think of Google, Facebook, and Twitter as offering us services, but we are still called to serve others.

Social networks are great for connecting us with friends who are like us, with shared values and socioeconomic backgrounds. The noosphere that Teilhard envisioned is strengthened by diversity. Do we dare to connect with people not like us? Jesus calls us beyond our filter bubbles—to love our enemies and befriend those we don't like. The internet is a patchwork quilt—as colorful as God's creation—but we'll see it only if we're willing to explore. Original knowledge was about the natural world—how things work. Now, we are exploring a virtual world. But the noosphere is still informed by the Creator behind us. YouTube reflects our capacity to be fruitful and multiply, to upload our creativity every single day. It reflects the pettiness and triviality of humanity (especially in the comments), but it also captures the joy and wonder of creation (such as goats that sound like people).

Our devices can connect us to others, but they can blind us to the person sitting next to us. Jesus's timeless question, "Who is my neighbor?" shifted in the internet era. It could be a friend on Facebook whom we've never met in person. It could be the person in our World of Warcraft guild, an avatar we respect and cooperate with on a regular basis. In the digital era of virtual relationships, we might need to ask, "Who is sitting next to me—on the bus, in the classroom, on my living room couch?" We must detach from the noosphere on occasion to become aware of our surroundings. Instead of asking our Google glasses to inform us, perhaps we can rely on old-fashioned wits—and be willing to be surprised by what we see.

Our devices are great for connecting us to the world at large—Google Earth answers questions about stars, planets, rain forests, species. But we must not confuse digital data for the lived experience. As embodied people, it is one thing to see a picture of Chilean Patagonia—quite another to go there. When I traveled to Torres del Paine in Chile, I was humbled by how long it takes to get there. The flight to Santiago is only the beginning of the planes, trains, and automobiles necessary to reach that end of the earth. The size of the king crabs offered in roadside diners en route was staggering. The scope of the tundra before reaching the mountains was mind-numbingly monotonous. Who would have ever dared to traverse this on foot or even horseback? The trip was made so worthwhile by the site of the peaks glistening on the lakes. What majesty, to look up and see the Southern Cross for the first time (no wonder Crosby, Stills, and Nash rhapsodized about it!). How amazing to see different birds and flora and fauna. While marveling at the glaciers, I was also struck by how far away I was from my family. If there was an emergency, and if they could reach me via cell phone, it would take at least twenty hours (and up to two days) to get back to California. I was as close to off the grid as humanly possible. While technology like Google Earth makes our world seem small, the physical space from the peaks of Torres del Paine to Southern California felt massive. My body was a tiny speck in a vast, vast globe.

I could have stayed home and studied all of this on the internet. I would know about Patagonia in the sense of the Spanish word, *saber*—to know a fact or possess knowledge. But I wouldn't know Patagonia in a personal, intimate, and embodied way, how it all fit together in a glorious whole. This is knowing as *conocer*, the Spanish word for personal knowledge, a familiarity rooted in experience. The web has introduced us to far-flung corners of the globe and of human experience. It makes the world seem small and knowable. The physical work of getting out there, of meeting people not on the web, of feeling the sun, and of breathing in the crisp mountain air is a far more intense and immediate knowledge. It gets into our bones. It changes us. As a paleontologist, Teilhard must have surely appreciated the difference.

Teilhard is to be commended for celebrating our social selves long ago. He was a priest who didn't fear science and technology but instead saw it as our future connective tissue. Half a century later, he reads as a remarkably prescient theologian and environmentalist. I would love to buy into his utopian views of where we are headed. I do feel far more connected to people around the world, particularly Christians from different continents, than I did before the internet. The noosphere has been a good thing. But I don't see an Omega Point coming without the Alpha and Omega, Jesus the Christ, at the center. Incarnation was so important to God that I cannot imagine that it is unimportant to us. While many technologists prefer the brain to the body, we must not fall into old gnostic heresies, preferring mind over matter. The noosphere has been built. The Omega Point hasn't arrived. When the resurrection comes, it will affirm our bodies, not deny them. That is why the bodily resurrection of Jesus is so important. He did not come back to life as a ghost, but as someone whose wounds we could examine. In the resurrection of the dead, the apostle Paul affirms, "The body that is sown is perishable, it is raised imperishable; it is sown in dishonor, it is raised in glory; it is sown in weakness, it is raised in power; it is sown a natural body, it is raised a spiritual body."[28] This is the kind of mystical language that Teilhard employs so often. It is a spiritual vision, rooted in a physical reality. I believe in the noosphere, but every Sunday we also affirm via the Apostles' Creed that we believe in "the resurrection of the body and the life everlasting."

Singularity as Eternity

What is the goal behind newer, faster, and smaller machines? At one point, we might have answered, "Walking on the moon." We won the second round of the space race, but colonies on the moon have yet to materialize. Another wave of technologists pursued artificial intelligence with gusto. They sought to pass the Turing test—can machines do what we can do? Could a computer answer an interrogator's questions as well as a human? Some might point to 1997, when IBM's computer Deep Blue defeated reigning chess champion Garry Kasparov, as the triumph of artificial intelligence. Jeopardy champion Ken Jennings was humbled by the supercomputer Watson in 2011.[29] He left the competition feeling obsolete, like a Detroit assembly line worker watching a robot replace him. How do machines fare in the interpretation of emotion or an appreciation of art? For forty years, philosopher Hubert Dreyfus has pointed out "what computers can't do." He stressed that much of our decision making is rooted in intuition, an innate background and understanding that resides beyond programming. Robots may be assembling our cars, but they still can't cook a gourmet dinner without following a recipe.

Artificial intelligence researchers celebrate the mind but view the body as a distraction or even a prison to escape; they refer to the body as "meatspace." Historian David Noble researched the religious fervor and longing for eternity that drive AI and denigrate the body. Marvin Minsky, director of MIT's Artificial Intelligence program, called the human brain "a meat machine" and denigrated our bodies as a "bloody mess of organic matter." He attempted to divorce the body from the self, insisting "the important thing in refining one's own thought is to try to depersonalize your interior."[30] Danny Hillis, founder of the Thinking Machines Corporation, suggested, "What's valuable about us, what's good about humans, is the idea thing. It's not the animal thing. . . . If I can go into a new body and last for 10,000 years, I would do it in an instant."[31] In *Beyond Humanity*, Earl Cox suggested, "Technology will soon enable human beings to change into something else altogether" and thereby "escape the human condition."[32] If we are primarily brains trying to escape our bodies, then Cox envisions a day when "humans may be able to transfer their minds into the new cybersystems and join the cybercivilization," ensuring an eternal existence. He celebrates a future when we shall be "freed from our frail biological form, human-cum-artificial intelligences will move out into the universe. . . . Such a combined system of minds, representing the ultimate triumph of science and technology, will transcend the timid concepts of deity and divinity held by today's theologians."[33] What an unabashed bid for eternity via technology. Such disdain for the body hearkens back to the ancient heresy of gnosticism. In the incarnation, Jesus honored the body and embraced the material world. Eternal life came through pain, suffering, and life lived among us.

Perhaps our relentless pursuit of scientific breakthroughs has always been rooted in a longing for transcendence. Philosopher Michael Heim suggests, "Our fascination with computers . . . is more deeply spiritual than utilitarian. When on-line, we break free from bodily existence, from earthy, earthly existence and emulate the *viseo dei* the perspective of God, the 'all-at-oneness' of divine knowledge."[34] In *The Metaphysics of Virtual Reality*, Heim insists, "What better way to emulate God's knowledge than to generate a virtual world constituted by bits of information. Over such a cyber world human beings could enjoy a god-like instant access."[35] Is the goal of technology to make us all iGods? Tom Furness, founder of the Human Interface Technology Laboratory, envisioned a future where "on the other side of our data gloves, we become creatures of colored light in motion, pulsing with golden particles. . . . We will all become angels, and for eternity. . . . Cyberspace will be like Paradise . . . a space for collective restoration of the habit of perfection."[36] The more time I spend online, checking people's comments, the less it feels like perfection. Daniel Crevier saw artificial intelligence as offering a machine-based transcendent soul consistent with the Christian belief in resurrection and eternal life.[37] The uploading of the mind is comparable to the survival of the soul after death into an immutable, unending system. Can we escape this mortal coil by uploading our thoughts? Noble suggests, "These technologies have not met basic human needs because, at bottom, they have never really been about meeting them. They have been aimed rather at the loftier goal of transcending such mortal concerns altogether."[38] Artificial intelligence is both an effort to play God and become (i)gods. But it foolishly drives a wedge between brain and body, the self and the spirit.

The clearest prediction of how and when we will rise above our physical limitations comes from technologist Ray Kurzweil. As an engineer, Kurzweil invented the first print-to-speech reading machine for the blind. Musicians like Stevie Wonder have reveled in his synthesizers. His reputation expanded with his optimistic predictions regarding the future of technology. In *The Age of Spiritual Machines* (1999), he describes advances in computing that have largely been realized in the decade since (although we're still a long way from the day when robots would so long for our spirituality that they would attend worship services!). Although his parents were Holocaust survivors, they exposed Kurzweil to a variety of faiths through a Unitarian Church.[39] His writing has pointed toward a new form of immortality and life everlasting. Kurzweil sounded like a fervent street preacher when he declared in 2005, "The Singularity is near."

What is the Singularity? Kurzweil welcomes a future where the distinctions between human and machine vanish. The physical and the virtual will merge; technology will trump biology. Kurzweil writes,

> The Singularity will allow us to transcend these limitations of our biological bodies and brains. We will gain power over our fates. Our mortality will be in our own hands. We will be able to live as long as we want (a subtly different statement from saying we will live forever). We will fully understand human thinking and will vastly extend and expand its reach. By the end of this century, the non-biological portion of our intelligence will be trillions of trillions of times more powerful than unaided human intelligence.[40]

These are massive statements of faith, a vision of a golden age when "our technology will match and then vastly exceed the refinement and suppleness of what we regard as the best of human traits."[41] We may think of designer babies, ordered by parents who want children with superior genes. Kurzweil's confidence resides in smarter machines that will create smarter people. Advances in technology have expanded our life expectancy. With our artificial hips, pacemakers, internal cardiac defibrillators, and cochlear implants, we are becoming grateful semi-cyborgs. Kurzweil goes further, seeing evolution as a move toward greater complexity, intelligence, beauty, creativity, and love. He stops just shy of infinite knowledge, leaving a little space for God.[42]

Kurzweil's ideas have gained such traction in technological circles that he has been celebrated with documentaries like *Transcendent Man* (2009) and the founding of Singularity University on a former NASA campus in Silicon Valley (also 2009). As Google's new director of engineering, Kurzweil hopes to tap their massive database to build a cybernetic friend "that knows that you have certain questions about certain health issues or business strategies. And, it can then be canvassing all the new information that comes out in the world every minute and then bring things to your attention without you asking about them."[43] As the Singularity draws near, we seemingly don't need to waste our time searching for answers. They come to us before we even ask—intelligent computers as revelation.

Kurzweil responds to critics of his techno-optimism with force and precision. He engages their arguments and draws on a broad array of biology, philosophy, and theology in his retorts. I resonate with his longing for immortality. I share the values of TEDsters who want to erase poverty, eradicate disease, and democratize education. We should all seek peace. Yet, despite Kurzweil's erudite enthusiasm, I cannot place as much faith in technology (or in our handling of technology). The specter of the errant HAL 9000 in *2001: A Space Odyssey* sticks with me. The intelligent and malevolent machines in *Blade Runner* and *The Terminator* did not give me confidence in a bioengineered future. Perhaps I need to embrace the ending of *The Matrix* trilogy where humanity and machine lay down their arms and learn to prosper in peace. It is not the machines I am worried about. It is the people who invariably create new uses for technology and chemicals such as guns and bombs. Our track record at extending life is only surpassed by our ability to take lives. The lessons of the twentieth century still haunt my dreams. I have watched too many hours of *The Lord of the Rings* to think that the future will be secured without a fight. A handshake across the internet may not bring about easy global understanding. Proximity may increase tension and amplify our attacks on each other. We will create new defense systems and inoculations to combat microthreats. I'm sure we will extend our life spans. We can respect and benefit from nanotechnology without placing our eternal hope in it.

I am compelled by the caution of Jaron Lanier, a pioneer in artificial intelligence who challenges Kurzweil's cyber-utopianism. Lanier asserts,

> The intentions of the cybernetic totalist tribe are good. They are simply following a path that was blazed in earlier times by well-meaning Freudians and Marxists. . . . Movements associated with Freud and Marx both claimed foundations in rationality and the scientific understanding of the world. Both perceived themselves to be at war with the weird, manipulative fantasies of religions. And yet both invented their own fantasies that were just as weird.[44]

Although seemingly a card-carrying member of the faith-in-technology club, Lanier points out, "A self-proclaimed materialist movement that attempts to base itself on science starts to look like a religion rather quickly. It soon presents its own eschatology and its own revelations about what is really going on—portentous events that no one but the initiated can appreciate. The Singularity and the noosphere, the idea that a collective consciousness emerges from all the users on the web, echo Marxist social determinism and Freud's calculus of perversions."[45] Lanier sees digital Maoists exhibiting as much blind faith as fundamentalist Christians. Lanier notes, "Singularity books are as common in a computer science department as Rapture images are in an evangelical bookstore."[46] Lanier is scared that the same short-term thinking that causes some Christians to imperil the environment (it is all going to burn anyway!) could cause technologists to make choices that imperil humanity. Those who don't value the body may create programs that fail to consider the consequences of our code.

How do we resist the temptation to put machines before humanity? Lanier suggests we slow down enough to adopt long-term thinking.[47] We could create videos that take one hundred times longer to create than they do to view. We could only post blogs that took weeks of reflection. On Twitter, we would post creative, internal feelings that defy easy categorization. Overturn the metrics. Frustrate the machine. We also must resist the temptation to check our phones for updates first thing in the morning and last thing at night.[48] Perhaps the ancient cycles of prayer can better prepare us to meet the day and ease into sleep. Poet Wendell Berry writes,

> So friends, every day do something
> that won't compute. Love the Lord.
> Love the world. Work for nothing.
> Take all that you have and be poor.
> Love someone who does not deserve it.[49]

Resisting the drumbeat of technology is not easy. Our Google news feed includes updates on the latest and greatest gadgets. Magazines reserve cover stories for Apple's and Amazon's products. These idols are so pervasive that it is tough to see the sway they hold over our hearts and minds. Jesus warned that the casting out of a demon made space for seven times as many to enter.[50] With each new innovation that is faster, another "essential" service seems to follow. We may be tempted to unplug from the noosphere and skip the Singularity altogether. So where can we find peace?

Escaping Technology: To the Wilderness

Two hours west of the Belize City airport, beyond where the rivers converge in San Ignacio, a sign announces the Black Rock Lodge. Turn left. Seven bumpy miles follow alongside farms, through orange groves, around Teak forests. The car shimmies, your body shakes. As you reach a dramatic bend in the pristine Macal River, Black Rock Lodge finally appears. A thatched roof emerges from a thick canopy of jungle trees. The main lodge sits above the river and several thousand feet below the cliffs. A dozen cabins are available for families, couples, or solo travelers seeking to get back to nature. A tarantula or scorpion might crawl into your footpath. Howler monkeys might let out their ferocious, Jurassic Park–sized roar. Keel-billed toucans, straight from the Froot Loops box, fly overhead. It is a close encounter with nature as God created it. And yet, the Black Rock Lodge still has a wi-fi signal in their dining room.

A creative director for the Grey Group in New York, a Travelex executive from London, and a Swedish engineer with Ericsson are responding to email on their iPads. Teenagers are playing with their cell phones. Nobody finds it the least bit surprising or incongruous. We are deep in the jungle, surrounded by miles of rain forest, and yet, I can check in with Facebook or Twitter or Foursquare.

How far do we have to travel to escape technology? Mobile phone coverage feels nearly ubiquitous. Wherever cellular signals travel, the internet is close at hand. It is tough to get perspective on something that surrounds us. Fish may not notice the water. All too often, we don't notice how many electronic messages we're processing via our smartphones. So stepping outside our zone of coverage might offer a unique opportunity to question our dependence on technology. Going offline may test our commitments (and our patience), but it may also help us recall what matters most. As we hurtle toward an unknown future with technology, we must plan some conscious pauses and be willing to use a mute button in our lives. Surely, if Jesus felt the need to seek time away from the crowds, we could survive a day or even a week without social media, right?

I asked Cameron Boyd, owner of the Lodge, how he gets internet service so far down a box canyon. He responded without hesitation: "From the Mennonites. They bounce it down from their mountain." I'm not sure what kind of answer I expected, but it probably didn't include Mennonites with internet service. But Cameron explained further: "We get everything from them—our cheese, our ice cream, our chocolate. Look them up online." Spanish Lookout is a Mennonite community founded by Canadians who came to Belize in the fifties.[51] They still speak Plattdeutsch, a dialect from the old country, and the men wear overalls. In addition to providing dairy and vegetables for a large portion of the country, these Mennonite farmers are also big on technology. They sell auto parts and internet service. Clearly, the Evangelical Mennonite Mission Conference has made peace with technology. Can we?

I started this book while I was teaching in China, where I gave up the internet. Or at least, the ability to get what I want and send what I wish. It made me appreciate our freedom of speech but also made me realize that I didn't need to know what everyone was thinking and doing moment by moment or day by day to experience the wonder of life. I discovered I didn't miss Facebook as much as I expected. News reached me with or without a Twitter feed. I discovered countless other sources of entertainment and enlightenment. There are so many different places to visit and foods to taste. And so many people I couldn't meet on the internet because Facebook hadn't come to their village (yet).

I finished this book in Belize, writing in a rain forest. Yes, there was a cell phone signal and slow wi-fi service that made rich text formats problematic. The jungle also included glorious vistas that sharpened my senses and broadened my understanding of the world. I saw new species of birds (that I could follow up with research on Google). I captured photos and videos that I could share with friends via Facebook (after I got home). I climbed in caves and tubed down the river (and have no photos on Instagram to prove it)—only rich, shared memories. No need to worry about privacy settings in those cases. Those family memories are known only to us and to God.

In arguments about preserving wilderness and protecting natural areas, we almost always resort to the tensions inherent in the biblical book of Genesis. Should we mine nature for its resources (oil, gas, minerals) or protect and keep it pristine? In both cases, we are in the position of power, deciding the fate of untapped acreage. This is our God-given position in the world. We end up arguing about whether spotted owls or horned frogs are worth saving. As philosopher Albert Borgmann (who lives in Montana) suggests, perhaps we overlook the restorative effects that the wilderness provides us.

The rise of technology has reminded us what it means to be embodied, to walk this earth, to breathe this air, to swim in these oceans and streams. The wilderness used to be something we feared. It was wild and tested our mettle and resilience. We traveled the high seas and scaled the heights. Our engineers learned how to harness and corral the wilderness to generate power. In the developing world, they're still busy altering their environment to fuel their burgeoning industries. The Three Gorges Project in China is a massive undertaking to keep up with their enormous energy needs. Belize has been more vigilant about preserving their wilderness while still obtaining valuable power. Black Rock Lodge is downstream from a hydroelectric dam. It was encouraging to see Belize adopting Wendell Berry's ecological dictum, "Do unto those downstream as you would have those upstream do unto you."[52] In the developed world, we have more of the luxury of preserving nature. We are shifting from dominion (ruling) to cultivation (keeping). We are coming to see how fragile and vulnerable the wilderness can be. We now care for it in the same way we protect and care for our aging parents. Borgmann notes that while technology often adopts a shallow or disposable view of things, "The wilderness is eminently deep."[53] It is worth nurturing, cultivating, and caring for. However, the Bible does not end in a garden.

Embracing Technology: To the City

I was in Belize around the same time as the conclusion of the Mayan calendar. This is their famous calendar that has tracked time over the past five thousand years. The Mayan understanding of mathematics and astronomy was so advanced that scholars have been able to count backward (and forward) on their calendar to December 21, 2012. Enterprising Americans cashed in on the opportunity to promote a new date for doomsday. Many postapocalyptic references crept into pop culture as the deadline approached. The popular fervor could have been tied to Mayan myths, but I think it is more about our dependence on technology.

Consider key television series of the past decade. We wanted to know: Could we rebuild society on a deserted island? *Lost*. Will we pull together as a community or engage in voting each other off the island? *Survivor*. What happens if electricity fades? *Revolution*. Will we all be consumed by the rise of zombies? *The Walking Dead*. Clearly, we have lots of angst about where all this technology is headed. What is the *telos* of our electronic progress? These pop culture touchstones suggest that we may feel the need to turn back the clock, to stop our forward march. These shows are about starting over, getting back to the land, learning how to survive. They take us to the jungle, to deserted islands, far away from the maddening crowds. The resulting series were not about technology saving us but about learning to trust our instincts, to rebuild community from the ground up. They are about life after technology. It is slower, more primitive, scary but satisfying.

Christians call the study of final things "eschatology." Enterprising televangelists have made a lot of money preaching fear from passages in the biblical book of Revelation. This book was written as an encouraging word to a persecuted people. The Roman Empire exerted immense pressure on the nascent Christian movement. Their destruction of Jerusalem in 70 AD resulted in so many questions of God. The Revelation of John is a veiled word of comfort to a fearful and persecuted people. It takes the long view of history. Yes, times are tough. Faith is mocked. Persecution is rampant. Hold on, because what we're experiencing now isn't the end of the story. The apocalyptic language of John may have made the allusions cryptic to the Romans but easy to sort out for his audience, the early Christians. Time has shrouded our understanding of dragons, lakes of fire, and the antichrist.

Our popular notions of the rapture and end times are a comparatively recent invention of John Nelson Darby. As a leader in the Plymouth Brethren movement in Ireland, Nelson focused on the interpretation of biblical prophecy. His translation of the New Testament in 1867 served as the basis for dispensationalism, which divided history into distinct eras, culminating in a second coming for the church (commonly known as the rapture) followed by a period of tribulation—a thousand-year (millennial) reign of Christ—before the antichrist is released, a final battle is waged, and judgment is delivered (Armageddon). Darby's understanding of the book of Revelation was popularized in America via Charles Scofield's Bible. These vivid and cataclysmic interpretations of Revelation have resulted in bestselling books like the Left Behind series and countless end-times movies. Dispensationalism has also influenced American foreign policy toward Israel and throughout the Middle East.

Unfortunately, Darbyites also encouraged a relative indifference toward our calling in Genesis to care for the earth. Dispensationalists often focus on judgment to come, fueling visions of a lake of fire, rather than the wedding banquet that actually ends the book of Revelation. Bestsellers like the *Late Great Planet Earth* heightened fears of the end of the world instead of pointing toward the city of God, full of streets paved with gold and trees whose leaves offer healing for the nations. Far too few people realize that the Bible ends with a vision of heaven come down to earth, rather than earth incinerated and people transported to heaven. We anticipate a disembodied experience rather than a robust vision of a blessed city and a hearty banquet. We preach weeping and gnashing of teeth when the Bible promises a party free from tears and fears. Misunderstandings of our future can radically alter our sense of purpose today.

In my research for this book, I discovered that Jesus was a *tektōn*. The word that was once translated as "carpenter" may be rendered more faithfully as "builder." In Hebrews 3, Jesus is described as the builder of the house of Moses, essentially the architect of Judeo-Christian faith. In Hebrews 11, Abraham is described as a tent dweller, but he looked "forward to the city with foundations, whose architect and builder is God."[54] The Father, Son, and Holy Spirit are builders, bringing order to chaos, form to faith. We are called to be an embodied people, living in the real world, caring for creation via technology. So what is God building and what kind of technology should we be investing in?

In Revelation 21, John foresees the Holy City, the new Jerusalem, coming down from heaven, dressed as a bride. This is the opposite of Nimrod's presumption in building a tower to heaven.[55] Nimrod tried to build a platform to elevate himself. Here, God promises that the new Jerusalem, like Jesus, will descend. God will dwell with his people, wiping tears, conquering death, eradicating pain. Technology that heals is a great thing, a God-given gift. The breakthroughs that will arise from Francis Collins and his team mapping the human genome will bless millions of people as long as we don't turn such knowledge into an idol, a chance to elevate our genius rather than elevating the Designer who wrote the code. I am eager to see what kinds of alternative types of energy tomorrow's engineers will envision. Note that in Revelation, God's *presence* is the power source, the only illumination we will need. Our technologies can be costly to create, our building programs and supply lines can tax the resources we've been given. Jürgen Moltmann celebrates the "cosmic Shekinah" that emanates from God.[56] This is the kind of glory that short-circuits our understanding—the majesty of God that shines like nuclear fusion, without the destructive capacity. Peter Rollins describes this fullness:

> In the same way that the sun blinds the one who looks directly at its light so God's incoming blinds our intellect. This type of transcendent/immanence can be described as "hypernymity." While anonymity offers too little information for our understanding to grasp, hypernymity gives us far too much information. Instead of being limited by the poverty of absence, we are short-circuited by the excess of presence.[57]

This is the source of an endless supply of energy and inexhaustible resources.

This heavenly vision was foreshadowed by the Sabbath rest in Genesis. There was no pain or death in the garden. Our future involves ceasing from striving, rising above travail. Geographer Yi-Fu Tuan writes, "To build is a religious act, the establishment of a world in the midst of primeval disorder."[58] We've been called to follow God's lead in holding the chaos at bay. We are attempting to build livable cities and sustainable economies as an expression of our faith, a sign of our stewardship. Rather than retreating to a pastoral setting, the Revelation of John includes jewel-encrusted walls, pearly gates, and streets of gold.[59] For those artisans engaged in creative endeavors, they should be encouraged by reports that "the glory and honor of the nations will be brought into it [the city]."[60] Ostensibly our finest achievements in art, music, drama, and literature may make the cut. This encourages us to create something beautiful.

While we must not overestimate our contributions to eternity, we can take some pride in what we have introduced. Kevin Kelly takes the long view of technology and progress and proclaims it blessed by God. Sure, the temptation to build a platform to heaven like Nimrod can result in a load of presumption and confusion. Kelly told *Christianity Today*, on the whole,

> the fallibility of the human condition means that we tend to destroy as much as we create every year. We cannot even begin to be mostly good. But the good news is that by God's grace we can, and should, improve our lives a little tiny bit over time. That incremental crawl in the direction of good is all we can expect theologically, and it's the reason almost no one gives up the advancements of today. In what way would Christ's redemption be at work if we moved a little bit toward evil every year?[61]

Thankfully, we are learning how to engage in new forms of accounting, measuring the triple bottom line: financial gains and losses, the community's gains and losses, and the environment's gains and losses.[62] We must build with an eye toward tomorrow.

What is our *telos*? We are invited to care for creation and join an overwhelming chorus of angels and archangels and all the company of heaven. Our voice doesn't need to be there, but it can be. We can join the choir, surrounded by a great cloud of witnesses, and contribute to the songs that compose an eternal playlist. Every day is an opportunity to celebrate the gift of life, to revel in the superabundance that surrounds us. We have so much that we absolutely, positively must share it. We can't eat it all. We can't hold it all. We can't store it all. Ellen Painter Dollar reflects on our cluttered lives that technology tries to liberate us from. She acknowledges,

> All of our stuff can distract and overwhelm us, but it can also provide context. Our clutter can remind us that matter matters, that the bodies we inhabit and tend, the food we make and eat, the clothes and toys and mementoes made or given or used with love can bind us to each other, and to those who came before and come after. Our clutter and all that it evokes in us can even, perhaps, help us guard against that old heresy of Gnosticism, which insists on the separation of the spiritual and the material, and the elevation of the former over the latter. Matter matters.[63]

As embodied and limited creatures, we all need food and water, clothing and shelter. After the fall, God clothed Adam and Eve. Technology provided consolation and comfort. We have been planting and harvesting, weaving and building ever since. From our abundance, we have a profound opportunity to share, to give thanks by giving. In God's economy, there is plenty to go around. We need not try to possess or hoard.

We celebrate technology as a gift but resist the temptation to prostrate ourselves before it. We must not let it fashion and mold us into its insistent (now!), efficient (faster!), and greedy (more!) image. We are made for more than information processing. When it comes to technology, our challenge is not to succumb to the temptation to know or possess everything as self-anointed iGods. We must embrace our limits while expanding our hunger for knowledge and understanding; that's practical wisdom. Trying to get our arms around the internet nearly drove us crazy. Thanks to Google we can step back, marveling at the vastness, measuring our minutia, tapping into the knowledge contained therein. Amazon's cloud removes the pressure to stuff our homes with stuff. Instead of trying to see how many people we can reach via Twitter, how many pingbacks our posts receive, or how many "likes" we can generate on Facebook, what if we focus on how much we can't grasp, letting go of that will to possess, organize, and know all?

The temptation of Google goes back to the garden—to become like God. The lure of Facebook, YouTube, and Twitter is to build a platform to elevate ourselves as iGods. The proper response remains just as timeless—resist temptation. Acknowledge how little we know despite the resources available. Practice humility because the fear of the Lord is the beginning of wisdom. Employ technology as a lifesaving ark, packed with God-given diversity, extending an olive branch. What if these values went viral? I'd love to see how many people might "like" that movement. In an accelerated culture, we can offer slow food and slow church.[64] A theology of abundance has an inexhaustible guest list and a bottomless cup. The wine keeps flowing. The bread keeps multiplying. Our mystic sweet communion never ends.

Discuss

1. Is technology serving you or enslaving you?
2. What kinds of practices can you adapt to keep technology from becoming an idol?

Notes

Introduction

1. Marshall McLuhan, *Playboy* Interview, 1969, quoted in "McLuhan at 100," The Technium, July 20, 2011, www.kk.org/thetechnium/archives/2011/07/mcluhan_at_100.php.

2. Rollo May, *The Cry for Myth* (New York: W.W. Norton, 1991), 57.

3. Clarke's oft-repeated Third Law first appeared in his revised edition to *Profiles of the Future: An Inquiry into the Limits of the Possible* (San Francisco: Harper & Row, 1973).

4. www.dailymotion.com/video/x8m5d0_everything-is-amazing-and-nobody-i_fun#.UYhx4YKR_x4.

5. Jean-Luc Marion discusses how idols act as a mirror, reflecting our gaze, in *God without Being*, trans. Thomas A. Carlson (Chicago: University of Chicago Press, 1991).

6. For an extended discussion of idols, see Tim Keller, *Counterfeit Gods: The Empty Promises of Money, Sex, and Power and the Only Hope That Matters* (New York: Riverhead Trade, 2011), xvii.

7. Exod. 20:3.

8. For a detailed analysis, see G. K. Beale, *We Become What We Worship: A Biblical Theology of Idolatry* (Downers Grove, IL: IVP Academic, 2008).

9. 1 John 5:21.

10. John Calvin, *Commentary on the Acts of the Apostles, Corpus Reformatorum*, 48.562.

11. Lam. 3:23 NLT.

12. Ps. 55:22.

13. Matt. 9:36.

14. Sherry Turkle, *Alone Together: Why We Expect More from Technology and Less from Each Other* (New York: Basic Books, 2011), 17.

15. William Powers, *Hamlet's Blackberry: A Practical Philosophy for Building a Good Life in the Digital Age* (New York: HarperCollins, 2010), 35.

16. Ibid., 43.

17. Sarah Evelyn Harvey, "Read All About It: The Facebook Effect," *Forbes*, December 5, 2012, www.forbes.com/sites/techonomy/2012/12/05/read-all-about-it-the-facebook-effect/.

18. Bruce Barton, *The Man Nobody Knows* (Indianapolis: Bobbs-Merrill Company, 1925), 140.

19. Kevin Kelly, "Nerd Theology," *Technology in Society* 21, no. 4 (1999): 391.

20. David Tracy quoted in the foreword to Marion, *God without Being*, xii.

21. Tertullian quoted in Frances and Joseph Gies, *Cathedral, Forge, and Waterwheel: Technology and Invention in the Middle Ages* (New York: HarperPerennial, 1995), 6.

22. Ibid.

23. Peter Rollins, *The Fidelity of Betrayal: Towards a Church beyond Belief* (Brewster, MA: Paraclete Press, 2008).

24. Gen. 11:9.

25. Martin Ford, *The Lights in the Tunnel: Automation, Accelerating Technology and the Economy of the Future* (Acculant Publishing, 2009).

26. Clay Shirky, *Here Comes Everybody: The Power of Organizing without Organizations* (New York: Penguin Press, 2008).

27. E. F. Schumacher, *Small Is Beautiful: A Study of Economics as if People Mattered* (San Francisco: Harper & Row, 1973), 33.

28. Russ Ackoff, "From Data to Wisdom," *Journal of Applied Systems Analysis* 16 (1989): 3–9.

29. Prov. 1:2–3.

30. Princeton Theological Seminary's website traces multiple instances similar to this sentiment, although none are quite as tidy as Barth's alleged quote from a *Time* magazine article published on May 31, 1963, which states, "[Barth] recalls that 40 years ago he advised young theologians 'to take your Bible and take your newspaper, and read both. But interpret newspapers from your Bible.'" www .ptsem.edu/Library/index.aspx?menu1_id=6907&menu2_id=6904&id=8450.

31. Prov. 4:6.

32. Sheryl Sandberg, *Lean In: Women, Work, and the Will to Lead* (New York: Knopf, 2013).

Chapter 1 Defining Technology

1. Kevin Kelly, "Nerd Theology," *Technology in Society* 21, no. 4 (1999): 392.

2. Mark 6:3 and Matt. 13:55.

3. "Tektōn," www.BiblyStudyTools.com, biblestudytools.com/lexicons/greek/kjv/tekton.html, accessed April 24, 2013.

4. I am indebted to provost Darryl Tippens for pointing this out following the 9th annual Frank Pack lecture I delivered on "faith and technology" at Pepperdine University on February 7, 2013.

5. Darryl Tippens, *Pilgrim Heart: The Way of Jesus in Everyday Life* (Abilene, TX: Leafwood Publishers, 2006), 159.

6. Ken M. Campbell, "What Was Jesus' Occupation?" *Journal of the Evangelical Theological Society* 48, no. 3 (September 2005): 501–19.

7. Kevin Kelly, *What Technology Wants* (New York: Viking, 2010).

8. Martin Heidegger, *The Question Concerning Technology and Other Essays*, trans. and introduction by William Lovitt (New York: Harper Colophon Books, 1977), lectures originally given in 1955, 13.

9. Kelly, *What Technology Wants*, 10–11.

10. Marshall McLuhan, *The Gutenberg Galaxy: The Making of Typographic Man* (Toronto: University of Toronto Press, 1962), preface.

11. Albert Borgmann, *Technology and the Character of Contemporary Life: A Philosophical Inquiry* (Chicago: University of Chicago Press, 1984), 27.

12. Ursula M. Franklin, *The Real World of Technology* (Toronto: House of Anasi Press, 1999).

13. Borgmann, *Technology and Character*, 47.

14. Joel Johnson, "1 Million Workers. 90 Million iPhones. 17 Suicides. Who's to Blame?," *Wired*, March 2011, www.wired.com/magazine/2011/02/ff_joelinchina/.

15. Borgmann, *Technology and Character*, 47.

16. Matt. 6:24.

17. Kevin Kelly, *New Rules for the New Economy: 10 Radical Strategies for a Connected World* (New York: Penguin, 1998), www.kk.org/newrules/newrules-thousand.html.

18. "The limits of plug-and-play development," *The Economist*, May 4, 2012, www. economist .com/blogs/freeexchange/2012/05/technology-and-development.

19. Scott Thumma, "Virtually Religious: Technology and Internet Use in American Congregations," March 2011, www.hartfordinstitute.org/research/technology-Internet-use.html.

20. Barna Group, "New Research Explores the Changing Shape of Temptation," January 4, 2013, www.barna.org/culture-articles/597-new-years-resolutions-temptations-and-americas-favorite-sins.

21. Borgmann, *Technology and Character*, 14.

22. Gen. 1:28.

23. James Limburg, "The Responsibility of Royalty: Genesis 1–11 and the Care of the Earth," *Word & World* 11, no. 2 (Spring 1991).

24. Cited by Frances and Joseph Gies in *Cathedral, Forge, and Waterwheel: Technology and Invention in the Middle Ages* (New York: HarperPerennial, 1995), 5.

25. Heidegger, *Question Concerning Technology*, xxvii.

26. Isa. 11:1–9.

27. Sallie McFague, *Life Abundant: Rethinking Theology and Economy for a Planet in Peril* (Minneapolis: Fortress Press, 2001), 72.

28. Gen. 2:15 NKJV.

29. William A. Stahl, *God and the Chip: Religion and the Culture of Technology* (Waterloo, ON: Wilfred Laurier University Press, 1999), 18.

30. Ibid., 2.

31. Acts 17:22–23.

32. Acts 17:29–30.

33. Cited by Gies in *Cathedral, Forge, and Waterwheel*, 5.

34. St. Thomas Aquinas, *Summa Theologica*, trans. the Fathers of the English Dominican Province, "Treatise on the Most Holy Trinity," Question 27, Article 1, Reply to Objection 3 (New York: Benziger Bros., 1947).

35. For much, much more, see Elizabeth L. Eisenstein, *The Printing Press as an Agent of Change: Communications and Cultural Transformations in Early-Modern Europe* (Cambridge: Cambridge University Press, 1979).

36. David F. Noble, *The Religion of Technology: The Divinity of Man and Spirit of Invention* (New York: Alfred A. Knopf, 1997), 94.

37. Ibid., 65; Num. 23:23 KJV.

38. Samuel Irenaeus Prime, *The Life of Samuel F. B. Morse* (New York: D. Appleton and Company, 1875), 510–11.

39. Thomas P. Hughes, *American Genesis: A Century of Invention and Technological Enthusiasm, 1870–1970* (Chicago: University of Chicago Press, 2004), 188.

40. Neil Postman, *Technopoly* (New York: Alfred A. Knopf, 1992), 51.

41. Noble, *Religion of Technology*, 106.

42. Hughes, *American Genesis*, 444.

43. Jean-Luc Marion, *The Idol and Distance: Five Studies* (New York: Fordham University Press, 2001).

44. Hughes, *American Genesis*, 453.

45. Theodore Roszak's *The Making of a Counter Culture: Reflections on the Technocratic Society and Its Youthful Opposition* (New York: Doubleday, 1969) names the technocracy as an enemy far more formidable than Vietnam, racial injustice, or poverty.

46. In the book *The Greening of America* (New York: Random House, 1970), Charles Reich also rebels against the pressures of time constraints, schedules, and rational connections.

47. E. F. Schumacher popularized the phrase in his groundbreaking book *Small Is Beautiful: Economics as If People Mattered* (San Francisco: Harper & Row, 1973).

48. Wendell Berry, "Think Little," *Whole Earth Catalog*, September 1970.

49. Stewart Brand, "The Purpose of the Whole Earth Catalog," *Whole Earth Catalog*, Fall 1968.

50. *Whole Earth Catalog*, accessed April 24, 2013, www.wholeearth.com/history-whole-earth-catalog.php.

51. Kelly, *What Technology Wants*, 233.

52. Fred Turner, *From Counterculture to Cyberculture: Stewart Brand, the Whole Earth Network, and the Rise of Digital Utopianism* (Chicago: University of Chicago Press, 2006), 134.

53. "Jobs: 'Find what you love,'" *Wall Street Journal*, October 6, 2011, www.online.wsj.com /article/SB10001424052970203388804576613572842080228.html.

54. "Stanford University," *Wikipedia*, accessed April 24, 2013, www.en.wikipedia.org/wiki /Stanford_University.

55. Hughes, *American Genesis*, xvii.

56. Ibid., xxii.

57. Thomas L. Friedman and Michael Mandelbaum, *That Used to Be Us: How America Fell Behind in the World It Invented and How We Can Come Back* (New York: Farrar, Straus and Giroux, 2011), 28.

58. Marcus Borg, *Jesus: A New Vision* (San Francisco: HarperOne, 1991), 195.

59. In Stahl, *God and the Chip*, 2.

60. Noble, *Religion of Technology*, 148.

61. Stahl, *God and the Chip*, 13.

Chapter 2 Apple

1. From "Steve Jobs rare footage conducting a presentation on 1980," posted on YouTube by the Computer History museum, www.computerhistory.org/atchm/steve-jobs/.

2. Walter Isaacson, *Steve Jobs* (New York: Simon & Schuster, 2011), xxi.

3. "The Evolution and History of the Apple Logo," *Edible Apple*, April 20, 2009, www.edibleapple.com/2009/04/20/the-evolution-and-history-of-the-apple-logo/.

4. Ivan Raszl, "Interview with Rob Janoff, Designer of the Apple Logo," *creativebits*, August 3, 2009, www.creativebits.org/interview/interview_rob_janoff_designer_apple_logo.

5. Ibid.

6. Jack Doyle, "Apple, Rising: 1976–1985," *The Pop History Dig*, May 10, 2010, www.pophistorydig.com/?tag=steve-wozniak-apple.

7. "A 1979 profile of Steve Jobs and Apple from *Time* Magazine," *Edible Apple*, October 30, 2009, www.edibleapple.com/2009/10/30/a-1979-profile-of-steve-jobs-and-apple-from-time-magazine/.

8. Doyle, "Apple, Rising."

9. William A. Stahl, *God and the Chip: Religion and the Culture of Technology* (Waterloo, ON: Wilfred Laurier University Press, 1999), 95.

10. "When Steve Met Bill: 'It was a kind of weird seduction visit,'" *CNN Money*, October 24, 2011, www.tech.fortune.cnn.com/2011/10/24/steve-jobs-walter-isaacson/.

11. Hans Urs von Balthasar, *The Glory of the Lord: A Theological Aesthetics—Volume 1: Seeing the Form* (San Francisco: Ignatius Press, 1982), 18.

12. Thomas L. Friedman and Michael Mandelbaum, *That Used to Be Us: How America Fell Behind in the World It Invented and How We Can Come Back* (New York: Farrar, Straus and Giroux, 2011), 140.

13. David Streitfeld, "Defending Life's Work with Words of a Tyrant," *New York Times*, October 6, 2011, www.nytimes.com/2011/10/07/technology/steve-jobs-defended-his-work-with-a-barbed-tongue.html.

14. I am grateful for the introduction to "Beautiful Code" provided by Joseph Hoffert of the King's University College in a paper titled, "Software Aesthetics and Human Flourishing," at Baylor University's Symposium on Faith and Culture, Waco, TX, October 2012.

15. "Jonathan Ive: Winner of the Design Museum's Inaugural Designer of the Year Award in 2003," Design Museum, 2007, www.designmuseum.org/design/jonathan-ive.

16. This video can been see at www.youtube.com/watch?v=r3EbwSOpw_A.

17. Doyle, "Apple, Rising."

18. Peter Elkind, "The Trouble with Steve," *Fortune* 157, no. 5 (March 17, 2008): 88.

19. In *West of Eden: The End of Innocence at Apple Computer* (New York: Viking Penguin, 1989), Frank Rose from *Wired* magazine chronicled the struggle for power between Jobs and the former PepsiCo CEO.

20. Elkind, "The Trouble with Steve," 88.

21. Jay Yarow, "The Full Text of Steve Jobs' Stanford Commencement Speech," *Business Insider*, October 6, 2011, www.businessinsider.com/the-full-text-of-steve-jobs-stanford-commencement-speech-2011-10.

22. Frank Rose, "The End of Innocence: What Happened after Apple Fired Steve Jobs," *Wired*, August 24, 2011, www.wired.com/business/2011/08/the-end-of-inno/.

23. "Jonathan Ive," Design Museum.

24. Ibid.

25. Alan Deutschman, *The Second Coming of Steve Jobs* (New York: Crown Business, 2011).

26. Ibid.

27. Leander Kahney, "Worshipping at the Alter of Mac," *Wired*, December 5, 2002, www.wired.com/gadgets/mac/commentary/cultofmac/2002/12/56674.

28. Isaacson, *Steve Jobs*, 329–30.

29. Tom Hormby, "'Think Different': The Ad Campaign That Restored Apple's Reputation," Low End Mac, April 9, 2007, www.lowendmac.com/orchard/07/apple-think-different.html.

30. Ps. 8:5.

31. 2 Pet. 1:3–4.

32. Shane Richmond, "Jonathan Ive Interview: Simplicity Isn't Simple," *The Telegraph*, May 23, 2012, telegraph.co.uk/technology/apple/9283706/Jonathan-Ive-interview-simplicity-isnt-simple.html.

33. "Jonathan Ive," Design Museum.

34. www.vitsoe.com/us/about/good-design.

35. Mark Prigg, "Sir Jonathan Ive: The iMan Cometh," *London Evening Standard*, March 12, 2102.

36. Steven Johnson, *Where Good Ideas Come From: The Natural History of Innovation* (New York: Riverhead Books, 2010), 170.

37. Richmond, "Jonathan Ive Interview."

38. Ibid.

39. Prigg, "Sir Jonathan Ive."

40. "Jonathan Ive," Design Museum.

41. Steven Levy, *The Perfect Thing: How the iPod Shuffles Commerce, Culture, and Coolness* (New York: Simon & Schuster, 2007).

42. Stephen Moss, "iPod—Therefore I Am," *The Guardian*, January 1, 2004, www.guardian.co.uk /technology/2004/jan/02/netmusic.gadgets.

43. Matt Buchanan, "Analyst: The iPhone Really Is the Jesusphone," *Gizmodo*, May 19, 2007, www.gizmodo.com/261886/analyst-the-iphone-really-is-the-jesusphone.

44. Heidi A. Campbell and Antonio C. La Pastina, "How the iPhone Became Divine: New Media, Religion and the Intertextual Circulation of Meaning," *New Media & Society*, May 18, 2010, www .nms.sagepub.com/content/early/2010/05/11/1461444810362204.

45. Brian Lam, "The Pope Says Worship Not False iDols: Save Us, Oh True Jesus Phone," *Gizmodo*, December 26, 2006, www.gizmodo.com/224143/the-pope-says-worship-not-false-idols-save-us-oh-true -jesus-phone?tag=gadgetscellphones.

46. Warren Kinsella, "The 'Jesus Phone' Cometh," *National Post*, www.nationalpost.com/news /story.html?id=7d385887-23c9-48ef-95c9-eaf61e9397de&p=1, accessed April 25, 2013.

47. Nancy Miller, "Minifesto for a New Age," *Wired* 15, no. 3 (March 2007), www.wired.com /wired/archive/15.03/snackminifesto.html.

48. S. Craig Watkins, *The Young and the Digital: What the Migration to Social-Network Sites, Games, and Anytime, Anywhere Media Means for Our Future* (Boston: Beacon Press, 2009), 160.

49. Ibid., 161.

50. Ibid., 165.

51. Ibid., 169.

52. Katie McDonough, "Welcome to Generation 'Fidgital,'" *Salon*, January 7, 2013, www.salon .com/2013/01/07/welcome_to_generation_fidgital/.

53. Watkins, *The Young and the Digital*, 187.

54. Tiffany Shlain, "Technology Shabbats," Tiffany Shlain website, www.tiffanyshlain.com/bio /tech-shabbats/, accessed April 26, 2013.

55. Ibid.

56. "About This Project," Sabbath Manifesto, www.sabbathmanifesto.org/about, accessed April 26, 2013.

57. Ibid.

58. Rachel Rettner, "Apple Obsession: The Science of iPad Fanaticism," *iPad News Daily*, May 4, 2010, www.ipadnewsdaily.com/56-apple-obsession-the-science-of-ipad-fanaticism-.html.

59. Kyle Smith, "Is Steve Jobs a Creative Genius, or a Tyrant?," *Forbes*, September 8, 2011, www .forbes.com/sites/kylesmith/2011/09/08/is-steve-jobs-a-creative-genius-or-a-tyrant/.

60. http://www.wired.com/business/2012/07/ff_stevejobs/all/.

61. Yukari Iwatani Kane and Ian Sherr, "Secret's from Apple's Genius Bar: Full Loyalty, No Negativity," *The Wall Street Journal*, June 15, 2011, www.online.wsj.com/article/SB10001424052702304563104576364071955678908.html.

62. For a detailed take on Apple's advertising and sales power, see Brett T. Robinson, *Appletopia: Media Technology and the Religious Imagination of Steve Jobs* (Waco: Baylor University Press, 2013).

63. Matt. 10:8.

Chapter 3 A Brief History of the Internet

1. Wendy M. Grossman, *net.wars* (New York: New York University Press, 1997), 18.

2. "Sir Timothy Berners-Lee Interview: Connecting All Humanity," Academy of Achievement, June 22, 2007, www.achievement.org/autodoc/page/ber1int-1.

3. Ibid., www.achievement.org/autodoc/page/ber1int-6.

4. Jennifer Cobb, *CyberGrace: The Search for God in the Digital World* (New York: Crown, 1998), 47.

5. Mark Pesce, "A Brief History of Cyberspace," 1995, www.cs.duke.edu/courses/spring01/cps049s /class/html/mp.history.html.

6. John Battelle, *The Search: How Google and Its Rivals Rewrote the Rules of Business and Transformed Our Culture* (New York: Portfolio, 2005), 58.

7. Ibid., 59.

8. Ibid., 61.

Chapter 4 Amazon

1. Jeff Bezos, "Quote of the Week," *Time*, June 3, 2008.

2. Clay Shirky, *Cognitive Surplus: Creativity and Generosity in a Connected Age* (New York: Penguin Press, 2010), 46.

3. "Self-Publish with Us," Amazon, www.amazon.com/gp/seller-account/mm-summary-page .html?topic=200260520, accessed April 26, 2013.

4. Shirky, *Cognitive Surplus*, 46.

5. John Geraci, "Amazon's Jeff Bezos Doesn't Want an Empire, He Wants the World," TechCrunch, February 18, 2013, www.techcrunch.com/2013/02/18/jeff-bezos-doesnt-want-an-empire-he-wants-the -world/.

6. Chip Bayers, "The Inner Bezos," *Wired* 7, no. 3 (March 1999), www.wired.com/wired/archive/7.03 /bezos_pr.html.

7. Ibid.

8. Ibid.

9. John Cook, "Meet Amazon.com's First Employee: Shel Kaphan," *GeekWire*, June 14, 2011, www.geekwire.com/2011/meet-shel-kaphan-amazoncom-employee-1/2/.

10. Ibid.

11. "Jeff Bezos Biography," Academy of Achievement, February 7, 2013, www.achievement.org /autodoc/page/bez0bio-1.

12. Cook, "Meet Amazon.com's First Employee."

13. "Jeff Bezos Biography," Academy of Achievement.

14. The first book-length history about the rise of Amazon.com was Robert Spector, *Amazon .com: Get Big Fast* (New York: HarperCollins, 2000).

15. Haim Mendelson, Philip Meza, and Mary Petrusewicz, "Amazon.com: Marching Towards Profitability," Stanford University Graduate School of Business, July 2001, www.gsbapps.stanford .edu/cases/documents/ec25.pdf.

16. Sharon Zukin, *Point of Purchase: How Shopping Changed American Culture* (New York: Routledge, 2005), 8.

17. Ibid.

18. James Marcus, *Amazonia* (New York: The New Press, 2004), 105.

19. Spector, *Get Big Fast*, xvii.

20. "Man of the Year: Jeff Bezos," *Wired*, December 20, 1999, www.wired.com/techbiz/media /news/1999/12/33176.

21. Mendelson et al., "Marching Towards Profitability."

22. Steven Levy, "Jeff Bezos Owns the Web in More Ways Than You Think," *Wired*, November 13, 2011, www.wired.com/magazine/2011/11/ff_bezos/.

23. Quoted repeatedly by James Marcus in *Amazonia*.

24. Jeff Bezos, "The Electricity Metaphor," TED, February 2003, ted.com/talks/jeff_bezos_on _the_next_web_innovation.html.

25. Josh Quittner, "The charmed life of Amazon's Jeff Bezos," CNNMoney, April 15, 2008, www .money.cnn.com/2008/04/14/news/companies/quittner_bezos.fortune/.

26. "Jeff Bezos Biography," Academy of Achievement.

27. Quittner, "Charmed Life."

28. Levy, "Jeff Bezos Owns the Web."

29. Mali74, "The Value of Customer Service: Lessons of Loss from Sprint," Yahoo! Voices, November 6, 2007, www.voices.yahoo.com/the-value-customer-service-lessons-loss-from-636559.html.

30. Mendelson et al., "Marching Towards Profitability."

31. "Jeff Bezos on Leading for the Long-Term at Amazon," *Harvard Business Review IdeaCast*, January 3, 2013, www.blogs.hbr.org/ideacast/2013/01/jeff-bezos-on-leading-for-the.html.

32. Ibid.

33. Greg Linden, Brent Smith, and Jeremy York, "Amazon.com Recommendations: Item-to-Item Collaborative Filtering," *IEEE Internet Computing*, January/February 2003, 79, www.cs.umd .edu/~samir/498/Amazon-Recommendations.pdf.

34. Marcus, *Amazonia*, 128.

35. Mendelson et al., "Marching Towards Profitability."

36. Kevin Kelly, "Chapter 9: Relationship Tech," from *New Rules for the New Economy*, Kevin Kelly, www.kk.org/newrules/newrules-9.html.

37. Ibid.

38. Chip Bayers, "The Inner Bezos," *Wired*, www.wired.com/wired/archive/7.03/bezos_pr.html.

39. Jessica Alpert, "Where to Worship? Church Reviews Go Online," National Public Raido, March 31, 2010, www.npr.org/templates/story/story.php?storyId=125394718.

40. John Drane, *The McDonaldization of the Church: Consumer Culture and the Church's Future* (Macon, GA: Smyth & Helwys, 2012).

41. Dietrich Bonhoeffer, *The Cost of Discipleship* (New York: MacMillan, 1963), 43–44.

42. Mic. 6:8.

43. Peter Rollins, *The Idolatry of God: Breaking Our Addiction to Certainty and Satisfaction* (New York: Howard Books, 2012).

44. Luke 9:23–25.

45. Chris Anderson, *The Long Tail: Why the Future of Business Is Selling Less of More* (New York: Hyperion Books, 2006).

46. Eli Pariser, *The Filter Bubble: What the Internet Is Hiding from You* (New York: Penguin Press, 2011), 30.

47. Bayers, "The Inner Bezos."

48. Quittner, "Charmed Life."

49. "Customer Success: Powered by the AWS Cloud," Amazon, www.aws.amazon.com/solutions /case-studies/, accessed April 27, 2013.

50. Quittner, "Charmed Life."

51. Dorrine Mendoza, "Amazon Outage Takes Down Reddit, Foursquare, Others," CNN.com, October 23, 2012, www.cnn.com/2012/10/22/tech/web/reddit-goes-down.

52. Levy, "Jeff Bezos Owns the Web."

53. Quittner, "Charmed Life."

54. Morten T. Hansen, Herminia Ibarra, and Urs Peyer, "The Best-Performing CEOs in the World," *Harvard Business Review*, January-February 2013, www.hbr.org/2013/01/the-best-performing -ceos-in-the-world/ar/2.

55. Shan Li, "Furor Surrounds Amazon's Price-Comparison App," *Los Angeles Times*, December 9, 2011, www.articles.latimes.com/2011/dec/09/business/la-fi-amazon-app-20111210.

56. Pariser, *The Filter Bubble*, 28.

57. Brad Tuttle, "Honoring the Enemy? Brick-and-Mortar Retailers Give Top Award to Amazon's Jeff Bezos," *Time*, January 16, 2013, www.business.time.com/2013/01/16/honoring-the-enemy -brick-and-mortar-retailers-give-top-award-to-amazons-jeff-bezos/.

58. Iain Mackenzie, "Amazon Launches New Kindle Reader," *BBC Newsbeat*, February 9, 2009, www.news.bbc.co.uk/newsbeat/hi/technology/newsid_7879000/7879927.stm.

59. Walter Brueggemann, "The Liturgy of Abundance, The Myth of Scarcity," *Christian Century*, March 24–31, 1999.

60. Ibid.

61. Ps. 104:27.

62. Brueggemann, "The Liturgy of Abundance."

63. Ibid.

64. Ibid.

65. Seth Fiegerman, "Jeff Bezos Explains Why He's Building a 10,000 Year Clock," Mashable.com, November 30, 2012, www.mashable.com/2012/11/30/jeff-bezos-10000-year-clock/.

66. Ibid.

67. John Newton, "Amazing Grace."

68. Fiegerman, "Jeff Bezos Explains."

Chapter 5 Google

1. Neil Postman, *Technopoly* (New York: Alfred A. Knopf, 1992), 61.

2. Ibid.

3. Steven Levy, *In the Plex: How Google Thinks, Works, and Shapes Our Lives* (New York: Simon & Schuster, 2011), 122.

4. John Battelle, *The Search: How Google and Its Rivals Rewrote the Rules of Business and Transformed Our Culture* (New York: Portfolio, 2005), 72.

5. Steven Johnson, *Where Good Ideas Come From: The Natural History of Innovation* (New York: Riverhead Books, 2010), 158.

6. Battelle, *The Search*, 76.

7. Eli Pariser, *The Filter Bubble: What the Internet Is Hiding from You* (New York: Penguin Press, 2011), 32.

8. Battelle, *The Search*, 76.

9. Ibid., 77.

10. Randall Stross, *Planet Google: One Company's Audacious Plan to Organize Everything We Know* (New York: Free Press, 2008), 9.

11. Sergey Brin and Larry Page, *The Anatomy of a Large-Scale Hypertextual Web Search Engine*, Seventh International World-Wide Web Conference (WWW 1998), April 14–18, 1998, Brisbane, Australia.

12. Battelle, *The Search*, 82.

13. Brin and Page, *Anatomy*.

14. Ibid.

15. Battelle, *The Search*, 84.

16. Ibid., 89.

17. Stross, *Planet Google*, 9.

18. Battelle, *The Search*, 106.

19. Bernard Girard, *The Google Way: How One Company Is Revolutionizing Management as We Know It* (San Francisco: No Starch Press, 2009), 31.

20. Battelle, *The Search*, 110.

21. Ibid., 115.

22. Levy, *In the Plex*, 122.

23. Ibid., 123.

24. Ibid., 131.

25. Ibid., 133.

26. Ibid., 135.

27. Megan Garber, "Google Keeps Paying Deceased Employees' Families for a Decade," *The Atlantic*, August 9, 2012, www.theatlantic.com/technology/archive/2012/08/google-keeps-paying -deceased-employees-families-for-a-decade/260897/.

28. Girard, *The Google Way*, 58.

29. Steven Johnson, *Where Good Ideas Come From: The Natural History of Innovation* (New York: Riverhead Books, 2010), 91.

30. Matt. 18:3.

31. Pariser, *The Filter Bubble*, 14.

32. Nicholas Carr, *The Shallows: What the Internet Is Doing to Our Brains* (New York: W.W. Norton, 2011).

33. Jaron Lanier, *You Are Not a Gadget: A Manifesto* (New York: Alfred A. Knopf, 2010), 32.

34. Ibid.

35. Jer. 29:13.

36. Matt. 7:7.

37. Dan Slater explores the big businesses behind online dating in *Love in the Time of Algorithms: What Technology Does to Meeting and Mating* (New York: Current, 2013).

38. Siva Vaidhyanathan, *The Googlization of Everything (And Why We Should Worry)* (Berkeley: University of California Press), 84.

39. Pariser, *The Filter Bubble*, 8.

40. Daniel Bell, *The Coming of Post-Industrial Society* (New York: Basic Books, 1973), 29–30.

41. Ibid., 30.

42. James Beniger, *The Control Revolution: Technological and Economic Origins of the Information Society* (Cambridge, MA: Harvard University Press, 1986), 48.

43. Ibid., 49.

44. J. David Bolter, *Turing's Man: Western Culture in the Computer Age* (Chapel Hill: University of North Carolina Press, 1984), 225.

45. Pariser, *The Filter Bubble*, 188.

46. Lanier, *You Are Not a Gadget*, 82.

47. Jacques Ellul, *The Technological Bluff*, trans. Geoffrey W. Bromiley (Grand Rapids: Eerdmans, 1990), 331.

48. Battelle, *The Search*, 20.

49. Ibid., 23.

50. Kevin Kelly, *What Technology Wants* (New York: Viking, 2010), 287.

51. Ibid., 12.

52. Ibid., 14.

53. Ibid., 86.

54. Thomas L. Friedman and Michael Mandelbaum, *That Used to Be Us: How America Fell Behind in the World It Invented and How We Can Come Back* (New York: Farrar, Straus and Giroux, 2011), 268.

55. Matt. 5:21–22.

56. Matt. 5:27–28.

57. Matt. 5:43–44.

58. Bolter, *Turing's Man*, 40.

59. Ibid., 219.

60. Postman, *Technopoly*, 113.

61. Ps. 46:10 and Phil. 4:6 NKJV.

62. Quentin J. Schultze, *Habits of the High-Tech Heart: Living Virtuously in the Information Age* (Grand Rapids: Baker Academic, 2002), 26.

63. Jacques Ellul, *The Technological Bluff*, trans. Geoffrey W. Bromiley (Grand Rapids: Eerdmans, 1990), 327.

64. Ibid.

65. James Beniger, *The Control Revolution: Technological and Economic Origins of the Information Society* (Cambridge, MA: Harvard University Press, 1986), 59.

66. Francis Collins, *The Language of God: A Scientist Presents Evidence of Belief* (New York: Free Press, 2007).

67. Michael Shermer, "Defying the Doomsayers," *The Wall Street Journal*, February 22, 2012, www.online.wsj.com/article/SB10001424052970203646004577213203698503484.html.

68. Kevin Kelly, "Nerd Theology," *Technology in Society* 21, no. 4 (1999): 391.

69. Battelle, *The Search*, 6.

70. These figures are from Peter Diamandis and Steven Kotler, *Abundance: The Future Is Better Than You Think* (New York: Free Press, 2012), reviewed by Shermer, "Defying the Doomsayers."

71. John 8:58.

72. Matt. 10:30.

73. Matt. 6:4.

74. Pariser, *The Filter Bubble*, 114.

75. Ibid., 135.

76. Ibid., 178.

77. Evgeny Morozov, "Don't Be Evil," *New Republic*, July 13, 2011, www.tnr.com/article/books/magazine/91916/google-schmidt-obama-gates-technocrats.

78. Stross, *Planet Google*, 200.

Chapter 6 A Brief History of Social Networking

1. Kurt Vonnegut, "Thoughts of a Free Thinker," Commencement Address, Hobart and William Smith Colleges, Geneva, NY, 1974.

2. Cited in Jennifer J. Cobb, *CyberGrace: The Search for God in the Digital World* (New York: Crown Books, 1998), 75.

3. Daniela Hernandez, "Facebook?! Twitter?! Instagram?! We Did That 40 Years Ago," *Wired*, December 24, 2012, www.wired.com/wiredenterprise/2012/12/social-media-history.

4. "PLATO (computer system)," *Wikipedia*, www.en.wikipedia.org/wiki/PLATO_%28computer_system%29, accessed April 26, 2013.

5. Brett Borders, "A Brief History of Social Media," Copy Brighter Marketing, June 2, 2009, www.copybrighter.com/history-of-social-media.

6. danah m. boyd and Nicole B. Ellison, "Social Network Sites: Definition, History, and Scholarship," *Journal of Computer-Mediated Communication* 13, no. 1 (2007), www.jcmc.indiana.edu/vol13/issue1/boyd.ellison.html.

7. "The History and Evolution of Social Media," *Webdesigner Depot*, October 7, 2009, www.webdesignerdepot.com/2009/10/the-history-and-evolution-of-social-media/.

8. For a helpful overview of this recent history, see boyd and Ellison, "Social Network Sites."

9. S. Craig Watkins, *The Young and the Digital: What the Migration to Social-Network Sites, Games, and Anytime, Anywhere Media Means for Our Future* (Boston: Beacon Press, 2009), 79.

10. Rebecca J. Rosen, "Facebook's Population Is Now as Big as the Entire World's Was in 1804," *The Atlantic*, October 4, 2012, www.theatlantic.com/technology/archive/2012/10/facebooks-population-is-now-as-big-as-the-entire-worlds-was-in-1804/263250/.

Chapter 7 Facebook

1. David Kirkpatrick, *The Facebook Effect: The Inside Story of the Company That Is Connecting the World* (New York: Simon & Schuster, 2010), 11. For an excerpt, see www.nytimes.com/2010/06/08/books/excerpt-facebook-effect.html.

2. Stephen Marche, "Is Facebook Making Us Lonely?" *The Atlantic*, March 2012, www.theatlantic.com/magazine/archive/2012/05/is-facebook-making-us-lonely/308930/.

3. Kirkpatrick, *Facebook Effect*, 9.

4. See Robert D. Putnam's poignant lament over our isolated postmodern condition, *Bowling Alone: The Collapse and Revival of American Community* (New York: Simon & Schuster, 2000).

5. Kirkpatrick, *Facebook Effect*, 25.

6. Ibid., 24.

7. Ibid., 14.

8. Ibid.

9. Ibid., 37.

10. Ibid.

11. Ibid.

12. Sherry Turkle, *Alone Together: Why We Expect More from Technology and Less from Each Other* (New York: Basic Books, 2011), 158.

13. Ibid., 160.

14. Ibid., 183.

15. Matt Richtel, "Wasting Time Is New Divide in Digital Era," *New York Times*, May 29, 2012, www.nytimes.com/2012/05/30/us/new-digital-divide-seen-in-wasting-time-online.html.

16. Lindsey Txakeeyang, "Facebook CEO Mark Zuckerberg Guest Lectures at Stanford's CS106A Class," *The Dish Daily*, December 6, 2012, www.thedishdaily.com/news/2012/12/06/facebook-ceo-mark-zuckerberg-guest-lectures-stanfords-cs106a-class.

17. Daniel Miller, *Tales from Facebook* (Cambridge: Polity Press, 2011), 170.

18. Gustavo S. Mesch and Ilan Talmud, *Wired Youth: The Social World of Adolescence in the Information Age* (East Sussex, UK: Routledge, 2010), 72.

19. Putnam, *Bowling Alone*, 19.

20. S. Craig Watkins, *The Young and the Digital: What the Migration to Social-Network Sites, Games, and Anytime, Anywhere Media Means for Our Future* (Boston: Beacon Press, 2009), 68.

21. Ibid., 70.

22. Mark Zuckerberg, "Our Commitment to the Facebook Community," *The Facebook Blog*, November 29, 2011, www.blog.facebook.com/blog.php?post=10150378701937131.

23. Christina Lopez, "$100 to Message Mark Zuckerberg?" ABC News blogs, January 11, 2013, www.news.yahoo.com/blogs/abc-blogs/facebook-charging-100-message-ceo-mark-zuckerberg-230014501.

24. Prov. 18:24.

25. John 21:1–19.

26. 2 Kings 2:1–6.

27. John 15:12–15 NKJV.

28. Prov. 14:7.

29. 1 Cor. 15:33.

30. Prov. 22:24–25.

31. Prov. 17:17.

32. Turkle, *Alone Together*, 176.

33. *Wired* magazine had a contest to elect the best self-promoter on the internet. Tim Ferriss, author of *The 4-Hour Workweek*, won. See Dylan Tweney, "Tim Ferriss Takes Wired.com's Self-Promotion Prize," *Wired*, March 31, 2008, www.wired.com/business/2008/03/tim-ferriss-tak/.

34. Deborah Vankin, "Taking It Public," *The Los Angeles Times*, July 28, 2012, D4.

35. Jen Doll, "Hello, Underbrag, the Best Dang Bragging in the Whole Wide World," *The Atlantic*, August 14, 2012, www.theatlanticwire.com/entertainment/2012/08/hello-underbrag-best-dang-bragging-whole-wide-world/55766/.

36. 1 Pet. 5:5.

37. Rom. 12:3.

38. Matt. 6:6.

39. Gen. 4:4–5.

40. Tim Ghianni, "Facebook 'Defriending' Led to Double Murder, Police Say," *Reuters*, February 9, 2012, www.reuters.com/article/2012/02/09/us-murders-facebook-tennessee-idUSTRE8182JY20120209.

41. Belinda Goldsmith, "Is Facebook Envy Making You Miserable?," *Reuters*, January 22, 2013, www.uk.reuters.com/article/2013/01/22/us-facebook-envy-idUKBRE90L0N220130122.

42. Alexandra Sifferlin, "Why Facebook Makes You Feel Bad about Yourself," *Time*, January 24, 2013, www.healthland.time.com/2013/01/24/why-facebook-makes-you-feel-bad-about-yourself/.

43. Goldsmith, "Facebook Envy."

44. Marche, "Is Facebook Making Us Lonely?"

45. Ibid.

46. Goldsmith, "Facebook Envy."

47. 1 Tim. 2:9–10.

48. 1 Cor. 8:13.

49. Luke 17:1–3.

50. Leah Pearlman, "I Like It," *The Facebook Blog*, February 9, 2009, www.blog.facebook.com/blog.php?post=53024537130.

51. Tom Whitnah, "I Like Your Comment," *The Facebook Blog*, June 16, 2010, www.blog.facebook.com/blog.php?post=399440987130.

52. Mike Krumboltz, "Things You Didn't Know about the Facebook Like Button," Yahoo! Finance, February 7, 2012, www.finance.yahoo.com/news/things-you-didn%E2%80%99t-know-about-the-facebook-like-button.html.

53. "Barack Obama," Facebook, www.facebook.com/barackobama, accessed on September 10, 2012.

54. "Mitt Romney," Facebook, www.facebook.com/mittromney, accessed on September 19, 2012.

55. Pariser, *The Filter Bubble*, 18.

56. Turkle, *Alone Together*, 168.

57. Ibid.

58. Anthony Wing Kosner, "Facebook Is Recycling Your Likes to Promote Stories You've Never Seen to All Your Friends," *Forbes*, January 21, 2013, www.forbes.com/sites/anthonykosner/2013/01/21/facebook-is-recycling-your-likes-to-promote-stories-youve-never-seen-to-all-your-friends/.

59. Lori Andrews, "Facebook Is Using You," *New York Times*, February 4, 2012, www.nytimes.com/2012/02/05/opinion/sunday/facebook-is-using-you.html.

60. Clay Shirky, *Cognitive Surplus: Creativity and Generosity in a Connected Age* (New York: Penguin Press, 2010), 123.

61. Jesse Rice, *The Church of Facebook: How the Hyperconnected Are Redefining Community*, (Colorado Springs: David C. Cook, 2009), 28.

62. Turkle, *Alone Together*, 172.

63. Ibid., 174.

64. Rebecca Cusey, "We Need to Break Up," Patheos.com, July 26, 2012, www.patheos.com/blogs/tinseltalk/2012/07/facebook-we-need-to-break-up/.

65. Turkle, *Alone Together*, 11.

66. Ibid., 14.

67. Ibid., 207.

68. Ibid.

69. Jaron Lanier, *You Are Not a Gadget: A Manifesto* (New York: Alfred A. Knopf, 2010), 17.

70. Ibid., 19.

71. Matt. 9:36.

72. Turkle, *Alone Together*, 202.

73. Kirkpatrick, *The Facebook Effect*, 287.

74. Luisa Kroll and Mike Isaac, "Facebook's Zuckerberg to Give Away Half His Fortune," *Forbes*, December 10, 2010, www.forbes.com/2010/12/09/zuckerberg-icahn-billionaires-business-giving-pledge.html.

75. Ryan Mac, "Mark Zuckerberg Finds Giving Spirit, Donates $500 Million to Silicon Valley Giving Foundation," *Forbes*, December 18, 2012, www.forbes.com/sites/ryanmac/2012/12/18/mark-zuckerberg-finds-giving-spirit-pledges-nearly-500-million-to-silicon-valley-education/.

76. Francis Heaney, "The Short Life of Flash Mobs," *Stay Free! Magazine*, www.stayfreemagazine.org/archives/24/flash-mobs-history.html, accessed April 28, 2013.

77. Sarah Evelyn Harvey, "Read All About It: The Facebook Effect," *Forbes*, December 5, 2012, www.forbes.com/sites/techonomy/2012/12/05/read-all-about-it-the-facebook-effect/.

78. Dietrich Bonhoeffer, *Life Together*, trans. John W. Doberstein (San Francisco: Harper & Row, 1954), 77–78.

Chapter 8 YouTube, Twitter, Instagram

1. Olivier Messiaen, *Saint Francois*, Act II, scene 58, (The Angel Musician).

2. To learn how this video became "the most viral political cause of all time," see the infographic at Ninja Shoes, "Kony 2012 Infographic," Analysis Intelligence, March 29, 2012, www.analysisintelligence.com/tag/kony-2012/.

3. Carolyn Davis, "'Kony 2012'—Effective or Just 'Slacktivism,'" *Philadelphia Inquirer*, March 14, 2012, www.articles.philly.com/2012-03-14/news/31164010_1_facebook-page-invisible-children-joseph-kony.

4. Nick Thompson, "'Kony 2012,' Viral Video Raises Questions about Filmmakers," CNN.com, March 12, 2012, www.cnn.com/2012/03/09/world/africa/kony-2012-q-and-a.

5. Erin Carlson, "'Kony 2012' Creator Jason Russell Addresses Nude Breakdown on 'Oprah's Next Chapter,'" *Hollywood Reporter*, October 8, 2012, www.hollywoodreporter.com/live-feed/kony-2012-jason-russell-breakdown-oprah-377041.

6. Joseph DeCaro, "Don't Get Violent over Viral Videos," Before It's News, October 12, 2012, www.beforeitsnews.com/christian-news/2012/10/dont-get-violent-over-viral-videos-2453124.html.

7. Clay Shirky, *Cognitive Surplus: Creativity and Generosity in a Connected Age* (New York: Penguin Press, 2010), 36.

8. Pelle Snickars and Patrick Vonderau, eds., *The YouTube Reader* (Stockholm: National Library of Sweden, 2009), 10.

9. Steven Johnson, *Where Good Ideas Come From: The Natural History of Innovation* (New York: Riverhead Books, 2010), 14.

10. Lev Grossman, "You—Yes, You—Are *Time*'s Person of the Year," *Time*, December 25, 2006, www.time.com/time/magazine/article/0,9171,1570810,00.html.

11. Johnson, *Where Good Ideas Come From*, 13.

12. Brett Molina, "YouTube: 72 Hours of Video Upload per Minute," *USA Today*, May 21, 2012, www.content.usatoday.com/communities/technologylive/post/2012/05/youtube-72-hours-of-video-uploaded-per-minute/1#.UVkx-hmR8Xw.

13. I appreciate the questions of commodification asked by Kate Shellnut in "The Problem with Christians Doing the 'Harlem Shake,'" *Christianity Today*, February 20, 2013, www.christianitytoday.com/women/2013/february/problem-with-christians-doing-harlem-shake.html.

14. www.voices.yahoo.com/top-3-viral-christian-videos-6759188.html.

15. Dave Urbanski, "'Why I Hate Religion but Love Jesus': Controversial Viral Video Logs 10 Million Hits in Four Days," The Blaze, January 15, 2012, www.theblaze.com/stories/2012/01/15/why-i-hate-religion-but-love-jesus-controversial-viral-video-logs-10-million-hits-in-four-days/.

16. Barbara Bradley Hagerty, "A Pulpit for the Masses: YouTube, Christians Click," NPR, February 7, 2012, www.npr.org/2012/02/07/146471341/wwjd-on-youtube-it-depends-who-you-ask.

17. James D. Davis, "The Word Made Video," *Sun Sentinel*, May 22, 2012, www.articles.sun-sentinel.com/2012-05-22/features/fl-jesus-video-20120522_1_youtube-video-religion-viral-video.

18. Hagerty, "Pulpit for the Masses."

19. See them both at Jeff Loveness's YouTube channel, "Prussian Sunsets," www.youtube.com/user/PrussianSunsets.

20. Henry Jenkins, "From YouTube to WeTube . . . ," *Confessions of an Aca-Fan*, February 13, 2008, www.henryjenkins.org/2008/02/from_youtube_to_wetube.html.

21. Shirky, *Cognitive Surplus*, 19.

22. "Christmas Food Court Flash Mob, Hallelujah Chorus," *YouTube*, November 17, 2010, www.youtube.com/watch?v=SXh7JR9oKVE.

23. JJ Starr, "31: The Sunrise Project," 2010, www.vimeo.com/7507367.

24. Roger Ebert, "The Most Beautiful Thing I've Ever Seen," *Roger Ebert's Journal*, September 16, 2010, rogerebert.com/balder-and-dash/the-most-beautiful-thing-ive-ever-seen.

25. For a robust elaboration of this notion, see Hans Urs von Balthasar, *Theo-Drama: Theological Dramatic Theory*, trans. Graham Harrison (San Francisco: Ignatius Press, 1989).

26. "Meet the Man behind Rebecca Black's 'Friday,'" *BillboardBiz*, March 30, 2011, www.billboard.com/biz/articles/news/1178532/meet-the-man-behind-rebecca-blacks-friday.

27. Rebecca Black, "Friday—Rebecca Black—Official Music Video," YouTube, September 16, 2011, www.youtube.com/watch?v=kfVsfOSbJY0.

28. Linda Holmes, "Ridiculed YouTube Singer Rebecca Black Grabs a Mountain of Bull by the Horns," NPR, March 18, 2011, www.npr.org/blogs/monkeysee/2011/03/18/134652534/ridiculed-youtube-singer-rebecca-black-grabs-a-mountain-of-bull-by-the-horns.

29. Shirky, *Cognitive Surplus*, 83.

30. Jack Dorsey, "twttr sketch," Flickr, March 24, 2006, www.flickr.com/photos/jackdorsey/182613360/.

31. Nicholas Carlson, "The Real History of Twitter," *Business Insider*, April 13, 2011, businessinsider.com/how-twitter-was-founded-2011-4.

32. David Sarno, "Twitter Creator Jack Dorsey Illuminates the Site's Founding Document," *Los Angeles Times*, February 18, 2009, latimesblogs.latimes.com/technology/2009/02/twitter-creator.html.

33. See Matt. 11:15; 13:9; Mark 4:9, 23.

34. Matt. 4:18–20.

35. Ashley Parker, "Twitter's Secret Handshake," *New York Times*, June 10, 2011, www.nytimes.com/2011/06/12/fashion/hashtags-a-new-way-for-tweets-cultural-studies.html.

36. Nate Ritter, "Helping People Everywhere through the San Diego Fires," *The Blog of Nate Ritter, Web Chef*, October 23, 2007, www.blog.perfectspace.com/2007/10/23/helping-people-everywhere-through-the-san-diego-fires/.

37. Alan Beard and Alec McNayr, *Historical Tweets: The Completely Unabridged and Ridiculously Brief History of the World* (New York: Villard, 2010).

38. Jana Riess/Twible @janariess, *Twitter*, www.twitter.com/janariess, accessed April 28, 2013.

39. Justine Sharrock, "How Facebook Plans to Make Us All Get Along," BuzzFeed, January 31, 2013, www.buzzfeed.com/justinesharrock/how-facebook-plans-to-make-us-all-get-along.

40. Susan Sontag, *On Photography* (New York: Penguin Books, 1977), 10.

41. Ibid., 14–15.

42. Roland Barthes, *Camera Lucida: Reflections on Photography*, trans. Richard Howard (New York: Hill and Wang, 1981), 11.

43. Ibid., 12.

44. Ibid., 13.

45. Ibid.

46. Ibid., 14.

47. Shirky, *Cognitive Surplus*, 26.

48. www.belarus.usembassy.gov/secretary_of_state_condolezza_rices_remarks_about_belarus_april_19-20_2005.html.

49. Evgeny Morozov, "Moldova's Twitter Revolution," *Foreign Policy*, April 7, 2009, www.neteffect.foreignpolicy.com/posts/2009/04/07/moldovas_twitter_revolution.

50. Andrej Dynko, "Europe's Last Dictatorship," *New York Times*, July 16, 2012, www.nytimes.com/2012/07/17/opinion/belarus-europes-last-dictatorship.html.

51. Andrew Sullivan, "The Revolution Will Be Twittered," *The Atlantic*, June 13, 2009, www.theatlantic.com/daily-dish/archive/2009/06/the-revolution-will-be-twittered/200478/.

52. "Iran, Tehran: Wounded Girl Dying in Front of Camera, Her Name Was Neda," YouTube, June 20, 2009, www.youtube.com/watch?v=bbdEf0QRsLM.

53. Matthew Weaver, "Iran's 'Twitter Revolution' Was Exaggerated, Says Editor," *The Guardian*, June 9, 2010, www.guardian.co.uk/world/2010/jun/09/iran-twitter-revolution-protests.

54. Blake Hounshell, "The Revolution Will Be Tweeted," *Foreign Policy*, July/August 2011, www .foreignpolicy.com/articles/2011/06/20/the_revolution_will_be_tweeted.

55. Ethan Zuckerman, "The First Twitter Revolution," *Foreign Policy*, January 14, 2011, www .foreignpolicy.com/articles/2011/01/14/the_first_twitter_revolution.

56. Saleem Kassim, "Twitter Revolution: How the Arab Spring Was Helped by Social Media," *PolicyMic.com*, July 2012, policymic.com/articles/10642/twitter-revolution-how-the-arab-spring -was-helped-by-social-media.

57. "Wael Ghonim: Creating a 'Revolution 2.0' in Egypt," NPR, February 9, 2012, www.npr .org/2012/02/09/146636605/wael-ghonim-creating-a-revolution-2-0-in-egypt.

58. Robert F. Worth, "Twitter Gives Saudi Arabia a Revolution of Its Own," *New York Times*, October 20, 2012, www.nytimes.com/2012/10/21/world/middleeast/twitter-gives-saudi-arabia-a -revolution-of-its-own.html.

59. Hounshell, "The Revolution Will Be Tweeted."

60. Anne Nelson, "The Limits of the 'Twitter Revolution,'" *The Guardian*, February 24, 2011, www.guardian.co.uk/commentisfree/cifamerica/2011/feb/24/digital-media-egypt.

61. Weaver, "Iran's 'Twitter Revolution.'"

62. Evgeny Morozov, *The Net Delusion: The Dark Side of Internet Freedom* (New York: Public Affairs, 2011), 293.

63. Ibid., 5.

64. Evgeny Morozov, "Iran Elections: A Twitter Revolution," *Washington Post*, June 17, 2009, www.washingtonpost.com/wp-dyn/content/discussion/2009/06/17/DI2009061702232.html.

65. Zuckerman, "The First Twitter Revolution."

66. Evgeny Morozov, "Muzzled by the Bots," *Slate*, October 26, 2012, www.slate.com/articles /technology/future_tense/2012/10/disintermediation_we_aren_t_seeing_fewer_gatekeepers_we_re _seeing_more.2.html.

67. Bill Wasik, "Crowd Control," *Wired*, January 2012, www.wired.com/magazine/2011/12 /ff_riots/.

68. Evgeny Morozov, "The Brave New World of Slacktivism," *Foreign Policy*, May 19, 2009, www .neteffect.foreignpolicy.com/posts/2009/05/19/the_brave_new_world_of_slacktivism.

69. Malcolm Gladwell, "Small Change: Why the Revolution Will Not Be Tweeted," *The New Yorker*, October 4, 2010, www.newyorker.com/reporting/2010/10/04/101004fa_fact_gladwell.

70. Dave Gilson, "The Tunisia Twitter Revolution That Wasn't," *Mother Jones*, January 27, 2011, www.motherjones.com/media/2011/01/evgeny-morozov-twitter-tunisia.

71. Ibid.

72. Shirky, *Cognitive Surplus*, 98.

73. James Surowiecki, *The Wisdom of Crowds: Why the Many Are Smarter Than the Few and How Collective Wisdom Shapes Business, Economies, Societies and Nations* (New York: Anchor, 2004).

74. Jonathan Salem Baskin connects social networking to earlier movements like the French Revolution, in *Histories of Social Media* (Chicago: Shadows on the Cave Wall, 2012).

75. "Sheryl Sandberg Interview: 'Wisdom of Friends Will Replace Wisdom of Crowds,'" *World Economic Forum blog*, January 19, 2012, www.forumblog.org/2012/01/sheryl-sandberg-interview -wisdom-of-friends-will-replace-wisdom-of-crowds/.

76. Caroline McCarthy, "Facebook: One Social Graph to Rule Them All?," CBS News, April 21, 2010, www.cbsnews.com/stories/2010/04/21/tech/main6418458.shtml.

77. Josh Constine, "Facebook Is Done Giving Its Precious Social Graph to Competitors," *Tech-Crunch*, January 23, 2013, techcrunch.com/2013/01/24/my-precious-social-graph/.

78. Matt. 18:15–17.

79. Matt. 14:22–23.

80. Luke 5:15–16.

81. Luke 9:18.

Conclusion

1. Ursula M. Franklin, *The Real World of Technology* (Toronto: House of Anansi Press, 2004), original Massey lectures given in 1990, 142.

2. Marshall McLuhan, "The Playboy Interview," *Playboy*, www.understandingnewmedia.com /mm1/class_materials/mcluhan-playboy.pdf, accessed April 28, 2013.

3. Bill Gates, "The Disappearing Computer," Microsoft News Center, reprinted from *The Economist*, 2003, www.microsoft.com/presspass/ofnote/11-02worldin2003.mspx.

4. Cornelius Plantinga Jr., *Not the Way It's Supposed to Be: A Breviary of Sin* (Grand Rapids: Eerdmans, 1995).

5. Lam. 3:22–24.

6. Isa. 43:18–19.

7. John 3:1–3.

8. Eph. 4:22–24.

9. 2 Cor. 5:17.

10. Rev. 21:4.

11. Bill McKibben, *Enough: Staying Human in an Engineered Age* (New York: Times Books, 2003), 109.

12. Matt. 10:8.

13. Graham Hill, "Living with Less. A Lot Less," *The New York Times*, March 9, 2013, www.nytimes.com/2013/03/10/opinion/sunday/living-with-less-a-lot-less.html.

14. Jeff Shinabarger, *More or Less: Choosing a Lifestyle of Excessive Generosity* (Colorado Springs: David C. Cook, 2013).

15. Jacques Ellul, *The Technological Bluff*, trans. Geoffrey W. Bromiley (Grand Rapids: Eerdmans, 1990), 258.

16. Albert Borgmann, *Technology and the Character of Contemporary Life: A Philosophical Inquiry* (Chicago: University of Chicago Press, 1984), 207.

17. Leander Kahney, "Design according to Ive," *Wired*, June 25, 2003, www.wired.com/culture/design/news/2003/06/59381.

18. E. F. Schumacher, *Small Is Beautiful: A Study of Economics as if People Mattered* (San Francisco: Harper & Row, 1973), 34.

19. Wendell Berry, "Think Little," *Whole Earth Catalog*, September 1970.

20. Luke 16:10.

21. Matt. 18:2–6.

22. Mark 10:13–16.

23. Pierre Teilhard de Chardin, *The Future of Man* (New York: Harper & Row, 1964).

24. Pierre Teilhard de Chardin, *The Phenomenon of Man* (New York: Harper & Row, 1961), 251–52.

25. Teilhard de Chardin, *Future of Man*, 165–66.

26. Jennifer J. Cobb, *CyberGrace: The Search for God in the Digital World* (New York: Crown Publishers, 1998), 91.

27. Pierre Teilhard de Chardin, *The Making of a Mind* (New York: Harper & Row, 1965), 119–20.

28. 1 Cor. 15:42–44.

29. www.ted.com/talks/ken_jennings_watson_jeopardy_and_me_the_obsolete_know_it_all.html.

30. David F. Noble, *The Religion of Technology: The Divinity of Man and Spirit of Invention* (New York: Alfred A. Knopf, 1997), 156.

31. Ibid., 162.

32. Ibid., 164.

33. Ibid.

34. Ibid., 159.

35. Ibid.

36. Ibid.

37. Ibid., 160.

38. Ibid., 206.

39. Ray Kurzweil, *The Singularity Is Near: When Humans Transcend Biology* (New York: Viking, 2005), 19.

40. Ibid., 23.

41. Ibid.

42. Ibid., 337.

43. Gregory Ferenstein, "Google's New Director of Engineering, Ray Kurzweil, Is Building Your 'Cybernetic Friend,'" *TechCrunch*, January 6, 2013, www.techcrunch.com/2013/01/06/googles-director-of-engineering-ray-kurzweil-is-building-your-cybernetic-friend/.

44. Jaron Lanier, *You Are Not a Gadget: A Manifesto* (New York: Alfred A. Knopf, 2010), 18.

45. Ibid.

46. Ibid., 25.

47. Ibid., 21.

48. Recommended by John Freeman in *The Tyranny of E-mail*, referenced in William Powers, *Hamlet's Blackberry: A Practical Philosophy for Building a Good Life in the Digital Age* (New York: HarperCollins, 2010), 217.

49. Wendell Berry, "Manifesto: The Mad Farmer Liberation Front," in *The Country of Marriage* (New York: Harcourt, Brace, Jovanovich, 1973), 14.

50. Luke 11:24–26.

51. www.gameo.org/encyclopedia/contents/S6803.html.

52. Wendell Berry, "Watershed and Commonwealth," in *Citizenship Papers* (Washington, DC: Shoemaker & Hoard, 2003), 135.

53. Borgmann, *Technology and Character*, 191.

54. Heb. 11:10.

55. Jürgen Moltmann, *The Coming of God: Christian Eschatology*, trans. Margaret Kohl (Minneapolis: Fortress Press, 1996), 312.

56. Ibid., 317.

57. Peter Rollins, *How (Not) to Speak of God* (Brewster, MA: Paraclete Press, 2006), 24.

58. Yi-Fu Tuan, *Space and Place: The Perspective of Experience* (Minneapolis: University of Minnesota Press, 1977), 104.

59. Rev. 21:18–21.

60. Rev. 21:26.

61. Kevin Kelly interviewed by Katelyn Beaty, "Geek Theologian," *Christianity Today*, July 15, 2011, www.christianitytoday.com/ct/2011/julyweb-only/geektheologian.html?start=2.

62. Franklin, *Real World of Technology*, 149.

63. Ellen Painter Dollar, "The Lessons of a Cluttered Life," Episcopal Café, October 4, 2010, www.episcopalcafe.com/daily/ethics/the_lessons_of_a_cluttered_lif.php.

64. Check out Chris Smith and John Pattison's "Slow Church" movement at www.patheos.com/blogs/slowchurch.

Index